Graduation
Masters of Divinity
Golden Gate - 1988

The Name Above Every Name

The Name Above Every Name

HERBERT C. GABHART

BROADMAN PRESS
Nashville, Tennessee

© Copyright 1986 • Broadman Press

All rights reserved

4250-32

ISBN: 0-8054-5032-7

Dewey Decimal Classification: 242.2

Subject Headings: DEVOTIONS, DAILY // JESUS CHRIST

Library of Congress Catalog Card Number: 85-28082

Printed in the United States of America

Library of Congress Cataloging-in-Publication Data

Gabhart, Herbert C., 1914-
  The name above every name.

  Bibliography: p. 382
  Includes index.
  1. Jesus Christ—Name—Meditations. 2. Devotional calendars. I. Title.
  BT590.N2G23 1986   232   85-28082
  ISBN 0-8054-5032-7

Credits for Biblical Paintings inserted between pages 162 and 163:
Mary Swadling Baby Jesus, © 1980, Convention Press.
Jesus Obeys Mary and Joseph, © 1981, Convention Press.
Mighty Works of Jesus, © 1981, Convention Press.
Jesus Showing His Love to the Children, © 1978, Convention Press.
Boat in a Storm, © 1979, Convention Press.
Pray to Your Heavenly Father, © 1980, Convention Press.
Between pages 192 and 193:
Jesus and the Samaritan Woman, © 1984, Convention Press.
Jesus Ministering, © 1977, Convention Press.
Walking on Water, © 1977, Convention Press.
Mary Anoints Jesus, © 1976, Convention Press.
Thy Will Be Done, © 1977, Convention Press.
Thou Art the Christ, © 1977, Convention Press.

Preface

Some things in life cling to us with unbreakable tenacity. Some ideas, thoughts, and experiences just won't let go. They float around in our minds, bobbing up now and then, with the same freshness and force that accompanied them at first. Frequently, they are like objects gathering additional matter en route, stalking and haunting our memories and consciousnesses with added impact.

It was more than thirty-five years ago, during my studies of the Bible and while preparing sermons for my parishioners, that I became impressed with the many different names Christ was called and the many different titles given Him or could be given to Him. The impression has grown, and I have pursued my interest with great desire and curiosity. Finally, I came to the point that I began to list the names and designations alphabetically. One day the thought hit me: Why not write a devotional book dealing with the names and descriptive titles given Jesus, using a different one for each day of the year? I did not know then whether I could—in good conscience and with good judgment—find enough for 365 days, but with constant diligence and much labor, I have amassed that number, plus one more for Leap Year.

My purpose is not to be sensational or unique or shocking, but to use this as a means to pay tribute and sincere homage to the one whose Name "is above every name" (Phil. 2:9). Personally and confessionally, it is my soul's tribute to Him, my Lord and Savior.

As I began this exciting endeavor, I did so with the prayer that He shall be glorified, for "Thou art worthy, O Lord, to receive glory and honour and power: for thou hast created all things, and for thy pleasure they are and were created" (Rev. 4:11).

This, then, is a book of devotionals about Him, His name and service titles. That name has been praised through the centuries by the singing of many songs and anthems and through the recitation of many poems. Nothing has ever fully unfolded—nor will this endeavor now fully unfold—the manifold meaning and redemptive work of Him who bore each name and title with love and grace. He is too big for mortal human beings to comprehend, yet His humanness draws us all close to Him.

Fairbairn was right when he wrote fifty-five years ago: "In less than eighty years, he (Pilate) sees in every city of the Roman world societies of men and women meeting in the name of this Jesus and singing praises to him as God; while so powerful has *his name grown* in some provinces that the very temples are deserted and the most famous governor of the day writes to ask the Emperor what policy he is to pursue."[1]

And what was true of Pilate during his day is even truer in our day.

---

1. Andrew Martin Fairbairn, *The Philosophy of the Christian Religion* (New York: The Macmillan Company, 1928), pp. 320 ff.

Introduction

Names are interesting, beautiful, significant, descriptive, and hereditary. Very few people name their sons Judas. With respect to many persons, their names and titles form a cadre, even a coterie, which might be likened to a well-orchestrated symphony under the direction of a conductor, accenting the upbeats and the downbeats, as in life.

The multiple names of Jesus and the many descriptive titles given Him run the gamut of everything from God Omnipotent to the terrible meek, from the One at whose name "every knee shall bow . . . and every tongue shall confess" Him to the One despised and rejected, and from the world's greatest revolutionary to the Prince of peace (Rom. 14:11).

His name has been gloriously proclaimed and ingloriously profaned. It has invoked fanatical loyalty and evoked pharisaical coldness. Seldom has the mentioning of it in any form or fashion produced only neutrality. There seems to be a self-generative genre associated with it. It usually rings some sort of bell with the human mind or the heart. Jesus cautioned His disciples thusly, "Why call ye me, Lord, Lord, and do not the things which I say?" (Luke 6:46).

So this odyssey of names touches base with each day of the year. I feel confident that my enthusiasm at the beginning of the odyssey will not have lessened when I come to the final page. On the contrary, I feel that it will have become even more alive and vibrant because I will have described Him in so many verbal frames, cameos, and contexts that I can say with Thomas, "My Lord and my God" (John 20:28). Were I a vocalist, I would more than likely burst forth in singing Charles Wesley's great hymn, *O for a Thousand Tongues to Sing*. I would sing especially the third stanza:

Jesus, the name that calms my fears,
That bids my sorrows cease;
'Tis music in the sinner's ears;
'Tis life and health and peace.

Prologue

A Name

I know of a land that is sunk in shame,
Of hearts that faint and tire;
But I know of a Name, a Name, a Name,
That can set that land on fire.

I know of a soul that is lost to God,
Bended down to the things of earth;
But, I know of a Name, a Name, a Name,
That can give that soul new birth.

I know of a life all steeped in sin,
That no man's heart can cure;
But I know of a Name, a Name, a Name,
That can make that life all pure.

So listen my heart, an angel speaks,
To save that life from dross;
Christ Jesus is the name,
He saves by the way of the Cross.

—Author unknown

1

Alpha

"I am *Alpha* and Omega, the beginning and the end, the first and the last" (Rev. 22:13).

Christ is the Alpha and the Omega, the beginning and the end, the first and the last. There was nothing before Him, and there is nothing after Him.

The word *alpha* is the name of the first letter of the Greek alphabet. *Aleph*, the comparable Hebrew word, stands for the first letter of the Hebrew alphabet. *Alpha* is also the brightest star of the starry constellations.

In calling Christ "Alpha," one is saying that He takes precedence over all others; He is foremost in rank, before, an original, and is in preference to anything else.

In our world today we are prone to establish categories of distinction. We refer to the "ten best-dressed" men or women. Jesus would certainly be first in that category because He wore the robes of royalty and righteousness. In the category of the "ten best-known" persons, He would head the list, for His name is spoken with reverence and praised with adoration daily more than any other. In the category of the wealthiest of the world, no sultan, sheikh, Wall Street giant, or oil magnate would even be within His shadow. He is joint owner with His Father of the heavens and the earth. He would stand out in the midst of these categories like a lone pine tree in a cotton patch.

Through Him all things were created. Through Him is creation redeemed. The pathway to glory begins at His cross. He is before all events, all history, and millions of millenniums.

Is He first in our lives? He is capable, worthy, and accessible. There is no acceptable substitute. He must never be relegated to the place of "second fiddle."

As the Alpha He should be first on every tongue, in every life, and in every deed.

2

Achiever

"There are also *many other things which Jesus did*, the which, if they should be written every one, I suppose that even the world itself could not contain the books that should be written" (John 21:25).

This has to be a hyperbolic statement. It is an intimation of the depth and breadth of His teachings and the immensity of His miraculous deeds, to say the least, about what effect His teachings and deeds have had upon the world.

Jesus wasted neither time nor words. He did not believe that one can achieve by sitting in the shade of a family tree. He set His face steadfastly. He knew where He was going, how to get there, and what to do along the way.

Achievement to Him was measured by what is finished, not by what is begun; yet He was an achiever on both counts. He did much, and what He began goes on and on, even now. He was somewhat of a traditionalist but more of a spiritual pioneer.

He had that rare capacity to see the invisible through faith, to feel the intangible through love, and to achieve the impossible through concentration of purpose.

There are many motivational books written today to "pump people up." They are good and helpful, but there is still no achieving without great labor and great love.

Jesus taught us how to knock the *t* off of *can't* thereby making it *can*. His goal is to redeem everyone—whosoever. His field is the whole world. He achieved what no one has ever achieved, before or since. He came down from heaven to bring God to humanity and went back to heaven to take humanity to God. What an achievement!

3

Adam, the Last or the Second Man

"The first man Adam was made a living soul; the last *Adam* was made a quickening spirit" (1 Cor. 15:45).

The term *Adam* means "from the red earth." It was given to the first man created by Almighty God from the dust of the earth. Man was God's masterpiece and crowning act of creation. He never created anything equal to or better than human beings. As if to set man further apart, He breathed into human nostrils the breath of life, and man became a living soul.

The apostle Paul was the only writer to refer to Christ as "Adam." In the passage from 1 Corinthians, Paul referred to Him as "the last Adam" and the "second man." In the first case there was no need for an Adam between the first and the last, and in the second case there could be no third man after the second man.

The first Adam was of the earth, a living soul, guilty of sin and subject to death. The last Adam, Christ, was from heaven, an eternal spirit, free of sin and the giver of life everlasting. Neither the first Adam nor the last Adam came by ordinary laws. The first was created by God from the earth. The last Adam shared in the creative acts and came to earth in righteousness and holiness.

As the first Adam was prophetic of the career and character of the race in its beginning, the last Adam was prophetic of the future of the race—a higher, more abundant life, an inheritance incorruptible filled with celestial and eternal joy.

Our inheritance from the first Adam is what he had and was. Our inheritance from the last Adam is what He had, was, and will be. All who are united to the first Adam by physical lineage will incur death which, by sinning, Adam introduced; similarly, all who by spiritual affinity are in Christ will enjoy the new life which He won in triumphing over death.

The term *second man* is a term both of association and action. Christ did become a man—the highest essence of humanity—in order to bring human beings into the fullness of God in heavenly places.

Oh, what an inheritance for all the redeemed: incorruptible, tax-free, sin-free, pain-free, forever!

4

Adonai

"And Abram said, *Lord* God, what wilt thou give me?" (Gen. 15:2).

Adonai is the plural form of the Hebrew word meaning "Lord." The Greek word *kurios* carries the same meaning of Lord.

As Lord, Jesus has the right to claim our lives, our love, and our loyalty. He, as Lord, is the only one worthy to claim all of each one of us.

Adonai-Jehovah, "Lord God" (Rev. 4:8), is the only one worthy to receive the glory and honor and power. As Lord, He has me and thee in His heart and hands. He has the tiny babes and men and women of power in His hands. As God, He has the whole world in His hands.

The many Hebrew names of the Triune God listed under the devotionals entitled "Elohim," "Adonai," and "Jahweh" are far from being all comprehensive as to the use of those names used singularly or compounded. Many other references and illustrations could be given.

Lydia Baxter wrote, during the previous century, a much-loved hymn entitled "Take the Name of Jesus with You." She seemed to sense that all through Hebrew and Christian history that Name above all names had found expression in a multitude of words which enlarged its meaning.

Precious Name, O how sweet!
Hope of earth and joy of heav'n.

There is no way to describe fully or to comprehend totally the beauty of that Name, Jesus, and the meaning of that Name, Christ.

We can fall prostrate at His feet—when our journey is complete.

5

Advocate

"We have an *advocate* with the Father, Jesus Christ the righteous" (1 John 2:1).

It has been said that the way to win a lawsuit is to have a good case, a good lawyer, and some good luck. That may work in the courts of earth but not in the court of heaven, for a good case and good luck are impossible to have.

In a somewhat lighter vein but with some truth, a wit exclaimed, "A lawyer is a learned gentleman who rescues your estate from your enemies for himself."

Once I spent almost a week in federal court as one of the defendants in a lawsuit. It was tiring, revealing, and emotional. Before going to court we searched and secured a lawyer of highest integrity, one knowledgeable and capable in the courtroom. We wanted an advocate who could plead our case well before the judge.

Christ is the Christian's advocate at the judgment bar of God. No better one ever stood before a judge. He is familiar with all the laws of sin and righteousness. He will plead our case.

The devil is a tough, persistent adversary. God is a just God. The stakes are high. No sinner can effect reconciliation with God; only a righteous advocate to a righteous God can. We—those redeemed by the atoning blood of Christ—are fortunate to be Christ's clients.

When Christians stand at the judgment bar, Christ will be there as our priestly advocate to represent us. He will say to the Judge, "Now they have known that all things whatsoever thou hast given me are of thee. For I have given unto them the words which thou gavest me; and they have received them, and have known surely that I came out from thee, and they have believed that thou didst send me. I pray for them: . . . which thou hast given me; for they are thine. And all mine are thine, and thine are mine" (John 17:7-10).

What an Advocate!

13

6

The Almighty

"Saith the Lord, which is, and which was, and which is to come, *the Almighty*" (Rev. 1:8).

It is mighty difficult to think of one being almighty. Some men are mighty; only God is Almighty.

The world has had some military men of power and valor, mighty in the eyes of their compatriots. By their actions Alexander the Great, Caesar, Hannibal, Charlemagne, Genghis Khan, and many other kings, sultans, and sheikhs have affected the destiny of millions who trembled when they spoke.

Christ, a man who walked the dusty roads of Palestine, was also the Almighty.

The Greek word for *almighty* is a composite of two words: *all* and *ruler*. The Almighty then means "ruler of all," not just a five-star general but one without possibility of equal. Christ's power was not measured by personal possessions or territorial claims but by His character, knowledge, and power to heal and forgive sins.

The wind and the waves obeyed His voice. The demons trembled at His commands. Death yielded up its victims. The sun, moon, and stars continue to move in their orbit in accordance with His laws.

The prophet Isaiah, in thinking of the Almighty God, said, "Who hath measured the waters in the hollow of his hand, and meted out heaven with the span, and comprehended the dust of the earth in a measure, and weighed the mountains in scales, and the hills in a balance?" (Isa. 40:12).

Job exclaimed, "Touching the Almighty, we cannot find him out: he is excellent in power, and in judgment, and in plenty of justice: he will not afflict" (Job 37:23).

The major difference in the might of Christ as opposed to human might is that Christ's power is enhanced by His being also all-loving. It takes real power to love all, lovely and unlovely alike. If one trembles at His power, is there an emotion adequate to respond to His love? Yes, one—reciprocal love of equal quality!

14

Ambassador from Heaven

"Now then we are *ambassadors* for Christ" (2 Cor. 5:20).
"God was in Christ, *reconciling* the world unto himself" (2 Cor. 5:19).

Christ was God's "Ambassador Plenipotentiary." I learned those two big, long words as a Royal Ambassador in our home church. I learned something else: an ambassador is one who represents his government or country at the court of another, and an ambassador plenipotentiary is the highest order—one who is invested with full power to act on behalf of his country.

Christ is God's Ambassador Plenipotentiary from heaven who came to earth to accomplish these things:

He came to represent God. He came with full authority to act for God. He was with full portfolio.

He came to give humanity a report on heaven . . . what it is like, what it takes to reside there, and what preparations need to be made in advance. Heaven is a beautiful, restful, healthy place where there is no sickness, sorrow, or pain. In order to reside there, a person must "lay up . . . treasures in heaven, where neither moth nor rust doth corrupt" (Matt. 6:20).

In order to get to heaven, a person must experience God's reconciliation through the ambassador, Christ. Christ is the one who puts our names on the guest list of heaven.

And the Ambassador Plenipotentiary of God came from heaven to redeem us from our sins so that we would be fit for heaven.

Mission accomplished! He has returned to His native land, heaven. He awaits our coming.

8

The Amen

"These things saith *the Amen,* the faithful and true witness, the beginning of the creation of God" (Rev. 3:14).

Christ is the God of Amen. He is our witness, the amplification of the tenets of our faith, which is rooted and grounded in Him.

In the Hebrew language, the word *amen* means "Truly, verily, so let it be." It is like saying, "So it was, so it is, so let it be." Or, "That's all for now; the truth has been told."

In referring to Christ as "the Amen," we are saying that He is the affirmation, the expression of approval, the source of strength and stability of our faith.

Many church congregations sing the Threefold Amen: "Amen, Amen, Amen." Many of the hymns of the church end with the word *Amen,* as is the case with most prayers. This expression of affirmation or assurance would not be very meaningful without Christ. He puts meaning into the word.

Thomas Chisholm's hymn "Great Is Thy Faithfulness" does about the best job I know in expressing what I consider to be the right reference of Christ as the Amen. In that hymn we find these phrases: "There is no shadow of turning with Thee;/Thou changest not, Thy compassions, they fail not;/As Thou hast been Thou forever wilt be." "Thine own dear presence to cheer and to guide." And, "All I have needed Thy hand hath provided;/Great is Thy faithfulness."

Amen, Amen, Amen.

But there is another threefold amen that every Christian could sing daily because of Christ's affirmation, helpfulness, and righteousness as the Divine One. Daily we can give utterance to:

Our redemption is secure through faith in Him. Amen.

Our daily lives are not without the ministry of His spirit. Amen.

Our heavenly home will be a hope come true. Amen.

So let it be. That is all for now. Have a good day!

9

Ancient of Days

"The Ancient of days came, and judgment was given to the saints of the most High" (Dan. 7:22).

To refer to Christ as the "Ancient of days" is to say, "He was there all the time."

The title "Ancient of days" also brings to mind the thought of Father Time, usually pictured in old almanacs as a very venerable figure, bald, gray bearded, and holding a scythe and an hourglass. The scythe indicates that sooner or later, Father Time will cut down every person in death. The hourglass suggests that time moves on, and time runs out for all of us.

Christ, as our Ancient of days, could be also our Father Time in the spiritual world with the exception that He does not age. He is not old. Human tribes come and go, dynasties rise and fall; and to Him they are like the meteorological changes on an April day. He sits, unchanged—the calm, deliberate monarch of the universe, the ruler of all nations and nature. His robes are as white as snow as befits the immaculate righteousness of His reign. He moves majestically in and through the centuries with the same posture of confidence as a plant owner who surveys the daily production of his employees.

Christ and His kingdom are always in intimate relations with God. For us He is the same yesterday, today, and forever. He is as familiar with the future as with the past and neglects not the present.

Let us repeat with our hearts what Alexander Pope wrote in "The Universal Prayer":

> To thee, whose temple is all space,—
>   Whose altar, earth, sea, and skies,—
> One chorus let all beings raise,
>   All Nature's incense rise!

The Angel of the Presence of the Lord

"And *the angel of his presence* saved them" (Isa. 63:9).

"So he was their Saviour. In all their affliction he was afflicted, and the angel of his presence saved them: in his love and in his pity he redeemed them; and he bare them, and carried them all the days of old" (Isa. 63:8-9).

The designation Angel of His Presence occurs nowhere else in the Bible.

I do not feel that it is a false assumption to assume that the angel here mentioned is none other than Christ. Who else meets such a description? About this angel it was said that He saved them; in His love and in His pity He redeemed them and bare and carried them. I cannot think of anyone who could do this for erring Israel save Christ.

In all their adversity He was no adversary. Doesn't this sound like Christ, our Advocate? He is still in that business, asserting love for the unlovely, guidance for and patience with the lonely.

Thoro Harris seemed cognizant of this when he wrote in his hymn "All That Thrills My Soul":

> Who can cheer the heart like Jesus,
> By his presence all divine?
> True and tender, pure and precious,
> O how blest to call him mine!

Most of the names and titles given to Jesus infer a service of ministry. Truly, throughout the centuries, He went about doing good. Are we content just going about? Going where? Going why? Going alone? No. Never, because Christ wants to accompany us. He stands ready with assurance, love, and succor. Ready to help us add hope and meaning to our journey.

11

Anointed of God

"The kings of the earth set themselves, and the rulers take counsel together, against the Lord, and against his *anointed*" (Ps. 2:2).

Christ is called the Anointed of God and the Anointed One. The former describes the fact of the anointing, the latter the purpose of the anointing.

Historically, the act of anointing was performed in connection with the setting aside of a prophet, priest, or king to his office. Symbolically, it denoted the receiving of spiritual gifts and endowments which would be needed in the performance of duties. When one was anointed, usually with oil, it was assumed that the individual was totally consecrated to the carrying out of those duties.

Christ was fully committed to His mission and, in a unique manner, equipped to carry out the tasks which He came into the world to execute: functioning as high priest, teacher, prophet, and king.

Christ was God stamped. He was set apart in the councils of eternity to perform His multiple roles in our redemption.

In our churches today we ordain persons who have felt called of God and send them forth to perform the tasks that come to them in response to the call. Many times there are commissioning services which add emphasis and awareness to the services to be rendered. Public ordination is usually reserved for ministers of the gospel. Christ's disciples were anointed through their union with Him (2 Cor. 1:21).

I think, however, it is not improper for each Christian to feel a sense of dedication to the calling of life. No task is inconsequential, none too minor; but each and every task should be taken seriously.

Since we no longer need an earthly priest to intercede for us, Christ being our High Priest, is it unreasonable to assume that our lives, too, should be set apart, ordained, and anointed of God? We sing, "Take my life, and let it be/Consecrated, Lord, to Thee."

Truly, we are on a great mission. We need to be God-stamped.

12

Anointed One

"The Spirit of the Lord is upon me, because he hath *anointed* me to preach the gospel" (Luke 4:18).

It is most certainly a high honor to be anointed, anointed of God, or even ordained of men. But the weighty purpose carries much more than honor.

Christ was anointed of God for a purpose. The Hebrew word *Mashiah,* for Messiah, conveys the idea of Christ as Deliverer. The Greek word *Christos,* for Christ, carries the idea of the Anointed One as Savior. He truly was Deliverer and Savior and much more.

Luke 4:18 tells us that Christ's anointment set Him apart for special purposes.

He was anointed to "preach the gospel," the good news, of salvation even to the poor. None was to be excluded from the good tidings. No one should be excluded today. We must see to that.

He was sent to "preach deliverance to the captives." He came to show people how to be free at last from the bondage of sin and Satan. His was an announcement full and free.

He came to heal the brokenhearted, to put all the pieces in their proper places.

His mission was to "set at liberty them that are bruised." He was wounded for our transgression and bruised for iniquities that we might be free from the wounds of sin.

He came also to "preach the acceptable year of the Lord" (v. 19). The blessings promised to Israel of old were summed up in the favors during the Year of the Jubilee which came every fiftieth year, falling on the year after a succession of seven sabbatical years. Those blessings consisted of liberty to all Hebrew bondsmen, ownership of all property which had been sold or leased reverting to the original owner, and the release of debtors from their penalties. It was a joyful year of blessedness.

With Christ, this year and every year is a year of the jubilee.

13

Appointed Emblem

"He that *hath seen me hath seen the Father*" (John 14:9).

Jesus came as the appointed Emblem of God. He came to show us the Father through Himself. He was not playing a role; He was a living example.

This eternal truth is borne out in His life in three special ways.

Through His life of purity, tenderness, devotion to right, and love for all persons, He displayed the moral perfections of God. No one ever came close to Him in this respect.

His healing ministry and triumph over death and the grave set Him apart—alone. His acts of healing were supernatural in effect, and His resurrection from the grave was a "first."

His blessed promises exceeded the bounds of former or latter convenants between persons. He promised eternal life to believers. He has yet to default on these promises. They are as good as the Word of God is good.

My minister told this story one Sunday morning: A chaplain was standing before his men trying to buoy them before the action started. He said, "I wish I knew what to give you this morning."

He paused for a moment, then heard one of the men reply, "Chaplain, just give us tomorrow."

The chaplain remained speechless. He could not promise the morrow.

But Christ can, and it will be better than today.

14
Apostle of Our Profession

"Wherefore, holy brethren, partakers of the heavenly calling, consider the *Apostle* and High Priest of *our profession*, Christ Jesus" (Heb. 3:1).

No other reference is made in the Bible to Christ as the Apostle and High Priest of our profession. We would be so much poorer spiritually if the author of Hebrews had not included such a reference to Him.

The two grand characteristics of Christ's character in this passage designating him as "Apostle" and "High Priest" describe His descent from heaven as God's ambassador of salvation and His reascent to heaven as humanity's interceding High Priest.

The author compares Him with Moses, a natural comparison: the Apostle of our confession with the apostle of the confession of ancient Israel. Jesus came as God's Apostle to call out His people from spiritual Egypt—to lead them into the promised land.

Likewise, there is a threefold exhortation in the passage. We are exhorted to *consider* Him. The word *consider* means much more than a casual glance. It means that we are to fasten our gaze upon Him. We are not to take our eyes off of Him, but we are constantly to turn our eyes upon Jesus. We are to keep Him in our sights with an awakened interest, a sharpened look, and a protracted gaze, not just with occasional snatches.

We are to *compare* Him with ourselves. We are to think of what He did for us and what we are doing for Him. We are to look at His sacrifice and consider our sacrifice, His suffering for us, our suffering for Him.

We are to *contemplate*—meditate upon—the fact that He bore the blows of sin for us; He bore the shame of sin for us; and He beat back the power of Satan for us.

This passage of Scripture tells us our Captain sustained the whole brunt of the assault of sin and conquered it. The Sent One, the Apostle of our Profession, is our victorious Lord.

15

Arbitrator

"Then went the Pharisees, and took counsel how they might entangle him in his talk" (Matt. 22:15).

Arbitrators have always filled an important role in disagreements even though some people have chosen at times to settle disputes by fighting duels. Parents arbitrate differences between children. Children sometimes resort to drawing straws to resolve their problems. Umpires and referees handle the calls necessary in making judgment decisions in athletic contests.

My Sunday School teacher is a retired law professor who has spent much time in labor and management arbitration. He chooses to call it "resolution of conflict." He arbitrates differences, attempting to bring each side to an agreement.

Jesus was a skilled arbitrator. The scribes and Pharisees, who had differences in interpretation and practice of the laws, tried to trap Him. Their interest was not primarily in knowing what was right; they wanted to discredit Jesus. Their courts of justice reeked with prejudice and bias.

It is hard to give a satisfactory decision as to truth if one is a party to the dispute. Neither is reason always capable of wading through the evidence, especially if a person is left to be the sole arbitrator of personal duties.

Jesus, having all knowledge and power, can be purely objective. Since He is love incarnate, He can quiet the restless pulse of care. If humanity is left to arbitrate solely human acts one toward another, Shakespeare may have been right when he wrote,

There shall your swords and lances arbitrate
The swelling difference of your settle hate.

But the Christian knows a fair and just Arbitrator, Jesus, the Christ. Without fear, favor, or fury, Christ can, when asked, move into the troubles between persons and calm the troubled waters, bringing peace and love. He is always available.

16

Artist

"Why take ye thought for raiment? Consider the lilies of the field, how they grow; they toil not, neither do they spin" (Matt. 6:28).

I have heard that a great artist checked the skill of his apprentices by how well they could draw a circle. Circles are hard to draw.

Christ's heart circled the globe. He had the soul of an artist. He could see the beautiful, perceive the minute, feel the delicate, and respond to the spirit.

He was to the soul of persons what Michelangelo was to art. As Michelangelo carved David from rough marble, Christ shaped Simon Peter from roughness of character. As Michelangelo painted the ceiling of the Sistine Chapel with imperishable beauty, Christ touched up the lives of broken souls with immortal glory.

Now, back to the idea of a circle in conjunction with an artist. Edwin Markham wrote a poem entitled "Outwitted," which underscores just how great an artist a person can become while associated in spirit and love with the Master Artist:

He drew a circle that shut me out—
Heretic, rebel, a thing to flout.
But Love and I had the wit to win:
We drew a circle that took him in!

We should be most grateful that in life we as Christians can enjoy the works of art which have been produced through the centuries by sensitive souls inspired by the Master Artist, while, at the same time, we are privileged to work with the Master Artist. Isn't that the best of two worlds? It is kinda like having your cake and eating it too.

17

The Ascended One

"It came to pass, while he blessed them, he was parted from them, and carried up into heaven" (Luke 24:51).

Christ, the One who descended from heaven's glory, became the Ascended One in glory.

In the Old Testament (Gen. 5:21-24), Enoch, the father of Methuselah, lived 365 years and "walked with God: and he was not; for God took him." The author of Hebrews tells us, "By faith Enoch was translated that he should not see death; and was not found, because God had translated him" (11:5). Enoch ascended from earth to heaven but did not pass through the portals of death. Jesus, however, passed through the portals of the grave to walk again upon the earth and to take His departure from earth by being carried up into heaven, borne on a cloud.

This was His occasion for going home. He left His earthly home to return to His heavenly home as He had come from His heavenly home to His earthly home. (He came to us from God; He went from us to God.) He came into the world differently from other people; He left differently from all who die.

His going home was not an occasion of a cloud of dust as people of earth ride off into the western horizon. It was not an occasion of the whirring of motors as is so commonly heard at airports where planes carrying our loved ones to distant destinations taxi down runways. It was the occasion of a finished job, a completed task. He was going back to report to the Father who had sent Him. He carried in His portfolio a suggestion that He should prepare places for His children and, at the Father's own time, return to receive them unto Himself. He has gone thus to prepare the places and the way.

Angels sang when He came to earth. Surely they must have burst forth into a celestial "Hallelujah" as He came again to the portals of heaven.

18

Author and Finisher of Faith

"Looking unto Jesus the *author and finisher of our faith*" (Heb. 12:2).

In this passage life is described as a race to be run, an enduring struggle. It is to be run with faith and patience, with eyes fixed on Jesus as the Author and Finisher of our faith.

No race can be run well without keeping the head high and eyes fixed straight ahead. No farmer can drill a straight row of corn while looking backward, sideward, or downward. No carpenter or brick mason can fashion a straight wall without a plumb line. For the Christian, Jesus is the leader, the Pioneer, the Trailblazer, the Example, and the Pattern Man, our Supreme Example. He has been down the path. He ran his race while on earth. He had faith as He took on the sins of the world and sin's captain, Satan. He had faith while in Gethsemane and while on the cross.

By His example, Jesus has given us the Ariadne's thread of faith to help us through the labyrinthine temptations of the world. He did not leave us after giving us the command but stayed with us, His people, to the finish line, and to victory and reward.

As our leader, Pioneer of our faith, He submitted to the cross without reservation. As the Perfecter of faith, He is now exalted at the right hand of God in order to exalt His faithful followers.

We together with other Christians have confessed our confidence in the Author of Faith using the words of Ray Palmer.

> My faith looks up to Thee,/Thou Lamb of Calvary,
> Saviour divine!
> Now hear me while I pray,
> Take all my guilt away,
> O let me from this day
> Be wholly Thine!

Palmer concluded the third stanza with these appropriate words, "Nor let me ever stray/From Thee aside."

Let us look constantly, with fixed gaze, unto Jesus, the Leader, Pioneer, Example, and Perfecter of our faith. Then we can win our race!

19

Author of Eternal Salvation

"Being made perfect, he became the *author of eternal salvation* unto all them that obey him" (Heb. 5:9).

It is amazing how many different roles some competent actors can play. That amazement fades into insignificance when we think of the many roles Christ lived out. In speaking of Him as our "author of eternal salvation," we are identifying Him as the source: the Procuring One, the One who made it all possible.

I have found in life that many times it is not what one knows but *who* one knows that causes doors to open. Once I was greatly favored by my pastor, who opened a door that provided an unusual relationship for me personally and most significantly for Belmont College for a quarter of a century. The friendship might have germinated, grown, and developed without my pastor, but I doubt it; and I feel the proper and timely introduction made much difference.

However, the observance of the church's ordinance, good deeds, or friendship with the clergy will not open the door to eternal salvation. Only Christ can do that. Many may point to the way, but the door can be opened only by the Author of eternal salvation.

Through Christ's experiences and sufferings in Gethsemane and at Calvary, He perfected His earthly efforts of redemption. It was wading through these sufferings in human form and going through temptation and death that brought Him finally up to glory. He gained the internal attributes of a perfect high priest and did for all humanity what the Levitical priest did symbolically.

Christ was the cause of temporal salvation once for Lazarus, but Lazarus would die again. He needed, through faith and obedience, eternal salvation which Christ provides for all who obey Him. It comes through trust and obedience, for there is no other way. These two things will lead us safely onward and upward through the doors to glory.

20

Authoritative One

"He taught them as one having authority" (Matt. 7:29).

My father spoke with authority. I tried him out once, much to my regret. The punishment was memorable and cathartic. I learned that I should respect him: his words and his instructions. He expected that of me. He expected the same respect to be shown Mother, and both commanded that respect.

Jesus spoke with greater authority. He was truth, and His words were true. He did not teach by using an overkill of quotation marks. He did know the teachings of the Old Testament, the rabbis, and tradition, but His teaching exceeded them all. He knew whereof He spoke. His words were final, and those who heard Him had that feeling of finality.

As One speaking with authority, He called forth respect and obedience. His utterances were authoritative in content, tone, and manner and, therefore, gave Him the right to command obedience, to expect action, and to direct people's lives.

The disciples felt His authoritative nature. He simply and unaffectedly called, and they left their families, friends, and successful careers to respond immediately. (See Matt. 4:20-22; Matt. 9:9; and Luke 5:27-28.)

Our response to the commands of Christ should carry the same application and challenge as expressed in the last verse of the poem "Dear Lord and Father of Mankind" by John Greenleaf Whittier:

> In simple trust like theirs who heard,
> Beside the Syrian sea,
> The gracious calling of the Lord,
> Let us, like them, without a word,
> Rise up and follow Thee.

21

Awesome Person

"But as many as received him, to them gave he *power* to become the sons of God" (John 1:12).

Jesus was not thought to be a physically awesome person. People looked at Him as a mere man, whose stature was not such as to make an unusual impression. But the Scripture refutes this first impression, for many whom He encountered were amazed and astonished at His words of authority and power. (See Luke 4:22,36-37; Luke 5:26.)

Awesomeness seems to attach itself to persons whose physical appearance is striking or huge, whose knowledge is full and frightening, whose power is extensive and usable, or whose money "talks" and produces wonders, mostly selfish.

Two individuals from history come to mind as being physically awesome: Goliath, the giant of the Philistines, and Temuchin, of the Mongols. Goliath was nine feet, six inches tall. He wore an armor of iron and brass, and his coat weighed 5,000 shekels (or 200 pounds). His iron spearhead weighed 600 shekels (or 25 pounds). What a monster of a man! The other, Temuchin, whose name was changed in 1206 to Genghis Khan, or the "Perfect Warrior," was known by his savage warfare. No opponent ever successfully challenged the mighty Genghis Khan. His empire stretched east and west across Asia.

Neither Goliath nor Genghis Khan could do what Christ, the Awesome Person, did. In the Gospel of Matthew we are told that He gave His disciples power to cast out evil spirits, to heal every disease and every sickness (Matt. 10:1). John, in his Gospel, tells us that as many as received Him, to them He gave power to become children of God. What awesome power! Then, too, even the winds and the waves obeyed His voice. Death yielded up its victims when He spoke.

People feared Goliath and Genghis Khan, but through the centuries, people have loved Christ, the Awesome One. What is the difference? Goliath and Genghis Khan devoted their strength and skill to killing people, while Christ lived and died to save people. He is still in the saving business.

Babe-Baby

"They came with haste, and found Mary, and Joseph, and the *babe* lying in a manger" (Luke 2:16).

It has been said that all the world loves a baby, but that has not always been true, especially of Herod when Christ was born of the virgin Mary.

Infanticide was practiced in the Graeco-Roman world. Children were killed, especially girls, weaklings, and the deformed, as a move to control the population growth. Some were sold or left exposed. Frequently, they were used for illegal sexual purposes and mendicancy. It was not unusual for a soldier-husband to leave word with his pregnant wife that if the child was a girl to get rid of her.[2]

Again, the birth of Christ put a new emphasis on a common experience and proclaimed to all ages that the birth of a child is a God-given privilege. Only God can give life, and all life belongs to Him.

Ages of piety and adoration have obscured the simple beginning of our Lord. He was not born full grown. His mother experienced the birth pangs of childbearing. He went through the stages of development and growth. He came as a baby. That is the way He made His entrance into human life, not as a king amid the riches of the world but as a baby born of humble parents who took a risk.

He was carried in Mary's womb, totally dependent upon her for life. Then He came out of her womb as a baby, an independent individual, an innocent infant. At birth His life separated itself from total dependence upon His mother, and He began the growing process of self-development.

Although we know very little about Jesus' infancy and childhood, we can be grateful that he did come to us as a babe—that he knew the growing pains and the joys of childhood. Every child is a miracle. But when we look at this babe and realize that in Him God has come to us, we are awed.

2. S. Angus, *The Environment of Early Christianity* (New York: Charles Scribner's Sons, 1932), p. 48.

23

Baptizer

"He that cometh after me is mightier than I, . . . he shall *baptize* you with the Holy Ghost, and with fire" (Matt. 3:11).

Once, while visiting the Holy Land, my party and I found ourselves at the place generally designated as the site where Jesus was baptized of John in the Jordan River. There was a group from the midwestern section of our country performing the rites of baptism for each other. My assumption was that it was being done with some nostalgic feeling of closer association with our Lord because of the tradition of the place.

Even though the wording of the passage in John's Gospel seems to infer that Jesus officiated in the act of baptism, He did not, but His disciples did that as part of their discipleship involvement. He did approve of John's baptism by being baptized of Him, and He did endorse baptism as a symbolic act of repentance from sin and "a death, burial, and resurrection to a newness of life," as pictured in the immersion process.

There is an old maxim that says, "What one does by another, he does himself." From that standpoint Jesus was a baptizer. But from another standpoint He was not a baptizer. He baptized not in water, for if He had done so, some of those receiving baptism from Him might have felt favored over others. He performed a greater baptism—He baptized His followers with the Holy Spirit. Such an immersion would provide for His followers the presence of the informing Spirit.

I believe that whenever the baptismal waters are stirred, Christ is both pleased and honored. Christ must have pleasure when His children follow His example. His gift of the Holy Spirit is another token of His utmost and careful concern for His followers.

The main question, therefore, is not where or by whom were we baptized, but what does our baptism signify, and what does it evoke from us?

24

Beginning and Ending

"I am Alpha and Omega, *the beginning and the ending,* saith the Lord, which is, and which was, and which is to come, the Almighty" (Rev. 1:8).

When Jesus is referred to as "Alpha and Omega" in these passages, there is an appositional phrase, "the beginning and the ending," which underscores a highly pertinent aspect of the subject.

The phrase "beginning and ending" denotes a continuation, a connection or the inseparability of the beginning from the ending. In other words, the total sweep is brought to the attention of the reader. Both are to be thought of at the same time along with all in between. An appositional phrase is therefore the layers in between. The subject gives the proper name, the phrase, the function.

My father was accustomed to saying to me: "Son, whatever you start, stay with it until you have finished. Do not stop in the middle of a task. Finish the row you are hoeing. Finish your work before you think of playing." I was cautioned about letting up; admonished to avoid distractions and deviations from the task and purpose.

The life and gift of grace in Christ begins, continues, and goes on and on, to wherever and whatever the end might be. Christ never steps aside or goes away from His task. He ushers us into the Kingdom of grace, and He will usher us into glory.

In announcing his candidacy for reelection as President, Ronald Reagan stated he did not feel he had finished the job. He wanted to be given another four-year term so he could finish what he had begun.

Thank God, Jesus was able to finish His task, but He cannot finish His redemptive mission in the human heart without the full consent of the individual. He wants to be the Beginning and Ending, but you and I make that decision. He stands ready to help us complete, to fill full, our lives.

25

Beginning of the Creation of God (Creator)

"Unto the angel of the church of the Laodiceans write; These things saith the Amen, the faithful and true witness, *the beginning of the creation of God*" (Rev. 3:14).

Children "tell it like it is." They sound off of the top of their minds without thinking ahead. Letters to God written by children are very interesting and provocative.

> Dear God, I'm afraid at night more than in the day. So, if you could keep the sun on longer, that would be a good thing (Joanne).

> Dear God, if you made the sun, the moon, and the stars as well as the rivers and lakes, you must have had a lot of big equipment (Paul).

When we think of the creation we are usually awestruck. How did God do it? He made something from nothing. He spoke, and the worlds came into existence. He had no mechanical equipment, no computers, and no task forces.

Our Scripture passage refers to Christ as "the beginning of the creation." Some ancient manuscripts have the word *church* instead of "Christ," but that does not correspond to the truths in John 1:3 and Hebrews 1:2. Only Christ is the head of creation. He was the creative force and is the Ruler and Prince of earth. That was one of His preincarnate relationships to the universe.

When I think of the creative acts of Christ in the beginning, I am more like the child. It is so mysterious, so comprehensive, so overpowering. Who but God and His Son could create such wonders: the beautiful world, the lovely heavens, and the laws that govern both?

May Riley Smith wrote:

> In the dark silence of her chambers low
> March works out sweeter things than mortals know.

And Christ knows all about it. He did it.

26

Begotten of the Father

"We beheld his glory, the glory as of *the only begotten of the Father*" (John 1:14).

I had just turned sixteen years of age when I left home to go to college. Upon my occasional return, invariably someone would say to me, "You must be Riley Gabhart's son. I haven't met you, but you look very much like him." And, of course, my answer would be yes.

When John referred to Jesus as the "begotten of the Father," He was not trying to establish His sonship necessarily. But He was saying that only the begotten son of God could act as God acted, talk as God talked, love as God loved. In other words, Jesus bore the weight of the glory of God.

As the only begotten of God, Christ was full of grace and truth. Grace reveals God's love; truth reveals God's light. These features were a part of Him from the beginning. But through His actions they became transparent. He was so full, so charted—today we might say "so overflowing"—that the glory which shone from Him gave the apostles the conception that it was that of the only begotten Son, for who else could He be?

Jesus came to reveal the Father. He dwelt among men—"pitched His tent"—among the people.

B. B. McKinney, one of Southern Baptists' greatest hymn composers, wrote these words in the first stanza of his hymn "Glorious Is Thy Name":

> Blessed Saviour, we adore Thee,
> We Thy love and grace proclaim;
> Thou art mighty, Thou art holy,
> Glorious is Thy matchless name!

Jesus wore the robes of grace and mercy and bore the truths that make us free with much poise and peace.

27

Beloved of God

"To the praise of the glory of his grace, wherein he hath made us accepted in the *beloved*" (Eph. 1:6).

Can you remember the times you served as distributor of the gifts around the Christmas tree in your home? I have watched the joy on the face of our granddaughter as she would take each gift to the proper person. She seemed to be as happy as if she had given the gifts, and almost as happy as if she were receiving them.

I, too, have run some errands of similar nature, distributing things to the members of my wife's Sunday School class or her DAR group so that I would have the privilege of making their acquaintance. What a joy!

Jesus was the distributor and dispenser of God's gifts to us. All of God's gifts come special delivery—even better than the most efficient of our delivery services. No gift is the same after it has been warmed by the kind hands of Jesus.

God so graciously bestows gifts upon His children. It is His plan that in the Beloved of God, the Giver and the recipient meet. What a rare and gracious occasion. For it is in Him, Jesus, that grace and salvation are found.

Think what it means to be on the receiving end of God's goodness and to have those good things brought personally by His Son. How would you feel—I know how I would feel—if you were to receive a message from the president of the United States saying he was sending a gift to you by his own personal ambassador? Wouldn't that be a thrill?

Frederick Hosmer captured this thought fully when he wrote in his poem "The Indwelling God":

Oh, gift of gifts,
Oh, grace of grace,
That God should condescend
To make thy heart his dwelling-place,
And be thy daily friend!

35

28

Beloved Son of God

"Behold a voice out of the cloud, which said, This is *my beloved Son*, in whom I am well pleased" (Matt. 17:5).

Most sons and daughters like to hear praise and commendation from their parents. I savored such times with my parents. As the father of three daughters, I saw how praise seemed to give them a lift. There is an old saying, "Honey traps more flies than vinegar." That is a bit extreme, but human beings yearn for approval. They are attracted and drawn upward by praise.

On two different occasions when God spoke of Jesus, "This is my beloved Son, in whom I am well pleased," He was not only putting His stamp of approval and approbation on what Christ was doing; He was saying: Jesus is greatly beloved by me, dear to my heart. His approval meant that the purpose and work of Christ met with divine favor.

When John baptized Christ in the Jordan River, the voice of the Spirit of God, saying, "This is my beloved Son, in whom I am well pleased" (Matt. 3:17), was the Father's means of stamping His approval for the beginning of Christ's ministry. God was saying that Jesus' work and mission met His standards. It was a celestial commendation of Christ to His contemporaries. It was His ordination to the high office of the Messiah of Israel and the Savior of the world.

In Matthew 17:5 when the same voice spoke the same words of commendation out of the cloud on the mount of transfiguration, three additional words were added: "Hear ye him." To those disciples with Christ, the voice was saying that Christ would speak with a divine authority for all which He would teach, all which He would do, and all which He would require of them.

At Christ's birth heavenly messengers identified the babe, and now, on these two additional occasions, His identity is made with the preexistent Logos for assurance to Him and to His followers in the trying days to come.

If God took time to praise Christ, why shouldn't we? Why not right now!

Bishop of Souls

"Ye were as sheep going astray; but are now returned unto the Shepherd and *Bishop of your souls*" (1 Pet. 2:25).

A little girl, when asked how she was able to ward off the devil, said, "When the devil knocks at the door of my heart, I take Jesus by the hand. I ask him to go with me to answer the door. When I open the door, the devil sees me and Jesus standing hand in hand, and he says, 'Excuse me, I must be at the wrong place.' He leaves."

Jesus plays a similar role with all believers. As Bishop of souls he is the spiritual Overseer of His flock. He is the Good Shepherd looking after the flock including the one that goes astray. His Holy Spirit is the "Paraclete" to guide us into all truth.

Since Christians have been cleansed by His blood, loosed from their sins, and made to become kings and priests, Christ is, to them, their Bishop. He wears no particular garb as bishops of the Greek, Roman, or Anglican churches. He wears only the robes of righteousness. Like the bishops of those churches, He does have special duties and powers over the priests. It is His purpose and mission to see that His followers grow and mature into the fullness of Himself.

His diocese is the kingdom of God where the rules of love, grace, mercy, and forgiveness place supreme responsibilities upon the priesthood of believers.

C. Austin Miles, the hymn writer of the early part of the twentieth century, expresses in the chorus of his hymn "In the Garden" what I consider to be a warm and pertinent relationship that exists between the Bishop of souls and His followers:

> And He walks with me, and He talks with me,
> And He tells me I am His own;
> And the joy we share, as we tarry there,
> None other has ever known.

What a glorious relationship. It makes the heart sing!

30

One Accused of Blasphemy

"Why doth this man thus *speak blasphemies?*" (Mark 2:7).

In my opinion, it is the height of blasphemy to call Jesus a blasphemer. But the scribes did.

In Capernaum friends came to Jesus bringing one sick of palsy but had to uncover the roof of the house to let down the sick man's bed. Seeing their faith, Jesus not only healed the man but said, "Son, thy sins be forgiven thee" (Mark 2:5). That really angered the scribes. To them, only God could forgive sins, and Jesus had taken unto Himself the prerogative of God. To them that was blasphemy, and they said so.

Why did they thus act? There was professional jealousy. Jesus was gaining much popularity, and theirs was waning. Quickly they spoke up; they wanted to be heard. "Why doth this man thus speak blasphemies? who can forgive sins but God only?" (Mark 2:7). Then, too, they stood on their impregnable legal principles and allowed no deviation. They blew a grand experience through envy and lack of perception.

To blaspheme is to revile impiously a sacred trust. It is to speak irreverently or in a defamatory manner. We may be guilty in our Christian demeanor; for whenever we sing: "Jesus is all the world to me," and "I'll go where You want me to go, dear Lord," then allow the weather to dictate our worship attendance at God's house, our innocence flees. In such action, we are like the young lover who wrote his girl friend saying, "I love you so much, I would swim the Hellespont or climb the highest mountain for one glimpse of your beautiful face. I'll be over tonight to see you if it doesn't rain."

The scribes gave no attention to Jesus' divinity. Their self-sufficiency and absorption in materialistic and legalistic trivialities shut their eyes to the truth that He was God manifested in the flesh. Truly, they were the blasphemers, not Jesus. Are we akin to them in any way?

31

Blessed and Only Potentate

"Which in his times he shall shew, who is the *blessed and only Potentate*, the King of kings, and the Lord of lords" (1 Tim. 6:15).

A potentate is one with great power, usually feared by some and admired by others. One might classify the great Mongol of China, Kublai Khan, and even Hitler as ones who have claimed such power, but never could the words *blessed and only* be placed before their names. Such words go only with Christ. Christ is the only One in the world possessed of independent right and absolute sovereignty, and this is brought about by the fact of His coming again with subsequent events such as the resurrection of the dead, the glorification of His own, and the damnation of the wicked.

Power in the hands of a potentate denotes great and excessive possibility. Lord Acton said that "power corrupts, and absolute power corrupts absolutely." Such power poses a great liability, certainly, if in the wrong hands; but in Christ's hands, it becomes a lovable asset.

Since there is only one God, there is only one blessed and only Potentate—His Beloved Son. He is worthy of all power, glory, and honor.

Isaac Watts wrote a hymn in 1719 entitled *Jesus Shall Reign,* and the words of the first and last stanzas seem most appropriate here:

> Jesus shall reign where'er the sun
> Does his successive journeys run;
> His kingdom spread from shore to shore,
> Till moons shall wax and wane no more.

> Let every creature rise and bring
> Peculiar honors to our King;
> Angels descend with songs again,
> And earth repeat the loud amen.

No earthly potentate ever had such a kingdom or was ever capable of handling such a kingdom—only the blessed and only Potentate. All praise and honor are due Him, for He is the fairest of all, ruler of all nature.

Branch of David

"Behold, the days come, saith the Lord, that I will raise unto *David a righteous Branch,* and a King shall reign and prosper, and shall execute judgment and justice in the earth" (Jer. 23:5).

The study of a family's genealogy and the eventual establishment of a family tree are interesting. My name, "Gabhart," is a German name, a derivative of "Gebhardt." At the height of the Hitler regime in Germany there was a Paul Gebhardt in Hitler's hierarchy. My grandmother on my mother's side was a Davenport. In the study of past connections, one of the Davenports was judge when John Brown, the American abolitionist, was tried and convicted of treason at Harper's Ferry, West Virginia, in the fall of 1859. Another Davenport stood on the riverbank as Robert Fulton's first steamboat sailed up the river and exclaimed, "Well, she moves, doesn't she?"

Now, let us take a look at the genealogy of Christ—a Branch of David—from David's line. Continuity is shown here. The word *branch* might well be translated "shoot or sprout," for either describes that which is connected to the root and contains as it were the springs of life.

By saying that Christ came as a Branch of David, Jeremiah was probably inferring that Christ came from human stock, showing His humanity; that He was of the house and lineage of David; and that He came quietly and grew gradually into manhood. His coming did not astonish the world with a sudden apparition or majesty. Coming as He did shows a close relationship to the circumstances of the world of sin and suffering.

There is no contradiction in saying that Christ was a Branch of David and then hearing Christ say in John 15 that He is the vine, and we are the branches. In the first part Christ's physical lineage is given, while in the second part, our spiritual relationship to him is described.

We could say, in modern parlance, he was well born, and his pedigree was good. But how much better it is to say that His spiritual connections were impeccable.

It is most important that He be a Branch in our spiritual family tree. We need His connections with the Father.

Branch of Righteousness

"In those days, and at that time, will I cause the *Branch of righteousness* to grow up unto David; and he shall execute judgment and righteousness in the land" (Jer. 33:15).

Yesterday we commented on Christ as a Branch of David, and today we are dealing with the statement that Christ is the "Branch of Righteousness." The relationship Christ bore with the house and lineage of David is significant, but being designated as the Branch of Righteousness is more significant. Each designation becomes increasingly important.

These designations remind me of a statement I have sincerely made to some of my friends in meeting their children for the first time, "It is amazing and great that each succeeding generation is improving over the previous one." How true that is in reference to Christ.

The ruin in Israel was due largely to the bad conduct of her leaders. Christ is the only perfectly righteous King, and that should call forth from us honor and obedience. Such a king as He deserves loyal service. As a righteous King, He is a type of what the righteous subjects should be.

Christ's government is built on righteousness. The character of the administration of His spiritual kingdom reflects the character of the ruling monarch, our King of kings. As a righteous King, He will do away with injustice and greed and rule with right and love, destroying wrong as He leads His subjects into the abundant life.

How grateful we are that He is not a descendant of Ahab, who stole Naboth's vineyard. How grateful we are that He was not like David in taking Bathsheba and having her husband, Uriah the Hittite, placed in the forefront of the army to be killed. How grateful we must be that He is not like the jealous Herod who had male infants slain. His rule of righteousness has made a vast difference.

He is not only a righteous King, but He is our priest-king, performing both functions so that we might grow into the likeness of the priest-king.

Bread (Living) from Heaven

"But my Father giveth you the true *bread from heaven*" (John 6:32).

It is true that we shall earn our living (our bread) by the sweat of our brow, but as Dr. Ellis Fuller, president of the Southern Baptist Theological Seminary in Louisville, Kentucky, said during the early forties, "Some people wouldn't accept manna from heaven unless it was buttered first." That was somewhat the problem Jesus had with the Jews as related by John's Gospel.

The manna that had come to the Israelites under Moses did not come from Moses but from God. The manna was characterized as life-giving, satisfying, and abundant.

When Jesus came, the Jews thought of celestial food, not of Jesus as giving life to the world. But on this occasion Jesus speaks one of His great I ams—"I am that bread of life" (v. 48) which will sustain your spiritual lives and satisfy the deepest wants of all people. His bread never runs out; there is ample for all at all times.

Just as the physical body hungers when healthy, so does the soul hunger. We have an ineradicable desire for the highest good, life beyond, which cannot be satisfied by mere earthly provisions. It is interesting that frequently carnal or physical indulgence can often cause spiritual emaciation.

The bread we eat daily sustains physical life, but the bread of Christ gives birth to eternal life. He is the manna—food—for a starving world. He came from the glory of heaven to the shame of earth to bring the living Bread to all who would partake, so they could be lifted from the shame of earth to the glory of heaven.

Just as we refer to bread as the "staff of life," we are more than justified in referring to Christ, our living Bread, as the staff and anchor of our spiritual lives.

"O taste and see that the Lord is good" (Ps. 34:8).

35

Bridegroom

"The days will come, when the *bridegroom* shall be taken from them, and then shall they fast" (Matt. 9:15).

Matthew, the author of the first book of the New Testament, employs a figure from nuptial ceremonies, bridegroom, in setting forth a relationship to Christ. A wedding is a happy occasion, and the bride and bridegroom are the most important characters of the ceremony and usually the happiest.

When the question was raised as to why Christ's disciples did not fast, Jesus spoke of a wedding ceremony and stressed that there was no time for fasting while the celebration was in progress. There should be joy and feasting instead. Guests at the wedding feast should be happy, not sad. The presence of the bridegroom should indicate the festivities were in progress.

In Matthew 25:10, in the parable of the wise and foolish virgins, the author is pointing out with urgency the need to be watchful and prepared, or else the door will be closed, and the wedding will proceed without an open-door policy for all.

Since no one knows the hour or day of Christ's coming, the admonition is quite clear, "Watch therefore, for ye know neither the day nor the hour wherein the Son of man cometh" (Matt. 25:13). Life is filled with expectancy regarding His return. But life must go on; we dare not sit down and wait. We must not, however, lose our enthusiasm regarding the coming of the Bridegroom.

A young man, about to be married, was fidgeting and nervously awaiting the wedding moment in the office of a minister. The minister noticed the groom but did not query him until the young man said, "I've lost, I've lost."

"Young man, have you lost your car keys?"

"No, preacher. I've lost my enthusiasm."

Let us anticipate His coming with joy, serving Him with the same joy, excitement, and enthusiasm until He comes.

Bright and Morning Star

"I am the root and the offspring of David, and the *bright and morning star*" (Rev. 22:16).

There is a rather humorous, catchy question that goes, "What happens to the pieces when the day breaks?" The answer, "They go into 'mourning.'" I think that answer is for the pessimist.

Are you grateful that Christ, our Savior, is the bright and Morning Star and that "mourning" becomes "morning" with Him? We tend to say morning and evening, while He says evening and morning. He is always pointing us to the dawn of a new day, a good day ahead because the darkness has vanished silently.

The morning star heralds the day. It is a symbol of promise: His presence and guidance. And that is what Christ is, the bright and Morning Star to the soul. Truly, a new day dawned for humankind when Christ was born, and a new day dawns for the individual heart when Christ comes in.

Aren't you grateful that Christ is never referred to as the "setting sun" or the "shades of night." As the Light of the world, He banishes darkness, and as the bright and Morning Star, He ushers in a new day of hope and light.

Reginald Heber wrote a hymn in the early nineteenth century entitled "Brightest and Best," and it is sung to the hymn tune MORNING STAR:

> Brightest and best of the sons of the morning,
> Dawn on our darkness and lend us thine aid;
> Star of the East, the horizon adorning,
> Guide where our infant Redeemer is laid.

As sailors of old followed the stars in the sky, we can follow the bright and Morning Star throughout the days of our lives, for He will be an unseen presence on our pilgrimage. Hold fast to him. Look up!

37
Brightness of the Glory of God

"Who being the *brightness of his glory,* and the express image of his person" (Heb. 1:3).

Let's think about brightness for a moment. The brightest thing we know is the sun. It is 93,000,000 miles from the earth, one astronomical unit. Sirius is a much brighter star than the sun, but its great distance from the earth means that it would take ten billion stars as bright as Sirius to equal the sunlight. In talking about distance, think of this: Sirius is 8.8 light-years from the earth, and one light-year equals 5,878,000,000,000 miles. But the star Rigel is 466 light-years from the earth.

Now that your head and mine are swimming, let us think about Christ as the brightest of the bright. He is the effulgence, the raying forth, the radiance of the glory of God. This tells of His transcendent glory. He is the brightest revelation, the eternal radiation of the splendor from God. This talks of Christ not just as an abstract action but as an independent existence also. Bright in His own right.

This unusual statement about Christ occurs nowhere else in the New Testament. It smites the human mind with awe. All of the brightness of the glory of humankind cannot equal the Son's brightness of the glory of God. As dewdrops and diamonds sparkle, the Son of God sparkles with inestimable brightness. No one is able to estimate the amount of candle power in His brightness.

His brightness, however, is in His revelation of God and of Himself. He is the image of the invisible God, and no one has seen God, but the only begotten Son has declared, or shown, Him. And the most wonderful thing about the brightness of the glory of God in Christ is not measured in terms of His distance from us but in terms of His nearness to us. He is nearer than the air we breathe, "a friend that sticketh closer than a brother" (Prov. 18:24). Then, too, we can reflect His light. Thank God.

38

Bringer of Joy

"I am come that they might have life, and that they might have it *more abundantly"* (John 10:10).

The world into which Christ came was a sad world. The Pharisees didn't do much to improve the joy that should come from religion. They were "killjoys," looking for the bad and the worst. But into that world came the Bringer of joy, Christ.

During the early days of our nation, Paul Revere rode to shout the news that the British were coming. But when Christ's advent was near, the heavenly host sang joyfully of His coming, and today we sing,

> Joy to the world! the Lord is come;
> Let earth receive her King;
> Let every heart prepare Him room,
> And heaven and nature sing.

We also sing,

> Joyful, joyful, we adore Thee,
> God of glory, Lord of love;
> Hearts unfold like flow'rs before Thee,
> Opening to the sun above.
> Melt the clouds of sin and sadness;
> Drive the dark of doubt away;
> Giver of immortal gladness,
> Fill us with the light of day!

It is said that just after Napoleon had fought at Waterloo, a signal corpsman began to send the news of the battle across the English Channel. He had sent the words *Wellington Defeated* before the fog settled over the channel for the night. He could not finish, and all England was bathed in gloom. But when the sun came up the next morning, he continued his signaling, and this was the message: "Wellington Defeated Napoleon."

What a difference that one additional word made. A world of difference is made in our lives when the word *Jesus* is added.

Brother of His Disciples

"Whosoever shall do the will of my Father which is in heaven, the same is *my brother,* and sister, and mother" (Matt. 12:50).

There was a very strong brotherly relationship between Jesus and His disciples. They were a close-knit brotherhood. One could correctly call them a "breed apart" from the Essenes of his day, or the Benedictines of the sixth century, or the Bridge-Building Brotherhood in south France during the latter half of the twelfth century, whose job it was to build bridges and keep ferries.

I think it would be more correct to call Jesus and His brother disciples a "brotherhood of burning hearts." They were, as Wordsworth once remarked, "Partners in faith and brothers in distress." Jesus said that His brothers were those who did the will of God. His life was motivated by a strong desire to do the Father's will, and His disciples should be likewise motivated.

Those who claim membership in this "brotherhood of burning hearts" will never think in terms of being a brother's keeper but of being a brother's brother, an equal. The ground is level at the foot of the cross. There are no different levels.

John Greenleaf Whittier wrote a hymn in the mid-nineteenth century entitled "O Brother Man, Fold to Thy Heart," and the third stanza sets forth a viable challenge for us today.

> Follow with rev'rent steps the great example
> Of Him whose holy work was doing good;
> So shall the wide earth seem our Father's temple,
> Each loving life a psalm of gratitude.

As disciples we can claim Christ as our brother, and we can call all who follow Him our brothers and sisters in Christ. He is the one who binds our hearts in Christian love. I do have a Big Brother.

40
Brothers' Brother

"Is not this the carpenter, the son of Mary, the *brother of James, and Joses, and of Judah, and Simon?*" (Mark 6:3).

The brothers of Jesus were named James, Joses, Jude, and Simon. What happens when five brothers get together? It would be hard to predict. Maybe they got along quite well, but maybe they didn't. Mark's Gospel says the same about His brothers as His neighbors and sisters, "They were offended at him." Maybe so!

Later, however, there is a general belief that James, His brother, is the one who wrote the Epistle of James and that the Jude who wrote the Book of Jude was also one of His brothers. If these assumptions are true, a cursory glance at the Epistle of James and the Book of Jude would certainly indicate that whatever caused them to be offended must have been long overcome because they both seem to be totally committed to Him. Look at James 1:1; 5:9; Jude 1:1,4,21,25.

It has been said that brothers will fight each other, then fight for each other. It has also been said that blood is thicker than water. A blood brother-brother relationship is a strong one. I have missed that experience in my family, for my only brother died when I was three years of age; but I have observed the relationship in other families.

When I think of Jesus and His brothers, there comes to my mind the story of a man passing down the road and seeing on the other side a lad carrying another lad. It appeared as if the one carrying the other was overloaded, whereupon the traveler remarked, "Sonny, isn't that lad you are carrying too heavy for you?"

"Oh, no, sir," came the reply. "He's not heavy. He is my brother."

It is never too late to think of our present family relationships and to try to deepen all relationships in accordance with brotherly and sisterly love. Love never fails (1 Cor. 13:8).

41

Brother of Sisters

"Is not this the carpenter, the son of Mary, . . . and are not *his sisters* here with us?" (Mark 6:3).

I grew up the younger brother of two sisters, one just eighteen months older than I. She and I spent much time together. Once at the country schoolhouse we were detained by a "bully." We had been told by our parents to come home immediately after school, but the bully would do something to prevent us from leaving. My sister got "fed up" with his antics and hit him rather hard with her metal dinner bucket. He let us go, and she grew mightly in my esteem.

I wonder if Jesus' sisters ever had to defend Him. I wonder what their relationship was with Him. Did they have the normal brother-sister experiences? Did they ever argue or bicker? Probably!

Unfortunately, we do not know how many sisters Jesus had (Matt. 13:56), nor do we know their names. One commentator thinks there might have been three or four. Family relationships are important; much grows out of these early years.

The passage in Mark 6:3 tells us the names of his brothers and refers to his sisters without any identification. It appears that His brothers and sisters "were offended at him" as well as those who were in the synagogue listening to Him. I wonder why? Did they find something in Him that caused them to hesitate and finally to refuse when asked to believe in Him? It is very hard at times to give full and due credit to our brothers and sisters.

It is not unreal to expect that Jesus had some growing-up pains and some unpleasant moments with His sisters and brothers. Such is family life. But He went through it all with a spirit of love, understanding, and forgiveness.

I have only one sister now; the older one has gone on to be with the Lord. I have great respect for my living sister. I must try harder to be a better brother.

Shouldn't we all?

42

Bruiser of Serpent

"And I will put enmity between thee and the woman, and between thy seed and her seed; it shall bruise thy head, and thou shalt bruise his heel" (Gen. 3:15).

This Old Testament prophecy concerning the life and death of Christ never waned or vanished from the mainstream of prophecy but continues to be fulfilled with each passing day. It is like a beam that steals through a gap in a thundercloud.

While my wife and I were driving to Memphis, Tennessee on a recent trip, the sky was overcast with clouds. It was about 4:30 in the afternoon. I saw the bright orange rays of the sun stealing through three gaps in the clouds. It looked as if there was a triplet of suns. We talked about its beauty and significance.

I want you to consider three beams of light that stole through the gaps of the clouds during Jesus' lifetime.

1. In Matthew 4:1-10 we have the three temptations of Jesus. In overcoming each temptation He gave the devil three bruising uppercuts.

2. In the Garden of Gethsemane the devil again asserted his power to tempt Jesus but the only response he got was, "Father, if thou be willing, remove this cup from me; nevertheless, not My will but Thine be done" (Luke 22:42). Again the devil's temptation was thwarted.

3. Jesus arose from the tomb of death, the last enemy the devil could throw at Him. He arose in fulfillment of prophecy, as prophesied on the third day (Luke 24:7).

John tells of the final bruising of the serpent by the Son: "That old serpent was bound . . . cast into a bottomless pit . . . into a lake of fire and brimstone" (John 20:2-3,10).

Jesus is still setting at liberty those who are bruised and wounded by sin. O glorious victory!

43

Builder of the Church

"And I say also unto thee, That thou art Peter, and upon this rock *I will build my church;* and the gates of hell shall not prevail against it" (Matt. 16:18).

About 1938-39, during the days when Hitler was at the height of his power, I saw in the morning issue of the Louisville, Kentucky *Courier-Journal* a cartoon depicting Mount Olympus, home of the ancient Greek gods, with a German swastika flying from the top. The cartoonist was suggesting that the German way of life under Hitler, the superman, had triumphed over the Greek religion. I looked at the cartoon and thought, "Thank God, the swastika will never triumph over the church which the Son of God established."

The church, either visible or invisible, is the only institution Christ established while on earth. It is permanent regardless of the power of evil. It will not cease to exist; it will not be swallowed up. No army can destroy faith implanted in the human heart.

The word *church* is used twice in the Gospels—in today's passage and in Matthew 18:17. The word in Greek means a called-out group, *ekklesia,* an assembly of Christians. The congregation of Israel was often called the "House of Israel," and, therefore, we are justified in calling a church the house of God.

Christ is not only the builder of the church; He has empowered and commissioned its members to go into all the world. He has promised that the church will triumph over the gates of Hades.

Timothy Dwight, at the beginning of the nineteenth century, expressed this feeling most appropriately in the second stanza of his familiar hymn, "I Love Thy Kingdom, Lord":

> I love Thy church, O God!
> Her walls before Thee stand,
> Dear as the apple of Thine eye,
> And graven on Thy hand.

There should never be any conflict between the spiritual congregation and the spiritual Builder; neither should there ever be more love for the physical building housing the congregation than for the Builder.

44

Burden Bearer

"For my yoke is easy, and my burden is light" (Matt. 11:30).

The story is told of a lady who was afraid she was going to miss her train because the hackman had not called for her trunk. Seeing her standing at the gate in tears, Abe Lincoln asked the trouble. He went for the trunk, put it on his shoulders, and said, "Wipe away your tears and come quickly." Down the street he went in long strides, carrying her trunk [burden] upon his back. He placed it at the track for departure and wished her a good time. It was a load off her shoulders.[3]

Christ is our burden bearer. He carries our concerns in His heart. We are to cast all our cares upon him (1 Pet. 5:7). There are two hymns that tell us about our wonderful burden bearer. The first one, written by Elisha A. Hoffman in the nineteenth century, is entitled "I Must Tell Jesus":

I must tell Jesus all of my troubles;
He is a kind, compassionate friend;
If I but ask Him, He will deliver,
Make of my troubles quickly an end.

The second one which Bertha Mae Lillenas wrote in 1934 is entitled "Leave Your Burden at the Place of Prayer." The third stanza reads:

Bring your load of doubts and fears,
All the burdens of the years,
You may meet your Saviour and his blessings share;
Bring your troubles not a few,
Jesus will your strength renew;
Leave your burden at the place of prayer.

When Jesus takes our burdens, they become to us as burdensome as wings to a bird, making it possible for us to soar into the blue sky of hope.

3. A. K. McClure, *Lincoln's Own Yarns and Stories* (Chicago-Philadelphia: The John C. Winston Company, n. d.), p. 29.

45

Captain of the Lord's Host

"The Captain of the Lord's host said unto Joshua, Loose thy shoe from off thy foot; for the place whereon thou standest is holy" (Josh. 5:15).

Alexander MacLaren wrote these provocative words in his *Expositions of the Holy Scripture:* "I believe, as the vast majority of careful students of the course of Old Testament revelation and its relation to the New Testament completion believe, that we have here not a record of the appearance of a created super-human person, but that of a preliminary manifestation of the Eternal Word of God, who, in the fulness of time, 'became flesh and dwelt among us.' "[4]

MacLaren goes on to picture Christ as the Leader of all the warfare against the world's evil. He further infers that no other power than His by His cross and meekness can overcome evil and bring the victory for right and truth.

Christ, as Captain of the Lord's host, calls His forces to lift high His banner and follow Him into the conflict. Frances Havergal, in the nineteenth century, expressed this truth in the third stanza of her hymn: "Who Is on the Lord's Side?"

> Chosen to be soldiers
> In an alien land,
> Chosen, called, and faithful,
> For our captain's band;
> In the service royal
> Let us not grow cold,
> Let us be right loyal,
> Noble, true, and bold:
> Master, Thou wilt keep us,
> By Thy grace divine,
> Always on the Lord's side,
> Saviour, we are Thine.

Isn't it time for us to click our heels, stand at attention, and salute, reverently and unselfishly, our Captain of the Lord's host!

4. Alexander MacLaren, *Exposition of the Holy Scriptures,* Book of Joshua (Grand Rapids: Wm. B. Eerdmans Publishing Co., 1932), p. 124.

Captain of Salvation

"For it became him, . . . to make the *captain of their salvation* perfect through sufferings" (Heb. 2:10).

A captain is usually considered the chief officer, one who has authority over others, or one who leads. A captain gives orders, sets the pace and example, and represents those under him.

The term *Captain of salvation* as used by the author of the Book of Hebrews means "founder, originator through suffering." Someone had to be responsible for our salvation. Someone had to make atonement for our sins. Someone had to die in our place because "the wages of sin is death" (Rom. 6:23).

One of the most amazing things about salvation available in Christ for all believers is Christ's willingness to become sin for us that we might become the righteousness of God in Him. He never turned His back on us.

There is an often-repeated remark that a certain captain of a group was shot in the back while running away from the battle. Not so with our captain. He willingly endured the total suffering of the cross. Our knowledge and remembrance of His suffering should keep us ever grateful.

On the occasion of the untimely killing of Abraham Lincoln by John Wilkes Booth, Walt Whitman wrote these immortal words in his poem "O Captain, My Captain!":

> The ship has weathered every rack, the prize we sought is won;
>
> ....
>
> The ship is anchor'd safe and sound, its voyage closed and done;
> From fearful trip, the victor ship, comes in with object won:
> Exult, O shores, and ring, O bells!"

Those words could apply to Christ's death also, but there is one major difference: Whereas Lincoln lay fallen, cold and dead, our Captain is more alive now than ever. He is risen. He is alive.

47

Carpenter

"Is not this *the carpenter*, the son of Mary?" (Mark 6:3).

The question raised by Mark in his Gospel: "Is not this the carpenter?" indicates that Jesus Himself was recognized as a carpenter. I imagine He was frequently called a carpenter.

It is not unreasonable to assume through references He made to a bushel basket, a lampstand, a yoke, and a plough, that these were objects He had made in the carpenter's shop.

I can do no better than to present here several stanzas from a poem written by George Blair entitled "The Carpenter of Nazareth."

> In Nazareth, the narrow road
>   That tires the feet and steals the breath
> Passes the place where once abode
>   That Carpenter of Nazareth . . .
> The maiden with the doll she broke,
>   The woman with the broken chair,
> The man with plough or yoke,
>   Said, "Can you mend it, Carpenter?" . . .
> "O Carpenter of Nazareth,
>   This heart, that's broken past repair,
> This life, that's shattered nigh to death,
>   Oh, can You mend them, Carpenter?"
> And by his kind and ready hand,
>   His own sweet life is woven through
> Our broken lives, until they stand
>   A New Creation—"All things new."

In His heavenly carpenter's shop He is still mending broken lives, shattered dreams, and making us over. The door to His shop is never closed.

Carpenter's Son

"Is not this *the carpenter's son?* is not his mother called Mary? and his brethren, James, and Joses, and Simon, and Judas?" (Matt. 13:55).

Through the centuries people have learned trades by becoming apprentices. Jesus was called the "carpenter's son." His father Joseph was a reputable carpenter of Nazareth, even though there is some evidence that this was an occupational title of reproach.

It was the custom of Jews, even of the wealthy families, to teach their sons a trade. A carpenter in those days was a maker of tools, household utensils, and generally considered a worker in wood.

Since Jesus belonged to a poor family, He did not eat the bread of idleness but took His place in Joseph's shop. He became accustomed to the sweat of honest toil. Such a trade did not provide much educational opportunity.

As an apprentice in Joseph's shop, was Jesus an apt pupil? I wonder if He was too much of a mystic or dreamer to keep His mind on the job. Did He ever have to be disciplined by His carpenter-teacher? Did He ever take jobs on His own? If so, did He have some of the rough-and-tumble problems similar to those of today?

I like the poem entitled "The Carpenter" by G. A. Studdert-Kennedy.

> I wonder what he charged for chairs at Nazareth.
> And did men try to beat him down
> And boast about it in the town—
> "I bought it cheap for half-a-crown
> From that mad Carpenter."
>
> ....
> I wonder did he have bad debts,
> And did he know my fears and frets?
>
> ....
> But that's just what I want to know.
> Ah! Christ in glory, here below
> Men cheat and lie to one another so
> It's hard to be a carpenter.

49
The Charismatic

"The Spirit of the Lord is upon me" (Luke 4:18).

A charismatic person is one who has a special divine endowment: an attractive personality with power. Some people hold that word in question, somewhat dubious of it in religious circles because it has been exploited and misused.

Jesus, in the true sense of the word, was charismatic. I quote the theologian Rudolf Otto: "The original tradition describes Christ as charismatic. We submit that this description is genuine, for in this way and only in this way can we explain the historical consequence; viz, the production of spirit-led, enthusiastic church. It is genuine, again, because its individual traits harmonize into a unity of the charismatic type. Yet, again, it is genuine because this whole charismatic type harmonizes with, and has the same meaning as, the message of the kingdom of God which is already breaking in, and which has been experienced as dynamis" [power].[5]

Some of the healings of Jesus took place at a distance from those healed. The doubter asks, "Can one believe in an operation at a distance?" One can if one believes in the power which Jesus possessed.

Jesus also had power to discern between good and evil spirits. That was a special gift. Read Luke 4:18 and you will sense that the one speaking had a special divine endowment. He always used that endowment not for Himself but for others.

His attractiveness drew crowds. His charm and presence held the crowds. It is true today.

As the sun in the sky draws water from the earth, the Son of God in the heavens still draws sinful hearts unto Himself to fill them with living water.

5. Rudolph Otto, *Contemporary Thinking About Jesus*, comp. Thomas S. Kepler (New York: Abingdon-Cokesbury Press, n.d.), p. 392.

50

Chef

"Jesus saith unto them, Come and dine" (John 21:12).

Seven men had fished all night and had caught nothing. Tired and discouraged, they rowed toward the shore only to hear a warm invitation, "Come and dine." A breakfast repast consisting of fish, bread, and possibly tea was awaiting them, having been prepared by the nail-scarred hands of the risen Lord. What a treat.

Breakfast is an important meal for fishermen, and it should be for each person. It provides energy for the day. Many say it is the most important meal of the day.

How good it was for the seven—Peter, Thomas, Nathanael, James, John and two other unnamed disciples, possibly not of the twelve but capable fishermen—to be able to gather at breakfast and fellowship with the Lord. What a good way to start a new day after a disappointing night.

Jesus had previously bidden His disciples to come and follow Him, to come unto Him if they were weary and heavy laden, and to come to Him for the Water of life. Now His final "Come" invitation is to "Come and dine." Was He saying by this act that He would provide daily sustenance, that He was the Bread of life, and that those who would be fishers of men could depend upon Him for their needs? Yes, I think so.

We can have the Lord as the Unseen Presence with us each morning at breakfast. While we eat of the physical food from the labors of our hands we can share with Him the spiritual food He, the Master Chef, has prepared for those who love Him.

We must be sure to reciprocate the invitation by inviting Him to "Come and dine with us."

Chief Cornerstone

"Jesus Christ himself being *the chief corner stone*" (Eph. 2:20).

Northwest of Jerusalem on the road to Gibeon in an old quarry is a stone set on its end. Looking from the road, one sees nothing wrong with it; but on going around it one is able to see the flaws that destroyed its value. It had been quarried, but it failed to pass inspection by the builders. It would strain our imagination to think of that stone as ever becoming a chief cornerstone in a grand cathedral. But, good friend, our Savior was rejected, yet He became the chief Cornerstone. The rejection was not due to a flaw in His life but the lack of the leaders of His day to see His true value. (See Matt. 21:42; Mark 12:10.)

Cornerstones are usually foundation stones. "For other foundation can no man lay than that is laid, which is Jesus Christ" (1 Cor. 3:11).

Cornerstones are frequently put in place at a formal inauguration of the erection of a building, and important documents for future generations may be placed either in them or behind them. Sometimes, however, references to the chief cornerstone may refer to the topmost or capstone which links the last tier together and, again, a very important stone.

Paul, in today's Scripture, gives us a somewhat different meaning of Christ as the chief Cornerstone. To him the chief cornerstone is laid beneath the two walls which diverge at right angles from each other, and the stone would bind both together, giving strength and cohesion to the whole. To Paul the two walls were the Jews and the Gentiles, and he saw in Christ the One who could reconcile them into one new Creation. He still can. One would not be straining the point to see also in this passage that Christ is designated as the foundation stone standing beneath walls, binding both the prophets and the apostles together. He does it all.

52

Chief of Ten Thousand

"For though ye have ten thousand instructors in Christ, yet have ye not many fathers: for in Christ Jesus I have begotten you through the gospel" (1 Cor. 4:15).

There is a popular song entitled "Seventy-six Trombones" which always catches my attention. Think of hearing seventy-six trombones playing simultaneously! But, more than that, years ago Thomas Kelly wrote a hymn called "Hark, Ten Thousand Harps." Imagine hearing ten thousand harps and voices! What a praise that many could sound for Christ.

Jesus is the chief of ten thousand, even ten thousand times ten thousand. The following Scripture passages indicate that truth from different perspectives.

In 1 Corinthians 4:15, the apostle Paul says to the Christians at Corinth that there may be ten thousand instructors, yet there are not many fathers, and I have begotten you through Christ Jesus in whom you have your salvation, and He is the chief of the ten thousand instructors.

In Revelation 5:11, John, while on the Isle of Patmos, could see in his mind an innumerable host of angels—"ten thousand times ten thousand, and thousands of thousands"—around the throne saying, "Worthy is the Lamb . . . to receive power, and riches, and wisdom, and strength, and honour, and glory, and blessing" (Rev. 5:12).

Could there ever be any doubt that Jesus Christ is the Chief of Ten Thousand? He could never be anything less.

May we this day pick up the refrain of that innumerable host and join our praise with theirs.

53

Child, Prenatal

"She shall bring forth a son, and thou shalt call his name Jesus: for he shall save his people from their sins" (Matt. 1:21).

It will be quite easy for those of you who are parents to recall those moments of joy and ecstasy when you knew for the first time that you were to become parents. I remember with acute recollection. "I was going to become a father. We were going to have a baby: Would the child be a boy or a girl? Should we think of pink or blue?" Oh, those things didn't matter. What mattered most was: Would there be ten little fingers and ten little toes, a cry, and normal breathing and eating.

During the nine months of waiting, my wife and I went through various stages together. We experienced the joy and pride that comes with the knowledge that a new life is being formed. What a period of gratification! Each day brought on greater anticipation. The excitement grew. Concern also grew. The seriousness of becoming parents began to dawn on us.

Then, the period of preparation really set in. We had some arrangements to make: a crib to secure, clothes to buy, and even books to read on how to be parents. We had to think of female and male names.

Don't you think Mary went through similar stages during the prenatal days? She, however, did not have to wonder if she was going to have a boy or a girl. The angel in the annunciation had told her that she would bear a son (Luke 1:31). She and Joseph did not even have to think of a name for the son because that same angel told Mary that His name should be "Jesus."

One thing was bad, but it had to be done. Mary and Joseph had to go to Bethlehem to be taxed during the time when she was great with child (Luke 2:5). A rather risky business, but there was no getting out of, of delaying, the taxing because an imperial decree had gone out from Caesar Augustus. But bear in mind that an imperial decree had gone out to Mary from God. Obedience is a great virtue.

54

Child (Newborn)

"When they were come into the house, they saw *the young child* with Mary his mother, and fell down, and worshipped him" (Matt. 2:11).

When Christ was born in the manger in Bethlehem, it started out as a rather inauspicious occasion (Luke 2:7). But it was not to stay that way. There were few, if any, for Joseph and Mary to share with. There was no nurse to bring the good news, but there was more.

W. H. Auden, in his work "A Christmas Oratorio, For The Time Being" brings two very important thoughts to our minds. First, but not according to chronology, he has the Wise Men coming to view the Christ child and, upon seeing all wisdom, which they sought, incarnate in the child, they exclaim, "Oh, here and now our endless journey ends." To them there was no need to look further.

But when the shepherds arrive at the manger in Bethlehem, they exclaim, "Oh, here and now our endless journey begins." Why did they say that? The answer is that they had found the Great Shepherd of all the lost sheep, and it behooved them as shepherds to go out and tell others that the Shepherd, the Messiah, had come. They had work to do.

Nahum Tate expressed this idea in his beautiful Christmas hymn: "While Shepherds Watched Their Flocks."

> All glory be to God on high,
> And to the earth be peace:
> Good will henceforth from heav'n to men,
> Begin and never cease.

It is still true that the arrival of a newborn child affects the lives of many. A birth may be far more significant than a battle. A baby brings hope, love, and opportunity.

Thank God for the miracle of birth and the joy the birth of a baby brings.

55

Child Jesus (First Public Appearance)

"The parents brought in *the child Jesus,* to do for him after the custom of the law" (Luke 2:27).

I have had many happy experiences through the years watching new parents bring their firstborn out for "public inspection," so to speak. "Oh, she looks like her mother." "He looks like both of you . . . so cute, so darling." "What a lovely baby!" Did you ever hear anyone say, "What an unattractive baby"? No, because only a few people don't respond affectionately to babies.

Joseph and Mary took the child Jesus with them to the Temple as, according to the law of Moses, it was necessary for the woman to participate in purifying rites within forty days after childbirth. It was also customary for the firstborn to be presented in the Temple of the Lord. Usually, an offering of about three dollars was also presented to the sacred treasury. But Joseph and Mary, being poor and finding such an amount burdensome, offered, as was allowable, a pair of turtledoves (Luke 2:22-24).

While there, aged Simeon, a just and righteous man, spoke of a revelation which had come to him through the Holy Spirit regarding their child. The parents "marvelled" at Simeon's sayings and predictions (Luke 2:33).

Charles Wesley, in the eighteenth century, wrote similar truths about Jesus when he penned these words in his hymn "Hail, Thou Long-Expected Jesus":

> Hail, thou long-expected Jesus,
> Born to set Thy people free:
> From our sins and fears release us;
> Let us find our rest in Thee.
> Israel's strength and consolation,
> Hope of all the saints Thou art;
> Long desired of ev'ry nation,
> Joy of every waiting heart.

The warm and heartfelt expectation of the coming Messiah that dwelt in Simeon's heart should likewise dwell in our hearts as we anticipate the return of Christ to claim His own. Let us so live each day as we wished we had lived when He comes.

56

Child, a Growing Infant

"The child grew, and waxed strong in spirit, filled with wisdom: and the grace of God was upon him" (Luke 2:40).

Children are born to grow on their own. They begin that process immediately after birth. Scales for weighing the child are among the most used of all household items at that period.

When our first child was born, I think I shared her weight with everyone with whom I chatted. She was fed according to the clock, even awakened at 2 AM to have a bottle stuck in her mouth. She was weighed daily. After six months the doctor said, "She is gaining too much. Slow down the process."

And the birth and development of Jesus troubled King Herod. He feared the growing influence of the child. Babies are not a threat to a kingly crown, but Herod thought so and ordered all male children two years of age and under to be massacred (Matt. 2:8-16). What a devilish thing for a king to do! So Jesus and His parents went to Egypt to avoid the wrath of Herod. Did Jesus remember that flight into Egypt? I wonder. What was His life like in Egypt and after returning to Nazareth?

John Banister Tabb, in his poem "The Boy Jesus," described what he thought it might have been like with Jesus in Nazareth.

> At evening he loved to walk
> Among the shadowy hills, and talk of Bethlehem,
> But if perchance there passed us by
> The paschal lambs, he'd look at them
> In silence, long and tenderly;
> And when again he'd try to speak,
> I've seen the tears upon his cheeks.

His growth was a joy to His parents, and I imagine God was also well pleased. In our spiritual lives do we remain babes, or do we keep on growing?

57

Chosen of God

"The rulers . . . derided him, saying, He saved others; let him save himself, if he be Christ, the chosen of God" (Luke 23:35).

The people and the rulers who were gathered around the cross derided Jesus by taunting Him to save Himself "if he be Christ, the chosen of God." Even though Christ was hanging on the cross, those who spoke these words put their own spiritual lives on a cross. They hung themselves with an *"if."*

It was hard for people in those days to present anyone who died on a cross as the Savior of humankind. Much more was needed. To them a savior would need to triumph over sin as well as physical suffering, so doubt took over at that time.

It is a very tragic situation when anyone's life hangs on an *if*. The word *if* is an interrogative particle casting doubt. Notice that the four-letter word *life* is one half "if"—the middle half (l *if* e).

Let me remind you:

If never accomplished much for God.

If never won many battles.

If never conquered the unknown.

If never brought back a lost day.

If never recalled an unkind word.

If never eased the pain of a hurting person.

If never turned a soul to repentance.

If can become the most useless, hopeless, and helpless word in the dictionary. Let us not say *if* in referring to Christ but, standing at spiritual attention, let us say, "You are the Christ, the chosen of God."

The world needs our affirmation of Christ as the chosen of God. Let us proclaim His deity by word and deed, following where He leads. Then, that will not let the *if* in life stand alone. It will put an *l* for *love* in front of the *if* and an *e* for *eternal* after it, making the word *life* eternal life because of the gift of the chosen of God.

58

Christt, The

"Thou art *the Christ*, the Son of the living God" (Matt. 16:16).

The name *Christ* is found as frequently in the Bible, if not more so, than any other name given Jesus. *Christ* designates Him as the Messiah, the Anointed One, the Savior. One could almost say that all of His major functions are contained in that name. So, that being the case, it is not an oversimplification to say that the choice today is the same as when He lived in Palestine—it is either Christ or chaos; the code of Jesus the Christ or the code of the jungles.

Around the turn of the century, Elisha A. Hoffman captured the significance of that name when he wrote his hymn: "What a Wonderful Saviour!"

> Christ has for sin atonement made,
> What a wonderful Saviour!
> I am redeemed, the price is paid;
> What a wonderful Saviour!

Spinoza said, "No one except Christ received the revelations of God without the aid of imagination, whether in words or vision." He is truly the Anointed One, and those who put Him to death in order not to receive Him as Messiah have given the final proof that He is the Messiah.

The Christ of the Nazareth's carpenter shop, the Christ of the raging sea, the Christ of the cross as well as the Christ of the vacant tomb, still confronts us with a supreme challenge, "Come, follow me." If we accept that challenge it means that we must be willing to take on His characteristics of meekness, love, and purity, and we must be willing to share His experiences of suffering, denial, rejection, and sacrifice. No one but Christ merits such adoration and loyalty.

59

Christ Jesus My Lord

"I count all things but loss for the excellency of the knowledge of *Christ Jesus my Lord*" (Phil. 3:8).

The apostle Paul, in a glow of heartfelt gratitude and love, wrote to the Philippians in endearing terms when he penned "Christ Jesus my Lord." In other words, he was saying, "He is mine: I am his." He wanted his identification with Christ Jesus known. He wanted to affirm Christ Jesus as "My Lord." He wanted all to know that he was willing to subordinate all things once valued in order to fully know Christ.

Christ Jesus was the greatest gain in Paul's life. He would count all other things as refuse, valueless. He had fallen in love with Christ: a love that would never depart. It was Paul's desire to be faithful and true to the love that had won his heart. He was willing to do his homework. He wanted to learn all he could about Christ Jesus, his Lord.

Bernard of Clairvaux was the abbot of a great Cistercian monastery in eastern France during the first half of the twelfth century. He was one of the most influential men of his time, an eloquent preacher and a great Christian. His hymn "Jesus, Thou Joy of Loving Hearts" is a warm expression of affection and admiration.

> Jesus, Thou joy of loving hearts,
> Thou fount of life, Thou light of men,
> From the best bliss that earth imparts,
> We turn unfilled, to Thee again.

But the expressions of the apostle Paul and Bernard of Clairvaux would be like a husband saying about his wife, "Jane, my loving wife" or a wife saying about her husband, "This is Jim, my wonderful husband." Both expressions are more endearing than just saying the name of the spouse.

Is not Christ Jesus a precious Lord? Why not, then, say so!

60

Christel of God

"He said unto them, But whom say ye that I am? . . . Peter answering said, *The Christ of God*" (Luke 9:20).

I agree with the words of the hymn "I Know Not How That Bethlehem's Babe" which was written in 1921 by Harry Webb Farrington:

I know not how that Bethlehem's Babe
Could in the Godhead be;
I only know that the manger Child
Has brought God's life to me.

It was a hard question to answer when Jesus asked His disciples, "Whom say ye that I am?" He was not interested in what others might say. He did not want their answers in quotation marks. He wanted their own hearts' reply.

As usual, Peter spoke up as the spokesman of the group. "The Christ, the Anointed One of God," he said (Matt. 16:16-18, author's paraphrase). And right he was. Christ was the One foreordained, predicted, promised, and given by God.

Today we are asked that same question of Christ. Others want to know whom we think He is. Christ is interested in our own personal acclamation of Him. A person who wishes to be a true disciple cannot hide under the proclamation of parents, the minister, or the church's articles of faith. Faith in Christ cannot be inherited or passed down. It is a very personal something, the revelation of the heart.

Even though we may fail to follow Him completely, let us never waver in our knowledge of who He is and what He has done for us. Let us not hesitate to acclaim Him as Savior and Lord.

Coleridge once remarked, "I believe Socrates and Plato, but I believe in Christ." That little word *in* makes a world of difference.

61
Christ of the Lord (The Lord's Christ)

"And it was revealed unto him by the Holy Ghost, that he should not see death, before he had seen *the Lord's Christ*" (Luke 2:26).

It is believed that Simeon, a venerable and righteous man of Jerusalem spoken of in the second chapter of Luke, had been long puzzled by the statement in Isaiah 7:14, "A virgin shall conceive." He had hoped to see the fulfillment of that prophecy.

When the Christ child was taken to the Temple to do for Him according to the law, this dear old man had obviously received a supernatural intimation that this child was the real one, for Simeon broke forth saying, "Lord, now lettest thou thy servant depart in peace, . . . For mine eyes have seen thy salvation, . . . A light to lighten the Gentiles, and the glory of thy people Israel" (Luke 2:29-32). The servant had seen the Master. As two unnoted worshipers entered the Temple, Simeon could not restrain himself, "It is He! That is He, the Lord's Christ."

What a beautiful sight to behold: an elderly, righteous man holding in his arms a child whom he believed to be the Savior. His remarks have been labeled as a song which has been given the name "Nunc Dimittis," the sweetest of the songs of the Nativity.

To the wondering mother, Simeon added this tragic word of prophecy, "Behold, this child is set for the fall and rising again of many in Israel; and for a sign which shall be spoken against; (Yea, a sword shall pierce through thy own soul also,) that the thoughts of many hearts may be revealed" (Luke 2:34-35). In other words, the ministry of Jesus would be the occasion for the fall and rise of many. It is either by accepting or rejecting Jesus that people reveal their true character.

May we sing the songs of joy and redemption because of "the Lord's Christ," the babe seen in the Temple by Simeon.

62

Comforter

"Let not your heart be troubled: ye believe in God, believe also in me. In my Father's house are many mansions: if it were not so, I would have told you" (John 14:1-2).

Many of us in our comforting role act like the person who went calling. "Say, you look terrible. Have you been ill? How do you feel?" Then, upon leaving, the visitor added, "Just wanted to come by and be of comfort to you."

Jesus predicated His comforting role upon belief in God. He offered much assurance by saying something in our Scripture verse which He never said on any other occasion, "If it were not so, I would have told you." The inference is that all things will eventually turn out for good to those who love God. Make no mistake about it. This faith and assurance lighten the loads of sorrow, bereavement, and discouragement.

During the first part of the nineteenth century, Thomas Moore wrote a very comforting and challenging hymn: "Come, Ye Disconsolate."

> Come, ye disconsolate, where'er ye languish,
> Come to the mercy seat, fervently kneel;
> Here bring your wounded hearts, here tell your anguish:
> Earth has no sorrow that heav'n cannot heal.

Now, if we will couple this with Horatius Bonar's hymn: "I Heard the Voice of Jesus Say," we will begin to sense and feel his comforting presence.

> I heard the voice of Jesus say,
> "Come unto Me and rest;
> Lay down, thou weary one, lay down
> Thy head upon My breast."
> I came to Jesus as I was,
> Weary, and worn, and sad;
> I found in Him a resting place,
> And He has made me glad.

Amen!

63

The Coming One

"I will come again, and receive you unto myself" (John 14:3).

As I was returning to my office from lunch one day, I stopped at a light and noticed on the back of the car just in front of me this statement, "Don't be caught dead without Christ." That hit me two ways.

First, I thought: *How true.* It would be awful to approach the river of death without having the assistance of Jesus Christ, else Jordan's crossing would be feared. With Him there is no fear in the crossover or in the valley and shadow of death.

Second, I thought of how bad it would be to be caught living without Christ when He comes again. If He should come unexpectedly, and it will be that way because His coming is not known, the person without Him then would be in a desperate and deplorable situation.

We should remember two things which are certain: He came to offer salvation, and He is coming again to gather all who have accepted this salvation to be with Him in glory.

The first time He came as a babe in the lowly manger of Bethlehem, and He is coming again as a glorious King on behalf of His Heavenly Father (Matt. 16:27). We are knowledgeable about His first coming, but we are not well informed as to His second coming. Therefore, the important thing is to be prepared for the Coming One.

The best way I know is to be like the little girl who was told by her father that if her hands and clothes were clean when he returned from a trip, he would give her a five-dollar bill. Normally, she just couldn't keep clean. When the father returned on a Thursday instead of the usual Friday, he found her spotless. He asked her, "How come you are so clean?"

"Well, Daddy, I wasn't sure when you were coming, so I just stayed clean." That is good advice.

71

64

Commander

"These twelve Jesus sent forth, and *commanded* them, saying, Go not into the way of the Gentiles, and into any city of the Samaritans enter ye not" (Matt. 10:5).

Jesus fulfilled the role of a commander many, many times. He was not a retired commander but one active in the fray.

A commander is one who gives orders, who has control or mastery of a group or situation. A commander expects obedience to the orders given.

As our commander, Jesus came not to destroy the law (the commandments) or the prophets, but to fulfill them (Matt. 5:17).

He commanded the unclean spirit to come out of the man in the synagogue in Capernaum (Mark 1:23).

He commanded the wind and the raging water of the Sea of Galilee to cease (Luke 8:24-25).

He commanded the damsel to arise from her sleep of death (Mark 5:41).

He commanded His disciples to go into all the world to preach, teach, and heal (Matt. 28:19-20).

He gave His disciples a new commandment that they should love one another (John 13:34).

He also told His disciples that if they loved Him, they were to keep His commandments (John 14:15).

So, it would be good for each one of us to stand at spiritual attention and salute our courageous, kind, and caring Commander. And whenever the orders come from Him, we should respond with a commitment which pledges our best to seeing that the orders are carried out.

One beautiful thing about Christ as our Commander is that amid all the vicissitudes of life, regardless of the tragedy and tension, He never forsakes His troops. And He is never without power to control the situation with proper resolution. He can take charge of any situation, but He must be given the chance.

Compassionate One

"Jesus went forth, and saw a great multitude and *was moved with compassion toward them,* and he healed their sick" (Matt. 14:14).

Lord Byron, the dashing, handsome English poet of the early nineteenth century, whose writings were characterized by a passionate intensity of emotion, said, "The dew of compassion is a tear." I agree!

Jesus was a compassionate person. The New Testament relates two incidents where Jesus is described as weeping. The first one is at the home of Lazarus, His friend, who had lived in Bethany, four days prior to his death (John 11:35). The second one is on the occasion of His triumphal entry into Jerusalem. As Jesus looked over the city, He wept (Luke 19:41).

Two days after His triumphal entry, in His last public discourse, He denounced the scribes and Pharisees and showed again His passionate emotion toward the city of Jerusalem. Many matters touched His heart deeply. He was not embarrassed to give expression to His emotions. He knew the fellowship in shared feeling. He was able to suffer with another. Christ could share mercy, give condolence, weep, and hurt with others. (See Matt. 23:37.)

The traditional "poker-face with ice water in the veins" seldom knows the warmth and pleasure of fellowship in feeling.

John Milton wrote in *Paradise Lost:*

> Beyond compare the Son of God was seen
> Most glorious, in him all his Father shone
> Substantially express'd, and in his face
> Divine compassion visibly appeared,
> Love without end, and without measure Grace.

Let us love one another with compassion, a fellowship in feeling. Tears sometimes will wash away grief and gloom. It is good to have an occasional cry. Tears are good for both body and soul, coming as the results of joy or pain.

Conqueror

"I say also unto thee, That thou art Peter, and upon this rock I will build my church; and the gates of hell shall not prevail against it" (Matt. 16:18).

One of the not-so-familiar hymns is "Conquering Now and Still to Conquer" by Sallie Martin. The first stanza pictures our Christ in the role of a conqueror.

Conquering now and still to conquer,
Rideth a King in his might,
Leading the host of all the faithful
Into the midst of the fight;
See them with courage advancing,
Clad in their brilliant array,
Shouting the name of their Leader,
Hear them exulting say: (chorus)
Not to the strong is the battle,
Not to the swift is the race,
Yet to the true and the faithful
Vict'ry is promised thro' grace.

The world has known many military conquerors: Darius, Alexander the Great, Caesar, Charlemagne, Napoleon, Hitler, and others of their ilk, but the world has never seen a conqueror equal to the Son of God. Jesus conquered people's hearts and called forth from them undying loyalty. Instead of conquering by destruction, He conquered by giving new and abundant life extending throughout eternity. He did subjugate His followers into a restricted slavery, but a slavery that brought freedom from restraint. His followers were made free through the truth. Even in death He became a greater conqueror because He conquered the last enemy —death—and came from the tomb with victory for His followers.

And He lives. His grave is famous because it is empty. He is still enlisting people to serve with Him in His kingdom. The world's greatest Conqueror was also the most compassionate one.

Consolation of Israel

"Behold, there was a man in Jerusalem, whose name was Simeon; and the same man was just and devout, waiting for *the consolation of Israel:* and the Holy Ghost was upon him" (Luke 2:25).

I recall once reading about a little girl who came home from visiting a neighbor's house where her little friend had died.

"Why did you go?" asked her father.

"To console her mother," said the little girl.

"What could you do to console her?"

"Oh, Daddy, I could get up in her lap and cry with her." A beautiful thought.

Dear old Simeon, who saw the Christ child for the first time in the Temple, had waited long for some consolation for the house of Israel. He looked for one to come who would offer that sympathy and comfort.

Consolation means the alleviation of misery, distress of mind and spirit. It is something or someone that consoles. Israel needed such a word or such a person. The prostration, ungodliness, and suffering that Israel was obsessed with needed alleviation. Israel expected the coming Messiah to do just that, and, fortunately, Simeon, unlike Israel, recognized Jesus, the babe in His mother's arms, as the Coming One who would bring such consolation.

Simeon's cry, expecting some relief from pressing needs, was the cry that Jacob gave to his sons before his death, "I have waited for thy salvation, O Lord" (Gen. 49:18).

J. Wilbur Chapman, at the turn of the twentieth century, wrote a lovely song "One Day" that summarizes it all:

> One day when heaven was filled with His praises,
> One day when sin was as black as could be,
> Jesus came forth to be born of a virgin,
> Dwelt among men, my example is He!
>
> One day the trumpet will sound for His coming,
> One day the skies with His glories will shine;
> Wonderful day, my beloved ones bringing;
> Glorious Saviour, this Jesus is mine!

Praise God!

68

Counsellor

"His name shall be called Wonderful, *Counsellor,* The Mighty God, The everlasting Father, The Prince of Peace" (Isa. 9:6).

There are all kinds of counsellors: free, expensive, good, and not so good. Many people will offer advice even when not asked.

If we paid attention to the counsel coming from advertisements, this is something of the advice we would receive:

If you are bored, buy an expensive car.

If you need romance, use a certain kind of toothpaste.

If you want money, use a credit card.

If you want a good time, use cigarettes and wine.

And I would respond with a loud, "Baloney!"

A good counsellor doesn't hand out advice in packages or capsule portions. A good counsellor will listen, try to understand, evaluate, make suggestions, and maybe offer some advice. The best counsellor is one who does all of those things but has the capacity to empathize with and inspire others.

Jesus had that capacity. He could see straight through persons. He could put His finger instantly on the problem. He knew the wiles of sin and the complexities of human nature. He was master of all situations.

He knew the art of kindness. He knew the sacred areas of life, and He never arbitrarily invaded those areas or trampled them down with stern reprimands except with those of excessive religiosity.

He was tender with children, kind to the outcasts, and loved all with meekness and mercy.

If we could only listen to Him as well as He is willing to listen to us, a marvelous counseling session would follow. He really knows how to speak to the human heart. Just try it.

Cousin, Second (Second Cousin of Elizabeth and Zacharias)

"Behold, *thy cousin Elizabeth*, she hath also conceived a son in her old age" (Luke 1:36).

Second cousins aren't always second-rate. I had a second cousin who was a first-rate cousin. We all called her "Cousin Margie." She taught the first grade in school for over forty years. She was the one who taught me to drive a car while I was a teenager. She had a Model T Ford. I learned on rough country roads. Cousin Margie made only one mistake in helping me learn to drive. Once she put her foot over on my foot, the one on the gas pedal, and said, "Go a little faster." I haven't been told that since!

Blood cousins usually form a part of family ties that build for family pride. There are frequently similar traits among cousins. The nature of the Jewish family would indicate that Jesus, no doubt, had rather close bonds with Elizabeth, Zacharias, and their son, John. There must have been back-and-forth visitation.

It would be most unnatural if "Cousin" Elizabeth and "Cousin" Mary did not talk time after time about the babe to be born of Mary and more especially about the growth and rearing of that special child.

Was He the talk of the larger family? How did that family react to His treatment later on? Did they think Him strange? These and a score of other questions could be raised.

Cousins can be of all kinds: feuding, fighting, jealous, or, on the other hand, they can be loving, caring, and concerned. The big question is: What kind of cousins did Jesus have, and what kind of a cousin was He? I don't think He shunned them. I feel, somehow, that He bonded them to His soul. He knew well His place in the life of the family and, more especially, the family of God. He can unite in the bonds of love all the family relatives.

Cousin, Third (Third Cousin of John the Baptist)

"Behold, *thy cousin Elizabeth*, she hath also *conceived a son*" (Luke 1:36). "The child grew, . . . and was in the deserts till the day of his shewing unto Israel" (Luke 1:80).

Jesus was a third cousin of John the Baptist. Second cousins seem farther removed from third cousins than from first cousins, but the relationship is there nonetheless.

I never visited my third cousins as I did my second cousins. I saw them only occasionally. But I had several. My grandmother was a Davenport. There were many of them. The family tree has been right well constructed and shows diversity of professions. Among my many cousins were a great college athlete, sheriff, law enforcement officer, minister, merchant, miller, realtor, and others.

As on yesterday we thought of Jesus as a second cousin, we think of Him today as a third cousin. This relationship might well raise some questions. Did He ever ponder His family ties of the past? Did He think of Himself as a descendant of King David? Did He rejoice in His family ties? Did He feel that the family name was good, and that He had something to live up to?

I wonder also if he ever called John the Baptist "Cousin John." Why not? The records suggest He held John in high esteem. For as much emphasis as He put on the family through the principles He enunciated, He no doubt thought well of His family. On the other hand, He knew when to draw the line between family "possession" and His loyalty and commitment to God.

The family was ordained of God that children might be trained for His service. The family was before the church, or we might call it the first form of church on earth. The ties of the family, however, were never meant to circumvent the church nor to become exclusive, ends in themselves. A happy family might well be a faint taste of what is in store for us in the heavenly family.

71

Covenant of the People

"I the Lord have called thee in righteousness, and will hold thine hand, and will keep thee, and give thee for *a covenant of the people,* for a light of the Gentiles" (Isa. 42:6).

During the Civil War, in the early summer of 1865, times were exceedingly hard for The Southern Baptist Theological Seminary. The picture of its continuing existence was bleak. Four of its leaders, Broadus, Boyce, Manly, and Williams, met together to discuss its plight. Broadus said, "Suppose we quietly agree [covenant] that the seminary may die, but we'll die first." The seminary did not die. They kept their covenant.

Covenants are made to be kept, not to be broken. A covenant is a very solemn agreement, or compact, between two or more people. Life is projected in covenant relationships: the covenant marriage vows, the church covenant, legal covenants, and, most of all, the covenant relationship a Christian has with God.

Just as was true during the time of Isaiah, Jesus is now a covenant of the people. He comes into the life of the Christian during the miracle of the new birth in a strong covenant relationship. We become His followers, He becomes our leader. His leadership is full of promises based on certain conditions—covenants. His presence is promised if we follow His way. Prayers are answered in accordance with His will. The abundant life is available through His commandments.

God and Christ have never broken a covenant made with their people. Time and time again, the second party of the covenant broke relationship with them. Time and time again, the pleading call to return came from the party of the first part. Periods of grace were nearly always present, giving the erring person or people time to come home.

Obedience to the covenant of the people can provide an infallible proof that our love for Him neither procrastinates nor questions.

72

Covert from the Tempest

"A man [he] shall be as an hiding place from the wind, and *a covert from the tempest*" (Isa. 32:2).

Life has its storms. I know. One night, as a teenager on the farm in west Kentucky, I was awakened by my parents, urging me to get up and seek shelter with them. A storm had come, and the fierce winds had blown over two barns. We could see the rubble in the flashes of lightning. Some of the shingles had been blown from the roof of the house, and water was coming into the rooms. In fear, we knelt to pray. The storm passed. We thanked God. It was a memorable experience that I have remembered each time the TV screen carries the words, "Tornado warnings until 10 PM, etc." I have been in other windstorms—frightening experiences, and now we talk of bomb shelters.

But there are other storms: psychological, emotional, winds of afflictions, and winds of adversity. At times we all have felt the need of divine guardianship. We want the assurance that God takes care of His vineyard.

Jesus, our God-man of many names and titles, is our coverture. He is as a shadow of a great rock in a weary land (Isa. 4:6). He is our Deliverer from the tempests of life.

William O. Cushing captured this great truth when he wrote his song: "O Safe to the Rock":

O safe to the Rock that is higher than I,
My soul in its conflicts and sorrows would fly;
So sinful, so weary, Thine own would I be;
Thou blest "Rock of Ages," I'm hiding in Thee.

Craftsman, Master

"We are *his workmanship,* created in Christ Jesus unto good works" (Eph. 2:10).

There aren't many master craftsmen left. They are few and far between. The Egyptians were probably the first great craftsmen, even though some work was done by the early Sumerians around 3000 BC. The great pyramids and the tombs of the kings are marvelous evidences of Egyptian craftsmanship. The *Discus Thrower* and *Venus de Milo* are examples of Greek skill. Michelangelo's *Moses* is a display for early Italian craftsmanship.

But though men have fashioned things from stone, bronze, gold, silver and wood, Christ did His craftsmanship on the hearts and souls of people. The Bible gives us a pretty fair chronology of His efforts in this direction. (See 2 Cor. 5:17; Gal. 6:15; Eph. 4:24; and Rev. 21:5.)

There are two poems which speak to us as we make ourselves available to the Master Craftsman. The last stanza of Oliver Wendell Holmes's "The Chambered Nautilus":

> Build thee more stately mansions, O my soul,
>> As the swift seasons roll!
>> Leave thy low-vaulted past!
> Let each new temple, nobler than the last,
> Shut thee from heaven with a dome more vast,
>> Till thou at length art free,
> Leaving thine outgrown shell by life's unresting sea!

and Longfellow's "The Builders":

> Let us do our work as well,
>> Both the unseen and the seen;
> Make the house, where Gods may dwell,
>> Beautiful, entire, and clean.

Enough said!

Creator of Israel

"I am the Lord, your Holy One, *the creator* of Israel, your King" (Isa. 43:15).

It is a distinct honor to be one of a kind. It is also a high honor to be the possessor of an original. Think of what it would mean to have an original painting by Picasso, an original piece of sculpture by Michelangelo, an original painting of Rembrandt, or one of Stradivari's violins! Any person in possession of any one of those works would be in a very select class.

Our Scripture verse for today states that Jesus was "creator of Israel." Israel was the special handiwork of the Master Creator. Even though we might say that He created everything, and He did, there is very special significance attached to the fact that He is mentioned as the Creator of Israel. Israel received special attention. Not every race of people received such attention. I doubt very seriously that Israel ever realized the full impact of such an honor. Maybe Israel did in desiring God's mercies, but what about doing God's will?

In one sense we are all "originals" created by the Master Creator. What an honor, but also what a responsibility! Just as Israel bore a special relationship and responsibility to the Creator, we likewise bear that same relationship, only two-fold: by virtue of creation and by virtue of redemption. We should, therefore, be less critical of Israel's erring ways and focus upon our own "doings."

Since we have been formed and fashioned by His tender hands and loving heart, we should seek to live out the prayer expressed by the psalmist in Psalm 51, given here in part with some paraphrasing:

O, Thou Master Creator of Israel and of all people and things, Create in me a clean heart, thou Master Workman of the ages. Renew within me a right spirit . . . and restore within me the joy of thy salvation.

A Nonpareil David

"I will set up one shepherd over them, and he shall feed them, even *my servant David;* he shall feed them, and he shall be their shepherd" (Ezek. 34:23).

The prophet Ezekiel referred to "a coming One, Christ" who could be called "a Better David," even a nonpareil David—one of unequalled excellence: a nonsuch. (The term *David* means "beloved of God.")

The David of the Old Testament has long been considered one of the world's greatest persons. David was a man after God's own heart. He was a masterful shepherd boy. He delivered his people from Philistine oppression by killing Goliath. He was a great king of all Israel. David placed his trust in the providence of God. He was a lover of peace and righteousness. However, there were two great calamities that marred David's life and reign: his adulterous relationship with Bathsheba, the wife of Uriah, when David allowed passion to dethrone conscience, and the rebellion of Absalom, David's son, when Absalom usurped the throne of David.

In reviewing this brief characterization of David, it is easy to see how Christ was a "better David," a "nonpareil David." Their lives had many parallels, but passion never dethroned the conscience of Jesus. His kingdom was in the hearts and lives of His followers. His reign is characterized by the spirit of love. As the Master Shepherd, He cared more for His flock than for Himself, even giving His life for His sheep.

The similarity was in evidence further when Jesus rode triumphantly into Jerusalem, the city of David, with the mob shouting, "Hosanna to the Son of David" (Matt. 21:9,15).

Irvin S. Cobb once remarked about Jesus, "Out of all history you'll find but one world conqueror who came with clean hands—and those hands the soldiers pierced with iron spikes when they nailed the Nazarene to the cross."[6]

6. Irvin S. Cobb, "Greatest Gentleman that Ever Lived," comp. Ralph Woods, *Behold the Man* (New York: The Macmillan Company, 1944), p. 15.

Daysman

"Neither is there any *daysman* betwixt us, that might lay his hand upon us both" (Job 9:33).

According to our Scripture passage, Job craved a daysman—umpire—between Himself and God because of the unequal terms on which they stood. Job was a man—a sinful creature—while God was infinitely powerful—a pure Creator. There was little common ground. A daysman was sorely needed, so Job felt.

Have you ever been in a situation where you felt the need of an umpire? During my college and graduate school days I played quite a bit of basketball. Once, while at the Seminary in Louisville, Kentucky, I became rather embroiled with a fellow player twice my size. He had an uncanny knack of shifting a part of his anatomy and knocking me to the floor. This occurred about three times without the detection by the umpire (referee). I longed for a better one to deal out justice. The territory didn't seem equal to me. So I made the mistake of trying to take things in my own hands, not a wise policy to pursue.

"Daysman," an archaic term, is properly defined as one who acts authoritatively for both parties and is free to impose conditions on both. We are far too frequently like Job in thinking of God as both the accuser and the Judge. Job was wrong. Satan was Job's accuser, and the game of life—the battle of life—is waged between Satan and the individual. Only Christ can lay His hands on both. For the repentant individual, Christ blew the whistle on Satan by giving His life for the sins of the world and made it possible for the individual to be free of condemnation. He made it possible, also, for the person to approach God on amicable terms.

Christ is our efficient Daysman. He officiates without bias or prejudice, so the game of life can be played according to divine rules.

Dayspring

"Through the tender mercy of our God; whereby *the dayspring* from on high hath visited us" (Luke 1:78).

Have you ever heard anyone say, "It was revealed in cold daylight"? However, in referring to Jesus as the "dayspring," we are saying that He was the daylight, the dawn, the beginning of a new era, or order of things, coming to us with a welcoming warmth. Dayspring, daylight, and dawn—the time when the bright present takes over from the dark past.

Thank God, that with the coming years ago of the Dayspring from on high, each breaking of the day ushers in a glorious morning: a gift from Him.

Some Bible commentators have felt that the reference in today's passage might refer to John the Baptist, but the heavier consensus is that it refers to the dawning of a new day, a new era, with the advent of Christ, the true Dayspring. Truly, a new order of things occurred with His coming.

The term *dayspring* picks up the beautiful imagery derived from the magnificence of an eastern sunrise. It is the picture of the sun pushing back the darkness of night. It also connotes the idea of a caravan which, during the darkness of night, has missed its way in the desert. The unfortunate ones are sitting down expecting the inevitable—death—when suddenly a light fills the horizon. So it was, and so it is, with the darkness of sin and the forgiving and loving light of the world, Jesus.

It was very dark when Jesus, the Dayspring from on high, came. Judaism was in the twilight zone with no pull of piety or acceptable spiritual service. Philosophy was peering toward pantheism and atheism. Idolatries were in the shadow of death. Into all of this came the Dayspring to illumine the blackness of the darkness of sin all the way to the glory of heaven.

So let us walk in the light as children of light in order that we may dwell in immortal glory. Our Dayspring from on high has brought the sunshine of salvation to a sin-sick world.

Day Star

"We have also a more sure word of prophecy; whereunto ye do well that ye take heed, as unto a light that shineth in a dark place, until the day dawn, and the *day star* arise in your hearts" (2 Pet. 1:19).

The day star is the morning star, the sun. Its arrival each morning pushes the night aside and ushers in a new day.

Roosters have a habit of crowing at the break of day. There is the story of the roosters who would crow at two o'clock in the morning. A bit unusual, but finally explicable. The owner noticed that the last streetcar to run at night would come around the corner with its lights perfectly positioned to shine through the cracks of the chicken house. The roosters mistook the streetcar's lights for the rays of the day star. Is there a lesson here for us?

Lamps and lights are good for the night, but how welcome and how precious to the traveler is the break of day, flooding the world with light. "Day star" is a very appropriate title for Christ, the herald of the dawn.

My father had the habit of rising early while it was still dark. He would come by my bed and say, "Get up, son. The sun will soon be up, and we will need to be in the fields." Daybreak for him was the bell sounding for work to begin. I didn't quite agree and hesitated once too long, much to my regret. He assured me by both action and words that he did not have time to call me more than once, and he expected me to respond. I promise you, I did thereafter.

But, oh, how many times I have failed to respond to the opportunities extended to me by the heavenly Day Star. My sins of omission could well exceed my sins of commission. He has called so many times.

May we this day, and in the days to come, welcome the dawn with an awareness that our Day Star comes early, asking each one of us to join Him in the fields which are white unto harvest.

Let us be up and doing. Time waits for no one!

Defender

"So when they continued asking him, *he lifted up himself,* and said unto them, He that is without sin among you, let him first cast a stone at her" (John 8:7).

Those self-righteous scribes and Pharisees thought they had a defenseless victim. The woman was caught in the act, and adultery was a serious offense against the law. With pride and scorn they brought her to Jesus as He sat in the court of the Temple in the Mount of Olives. They wasted no time and showed little courtesy as they blurted out to the Master Teacher, "Moses in the law commanded that such should be stoned. What do you say?" (author's paraphrase).

He immediately came to the defense of the helpless woman but said nothing, only stooping to write in the ground, and then looking up at them He said, "You who are without sin cast a stone." But no stones were thrown.

Truth and love were His only weapons of defense. He defended the woman by disarming her judges. He did not show disrespect of the law and the ordinances of Moses. The code remained, but who was qualified to execute it? No one among the group was able, so they tucked their heads and silently slipped away. Quite different from their boisterous approach.

The woman appeared to be truly penitent. Jesus was truly forgiving of her as a sinner, but He did not condone her sin; He condemned it. His interest was in freeing the sinner from her accusers and her sin. It is so sad that a few years later no one came to His rescue in freeing Him from His accusers.

He prevented mob action, an unpredictable thing. He thwarted it with truth and love—still our best defense.

Deliverer

"So all Israel shall be saved: as it is written, There shall come out of Sion the *Deliverer*, and shall turn away ungodliness from Jacob" (Rom. 11:26).

When man sinned, he did not catch God forgetful or unprepared. God had a plan and a Deliverer waiting in the wings. "And I will put enmity between thee and the woman, and between thy seed and her seed; it shall bruise thy head, and thou shalt bruise his heel" (Gen. 3:15).

And what a Deliverer there was, standing ready to come in the fullness of time. He would be the One who would free persons from the restraints of sin and provide liberty and release from the chains of sin.

While in the lion's den, Daniel was asked by the king, "O Daniel, servant of the living God, is thy God, whom thou servest continually, able to deliver thee from the lions?" (Dan. 6:20). The answer was in the affirmative.

In the Model Prayer, Jesus, the great Deliverer, taught His disciples to pray, "Deliver us from evil" (Matt. 6:13). He was offering himself for the job.

The apostle Paul, giving some parting advice and counsel to Timothy, his spiritual son in the ministry, said, "The Lord shall deliver me from every evil work, and will preserve me unto his heavenly kingdom" (2 Tim. 4:18). Paul was sure that he had not caught his Deliverer unprepared.

The hymn, written during the eighteenth century by William Williams, "Guide Me, O Thou Great Jehovah," speaks of the Deliverer in most expressive words:

> Open now the crystal fountain,
> Whence the healing stream doth flow;
> Let the fire and cloudy pillar
> Lead me all my journey through;
> Strong Deliverer, be Thou still
>   my strength and shield.

The Deliverer waits patiently with out-stretched arms and loving heart.

81

Desire of All Nations

"I will shake all nations, and *the desire of all nations* shall come: and I will fill this house with glory, saith the Lord of hosts" (Hag. 2:7).

Desire is a good, warm, and strong word. It denotes anticipation, expectancy, and fulfillment.

Homer, in the *Odyssey*, spoke of it as the "ache of longing." Shakespeare had Cleopatra say, "I have immortal longings." Desire is then rightfully defined as an aching, immortal longing.

In the context of our Scripture reference, "desire of all nations" meant that the one who would fulfill all desires would be versatile, capable of meeting the needs of every nation. He would be able to leave nothing undesired.

The history of all races, from antiquity until now, indicates that all the religions of people, from those in a most degraded condition to the most cultivated and civilized people, desired—longed for—the appearance of a visible Deity. They wanted a God at hand, not one afar off. They frequently expressed their desires in this respect by their worship of idols and kings, all attempts at incarnations of deity.

There have been four basic desires of nations regarding the appearance of a visible god. First, they have wanted a come-near god, not just one they could look up to. Second, there has been the desire for a god who could deliver people from their sins. Third, through the ages, people have wanted an authentic communication from God to humanity. They have longed for God's authentic One. Fourth, the desire for the assurance of afterlife—immortality—has always found itself in the practices and beliefs of all major religions.

Does Jesus meet all the criteria? Rather, I should ask, has anyone other than Jesus ever met these criteria? No! He is the prophesied Desire of all nations.

Despised and Rejected One

"He is *despised and rejected* of men; a man of sorrows, and acquainted with grief: and we hid as it were our faces from him; he was despised, and we esteemed him not" (Isa. 53:3).

It is a terrible thing to be unwanted, rejected. I have watched clumsy, uncoordinated youngsters weep when they were unwanted in the choosing of sides which took place before the game began.

It is far more terrible to treat God's Son in such a manner. But they did way back then (Ps. 22:6), and we still do. His overtures of grace are still rejected. His love is spurned. He has been left alone, purposely avoided. God forgive us! The poem "Indifference" by G. A. Studdert-Kennedy speaks to this matter.

When Jesus came in the days of old,
    they hanged Him on a tree,
They drove great nails through His hands
    and feet, and made a Calvary;
They crowned Him with a crown of thorns,
    red were His wounds and deep,
    For those were crude and cruel days,
    and human flesh was cheap.

When Jesus came to our town,
    they simply passed Him by,
They never hurt a hair of Him,
    they only let Him die;
For men had grown more tender,
    and they would not give Him pain
They only just passed down the street,
    and left Him in the rain.

Still, Jesus cried, "Forgive them, for
    they know not what they do,"
And still it rained the winter rain
    and drenched Him through and through;
The crowds went home and left the streets
    without a soul to see,
And Jesus crunched against the wall
    and cried for Calvary.

The Dew

"I will be as *the dew* unto Israel: he shall grow as the lily, and cast forth his roots as Lebanon" (Hos. 14:5).

Have you ever been wet by the dew? Have you ever plucked a cantaloupe right off the vine while it was still covered with dew? I have, many times, also watermelons. Cantaloupes and watermelons are better when plucked in that manner. There seems to be a freshness and deliciousness that refrigerators can't give.

Dew is refreshing, fertilizing, and reviving. It forms silently during the night. It is unseen and moves over the earth without the heralding of thunder or the display of lightning. It comes repeatedly; if it came only once, it would be of little value.

In lands where there is little rain, the dew fertilizes the earth, refreshes the languid plants, and revives all things of nature, making them grow. Dew thus becomes the source of fruitfulness.

In a spiritual context, the dew of God signifies temporal blessings and spiritual blessings by the refreshing of the soul and the bringing of the fruit of the Spirit.

The main point of the emblem of dew is the result of the Lord's gracious activity when He comes as the Dew of God. Over and over again, Christ, as the Dew of God's grace, spent much time trying to revive a spiritually parched world. He sought to bring the abundant life.

As the dew of earth is more likely to form on a clear, calm night than on cloudy or windy ones, so the dew of God's grace is more likely to descend upon those who are still and know Him.

My prayer today for myself and my readers is that God's dew will be as the "dew that covers Dixie" and the whole world. However, spiritual dew does not come automatically. It is always available, but it comes only in response to worship and commitment.

84

Diadem

"Thou shalt also be a crown of glory in the hand of the Lord, and a royal *diadem* in the hand of thy God" (Isa. 62:3).

One of the greatest collections of crown jewels the public has been free to view is that which resides in the Tower of London which was built in 1078 by William the Conqueror. There is quite a variety of jewels, and they are used by the royal family on special occasions. They are emblems of regal power.

What a contrast with the crown of thorns which was rammed down on the head of Jesus—the only earthly crown ever worn by the King of kings. Those who made Him wear it did so as an act of mockery and derision.

I have seen decorated soldiers from the battlefield, generals from the Pentagon, and leaders of nations garbed in precious medals. I do not question the sacrifices made by these. When I think of Christ—the souls He has redeemed, the lives He has put back together, the homes He has salvaged, and the peace and comfort He has given through the centuries—I am prone to feel that the crown most worthy of all is a crown of righteousness. It is the one that will not tarnish or decay throughout eternity.

The hymn written by Matthew Bridges in the mid-nineteenth century entitled "Crown Him with Many Crowns" and sung to the tune DIADEMATA expresses the spirit of what I would like to share with you.

> Crown Him with many crowns,
> The Lamb upon His throne;
> Hark! how the heavenly anthem drowns
> All music but its own:
> Awake, my soul, and sing
> Of him who died for thee,
> And hail Him as thy matchless King
> Through all eternity.

Diplomat

"Then came to him the mother of Zebedee's children with her sons, worshipping him, and desiring a certain thing of him" (Matt. 20:20).

A diplomat has been defined as one skilled in personal, interracial, and international diplomacy, using tact and artfulness in the conduct of affairs. One of the most tactful and diplomatic responses I ever read was that of Henry Clay, a leading statesman during the critical years just prior to the American Civil War. A lovely lady whom Clay had met previously seemed a bit taken back that he seemed to have forgotten her name. To which Mr. Clay replied, "My dear lady, when I met you a year ago I was so impressed with your beauty that I knew that ere I met you again you would change your name, and I just didn't bother to remember it."

Our devotional Scripture for the day shows Christ as a diplomat in the truest sense. Salome, the mother of James and John, and probably Jesus' aunt, approached Jesus asking that He grant her two sons seats of honor, one on His right side and one on His left side, when Jesus established His kingdom. This was a common practice of the Romans and Jews at banquets and still is. It is interesting to note that Salome did not use diplomacy. She commanded Jesus to respond affirmatively to her request. She thought that since there was a family relationship, then, too, her sons had been favored by going with Jesus to the mount of transfiguration and also of sharing in a special way the raising of Jarius's daughter, the request was reasonable and should be granted.

Jesus didn't respond with a harsh "No, indeed. I will not." He asked if James and John had considered the cost. Were they willing to drink of the bitter cup of suffering? Their response was yes (Matt. 20:22).

Jesus brought them to the real point of favored position in His kingdom as being that which comes from service. That is the real measuring rod of greatness. Greatness is not handed out or dispensed arbitrarily. It is earned. Have we learned that?

Disciplemaker

"He saith unto them, Follow me, and I will make you fishers of men" (Matt. 4:19).

Jesus spent a lot of time calling persons into His service and training them to become disciples. A disciple is a scholar, a learner, a follower who believes strongly in the doctrines and teachings of his master. Jesus called the twelve and gave them firsthand experiences and related to them many parables and exhortations.

He is still in the recruiting business. He is looking for followers, fishers of men, and witnesses. The disciple must never feel above his teacher or master and must be willing to subordinate self to the desires and commands of the teacher.

In this respect Carl Sandburg's poem "Prayer of Steel" does something for me. Maybe it will for you.

> Lay me on an anvil, O God,
> Beat me and hammer me into a crowbar.
> Let me pry loose old walls,
> Let me lift and loosen old foundations.
> Lay me on an anvil, O God,
> Beat me and hammer me into a steel spike,
> Drive me into the girders that hold a skyscraper
>   together,
> Take red hot rivets and fasten me into the
>   central girders,
> Let me be the nail holding a skyscraper
> Through blue night into white stars.

Disciplined disciples is the desire of the Disciplemaker.

87

Dissenter

"Ye have heard that it was said by them of old time, . . . *But I say unto you"* [I choose to dissent; I beg to differ] (Matt. 5:21-22).

Christ chose to differ with the established laws and customs. In that respect He was a nonconformist.

Our church history records for us that there were nonconformists regarding the Church of England and the church of Rome. The reformation was an outgrowth of such against the church at Rome. Free churchmen sprang up in England in revolt to the established church.

Jesus recognized the established laws and the traditional interpretation of those laws. He was aware of what the teachers and rabbis had taught their followers.

But as recorded in the fifth chapter of Matthew, Jesus chose to dissent—disagree—with the letter of the law. The Greek language emphasized the personal pronoun *I.* "I say unto you." Christ was speaking with the same and even more authority as those words of law once spoken by God. He therefore spoke as one with proper authority. He was not a recalcitrant rebel trying to get even with His critics. His dissent was in order to give a more perfect and far-reaching interpretation of their codes of conduct. Thought, motive, and intent were to be accounted for even as the act.

The world today needs to hear Him say, "But *I* say unto you" (author's italics). We tend to listen to too many other voices. I think He would cancel out many of those voices and say, "Look, let us get on with the important issues. *I* say this unto you. Follow Me!"

88

Divider

"He said unto him, Man, who made me a judge or *a divider* over you?" (Luke 12:14).

There are many legends about the Holy Grail. One is that it was the cup that Jesus drank from at the Last Supper. Another is that Joseph of Arimathea used it to catch the blood that dropped from Jesus' side as he hung on the cross. Still another, that it travelled all over the world on a beam of glorious light, and one night it came to King Arthur's court. Its effect upon the group is described thusly, "Then were all alighted of the Holy Ghost, and then each knight began to see his brother fairer than ever he saw him before."[7]

It is no false assumption to assume that each knight felt more kindly disposed toward his brother, more generous and serving. Something like that might have caused the brothers in our Scripture passage to make the division of the inheritance without bothering Christ. Obviously, there was no written will and not much will to divide the inheritance equally.

By coming to Jesus asking that He make the division of the inheritance, the man showed a willingness to have a third party involved. There must have been a strong element of covetousness in the situation. Jesus focuses the attention of the inquirer on the real issue: abundant life is not in things which a person possesses. Things will perish in this life, but life goes on. We live in a world of things. Have you ever thought about the number of radios, stereos, and televisions you have in your home? Count them, you will be surprised. Thing, things, things!

The person who lays up treasures for self is not rich toward God. Our possessions should never possess us. U-Haul trucks do not follow hearses to the cemetery to deposit things in the grave with the casket. The kingdom of God comes first.

7. Arthur E. Crowley, "Worship Opens Blind Eyes," *Treasury of the Christian Faith*, ed. Stanley I. Stuber and Thomas Curtis Clark (New York: Association Press, 1949), p. 806.

Divine Legate

"Jesus answered them, I told you, and ye believed not: *the works that I do in my Father's name*, they *bear witness of me*" (John 10:25).

In Indian folklore, there is the story of an Indian who, looking out across the plains, sees a figure on the horizon. At first he thinks it a wild animal. As it draws nearer, the Indian sees it is a man on a horse, but, believing the rider to be the enemy, the Indian prepares to shoot. The rider continues to come closer, and he realizes that it is not the enemy but one of his own tribe, so the Indian prepares to welcome the visitor. When the approaching figure comes closer, the Indian recognizes the visitor as his brother, and they embrace.

This parable speaks of Jesus as the divine Legate. He is God's envoy, God's ambassador with full power. The closer Jesus comes the more we recognize Him not only as a brother but as God.

What Jesus did, He did in the Father's name. What the Father does, the Son does in like manner, and the works of the Father are wrought by the Son. Some fathers and sons can't work well together, but not so with Jesus and His Father, God. They understood each other, and the work of One was the work of the other.

Would it be fair to refer to Jesus as a "stand-in" for God? I see nothing wrong with this. He stood *for God*, also.

I have a Bible which was presented to me in May, 1930, by a high school friend. I have kept a poem by Annie Johnson Flint on the flyleaf. The poem, "Jesus Christ—and We," suggests that we should represent Christ just as Christ represented God.

> Christ has no hands but our hands
> To do his work today;
> He has no feet but our feet
> To lead men in his way;
> He has no tongue but our tongues
> To tell men how he died;
> He has no help but our help
> To bring them to his side.

Just as Christ was a divine Legate of God, we are ambassadors for Christ.

Donor of Immortality

"I give unto them *eternal life*" [immortality] (John 10:28).
"For this corruptible must put on incorruption, and this mortal must put on *immortality*" (1 Cor. 15:53).

While I was a college president, fund raising was one of my most enjoyable responsibilities. I would frequently call it "fun raising" or "friend raising," for, to me, it was both.

It is easy to remember the first $50,000 gift I secured for the college. I well remember the first $250,000 gift, and, you can bet your life, I will never forget the time I asked for $1,000,000, and our most generous donor gave the college $1,200,000, and has since brought the total of his giving to over eight figures. Gifts of that nature are not easily forgotten.

How then could I, or anyone for that matter, ever forget or be less than deeply appreciative of our gift of immortality given to us by the Son of God, worth inestimably more than the millions given the college? Not only did Christ give Himself to make this immortality possible, but He forgave us, the recipients, of our sins. That is two-for-one giving.

Immortality is exemption from the sting or annihilation of death. It is "everlastingness."

There is an old German motto which says, "Those who live in the Lord never see each other for the last time." Believing this, we can die well, and we can live life to the fullest.

The resurrection of the body to immortality is one of the greatest and most glorious teachings of our Christian faith, and it is founded on the resurrection of Christ: a sure thing!

The Door

"Then said Jesus unto them again, Verily, verily, I say unto you, I am the door of the sheep. . . . I am the door: by me if any man enter in, he shall be saved, and shall go in and out, and find pasture" (John 10:7,9).

Most all buildings today have two kinds of doors: entrance doors and exit doors. In the first place, an entrance door provides access to an area while in the second place, an exit door is a causement means of leaving an area.

In our Scripture for the day, Jesus refers to Himself as the door of the sheep. He had in mind a very familiar situation in those days. When the sheep had been placed in an area called a "sheepfold," the shepherd would place Himself over the entrance to prevent any sheep from leaving or to prohibit wild animals from coming into the enclosure. Literally, the shepherd would lay down his life for his sheep.

The Pharisees thought of themselves as doors because of their confidence in the laws. They tried to teach salvation without the Messiah. They provided what we might call a "false door."

The whole thrust here is to distinguish between false and true teachers, using the parable of the shepherd and his sheep. Many false teachers have called out to the sheep, but the sheep of Jesus will not follow a strange voice.

As the Good Shepherd and the true Teacher, Jesus provides green pastures for His sheep. He leads them beside the still waters, so they can drink calmly and in peace.

As a Good Shepherd, Jesus provides for the safety of His sheep. John 10:28-29 says, "I give unto them eternal life; and they shall never perish, neither shall any man pluck them out of my hand. My Father, which gave them me, is greater than all; and no man is able to pluck them out of my Father's hand."

The door to His heart is always open!

Eagle

"As an *eagle* stirreth up her nest, fluttereth over her young, spreadeth abroad her wings, taketh them, beareth them on her wings" (Deut. 32:11).

Jesus can be compared to an eagle. This comparison in no way degrades Him but merely adds to His lustrous halo of titles and designations. The Deuteronomy passage gives us this privilege.

An eagle is a bird noted for its strength. It is graceful with a keen vision and the power to soar. It has been called "king of birds." The symbol of the eagle appears on the great seal of the United States. We speak of being "eagle eyed," sharp, and observing.

In referring to Jesus as an eagle, we come immediately into the care of Israel and the Israel of God as described in Deuteronomy 32:11 and Galatians 6:16. Through the centuries God had to discipline Israel, and Christ had to discipline His disciples and continues to discipline us as the Israel of God. Such discipline and training are needed for the work appointed to us to do.

A mother eagle takes good care of her young. She feeds them, trains them, and carries them for awhile on her wings. She knows when to push them from the nest.

The Christian life is filled with teaching, testing, and guarding. We are to listen, study, and learn. In the career of a Christian it is very important to keep on learning. We are never out of class, either formally or informally.

Testing is a part of Christian growth. Sooner or later we must place full weight upon faith. Sooner or later we must face up to the crossroads: the high way or the low way. Sooner or later the Christian will find it hard not to yield to temptation.

There is the beautiful remembrance that the eagle, the Lord, will guard us so that no evil can permanently befall us. He will carry us on His wings and hide us under His wings.

Ecce Homo

"Then came Jesus forth, wearing the crown of thorns, and the purple robe. And Pilate saith unto them, *Behold the man!*" (John 19:5).

I would like to refer your mind to what Charles Dickens wrote in *Pickwick Papers:*

"It's always best on these occasions to do what the mob do."

"But, suppose there are two mobs?" suggested Mr. Snodgrass.

"Shout with the largest," replied Mr. Pickwick.

And that was the action the crowd took when Jesus was standing before Pilate. Bystanders of a mob usually flow right into the spirit of the mob, maybe due more to fear than to compatibility.

When Pilate said, "Ecce Homo" ("Behold the man" or, "Lo, the man" or, "Look at this man"), he was trying to say to the mob, "Can this poor, bruised, battered, spiritless sufferer be dangerous or threatening? Is He worth such fear and hate? Does He look like a triumphant King? Can He engender much support? It seems to me there is too much ado about too little of a man."

But Pilate's words seemed to tee off the mob even more and the shouts were, "Crucify, crucify, crucify!" The mob was more like wild beasts ready to attack. The passion of the mobsters was intense, fierce, and irrational. They were very determined to make even His death as painful and disgraceful as possible.

Religious animosity is usually very bitter, very unrelenting, and atrocious. It takes on an intensity unknown to other causes. To underscore this fact one needs only to call to mind the Spanish Inquisitions and the witch hunts in Salem which were attempts to stamp out what was defined as heresy. Thousands were cruelly killed by the government.

It is interesting that in the presence of the Jerusalem mob, not a voice was raised in favor of Jesus. Could that still be true?

Elect and Chosen of God

"Behold my servant, whom I uphold; mine *elect*, in whom my soul delighteth; I have put my spirit upon him: he shall bring forth judgment to the Gentiles" (Isa. 42:1).

Matthew, in writing about Jesus as the elect and chosen of God, quotes from the Book of Isaiah. The Isaiah passage points out that the Messiah to come will be triumphant, without failure.

Failure is a part of human life. No one has scored an hundred on every examination taken. No one has done all the nice things that a husband and wife should do for each other. No one has been totally free of the bitter taste of failure. Christ is the only exception.

Governments have failed. Nations have fallen and continue to fall. Philosophies of life have come and gone. T. S. Eliot once remarked that Americans are looking for a system so perfect that no one needs be good. Here in our country, we think that way. We expect the virtues of our democratic way of life to carry us, as it has basically in the past, through all troubled water; but, that is not so. Democracy is no better than those who live under it and support it.

Matthew saw in Jesus One whom God had laid hold of, one beloved, chosen, elect, and precious: One who was well pleasing to God. He believed Him to be a very special person, especially equipped to handle all situations and to master all occasions. Matthew somehow envisioned the triumphant march of the Master through all the woes and temptations of life, emerging finally as the sinless, changeless and all-powerful one.

Jesus was the "elect and chosen of God" not to, as James Martineau once said, "persuade the Father," not to appease the Father, not to make a sanguinary purchase from the Father but simply to: "Shew us the Father." One cannot see Jesus without seeing God. One cannot understand God without understanding Jesus. They were and are inseparable.

95

Elias

"Some say that thou art John the Baptist: some, *Elias;* and others, Jeremias, or one of the prophets" (Matt. 16:14).

This very familiar passage is a miniature "Who's Who" or "What's What." It is sometimes very difficult to get persons properly identified.

When Jesus asked His disciples, "Whom do men say that I the Son of man am?" (Matt. 16:13), He tipped His hand. But the disciples were too interested to get on with quoting what others were saying. Aren't we all like that? Wouldn't we rather say, "Let me tell you what others have said," rather than saying something ourselves. We like to use quotation marks.

How could Jesus have been John the Baptist, one of His contemporaries? How could He have been Jeremiah without a special reincarnation? And, of course, Elias, or Elijah, was a very poor choice. Jesus was in no way like Him. But the disciples couldn't free themselves from the expectation of the Jews who looked for Elijah to come back to life and become a forerunner of the Messiah. The expectation had grown to an extent that every unusual person to appear on the horizon was expected to be Elijah.

I have heard and seen this episode reenacted time and time again as persons try to identify every evil leader as the antichrist. Someone once remarked that there have been enough antichrists to form quite an array of has-beens.

It is so important that we get clear in our minds just who Jesus was and is. It all begins right here, for our faith has that as the starting gate. Peter's confession, "Thou art the Christ, the Son of the living God" (Matt. 16:16), must be our daily confession. Once we make this confession, then we can behold Him as multifaceted in life, in purpose, and in action. All other names, titles, and designations have their rootage here.

El, Elohim, Etc.

"And *God* [Elohim] said, Let *us* [Elohim] make man in our image" (Gen. 1:26).

Elohim is the Hebrew word for God. It is a plural noun conveying the comprehensiveness of His person. It is used over 2500 times in the Old Testament and always with a singular verb. The plurality of the word indicates the Trinity, tri-unity: Father, Son, and Holy Spirit which existed from the beginning. The word denotes the Supreme One, the eternal One.

A short form of Elohim is *El,* which means the Mighty One. He is able to do anything according to His will (Ps. 19:1).

There are quite a number of derivations of Elohim. *Eloah* is the singular term and is found in Deuteronomy 31:15 where, in the King James Version, it is translated "Lord."

El Elyon is translated "the most High" (Ps. 91:1; Gen.14:19). The idea here is that God is high and over all.

El Gibbor means "the mighty God" (Gen. 49:24); "the mighty One" (Isa. 49:26). This name indicates the majesty, strength, and power of God, and David assumed that God, *El Gibbor,* would fight for Israel.

El Shaddai means "God Almighty, All Powerful" (Gen. 17:1). This strength, however, especially relates to the tender relationship God bears with His children as the adequate Protector and Provider. He is the One who supplies, sustains, and satisfies. A very popular song, high on the list of hits, is entitled "El Shaddai."

El Olam can be translated "the everlasting God" (Gen. 21:33; Rom. 16:26). He is a God forever available. He is exactly what His people need from age to age. He endures; He never forsakes.

The short form *El* is used extensively in proper names. Three illustrations: Dani-El, "Judge of God"; Ezeki-El, "God will strengthen"; and Beth-El, "House of God."

May this name of God in all of its aspects receive the honor and praise due it.

Emmanuel

"Behold, a virgin shall be with child, and shall bring forth a son, and they shall call his name *Emmanuel*, which being interpreted is, God with us" (Matt. 1:23).

God without humanity is still God while humanity without God is nothing, but humanity with God makes an awesome twosome. That is a good reason why we should be forever grateful that God sent His son, Emmanuel—God with us—into the world, so Emmanuel could bring man and God together.

The word *Emmanuel*, spelled with an *E*, is used more frequently in the Septuagint. It is not so much a name borne as a description of Jesus' character and position. However, early Christian writers and also modern writers have applied it to Him. The appellation spelled "Immanuel," affixed to Him, occurs in the Old Testament in Isaiah 7:14. (See also Isa. 8:8.)

Since Jesus came, Christians are never alone. His Holy Spirit took over where He left off. The hymns of our faith keep coming to me over and over. They pay great tribute to Christ and have been instrumental in helping me verbalize my faith. I am thinking now of the hymn "Never Alone." Its author is anonymous, but the late B. B. McKinney set it to music.

> I've seen the lightning flashing,
> And heard the thunder roll,
> I've felt sin's breakers dashing,
> Trying to conquer my soul;
> I've heard the voice of Jesus,
> Telling me still to fight on,
> He promised never to leave me,
> Never to leave me alone.

He will never leave us. Emmanuel came, and He came to be with us. Now we look forward to going to be with Him in the "land that is fairer than day."

The Empowering One

"When he had called unto him his twelve disciples, *he gave them power* against unclean spirits, to cast them out, and to heal all manner of sickness and all manner of disease" (Matt. 10:1).

In 1931 Frank S. Mead wrote a book entitled *The March of Eleven Men* in which he very pointedly tells of the powerful thrust the disciples made upon the Greco-Roman world.

"Truly the eleven men had swept the scholarship of the most impregnable citadels of ancient learning to the foot of the cross of the Nazarene, and made it worship there. Christianity took prisoner the finest learning of Athens, Alexandria and Antioch," he wrote.[8]

Mead indicated that the one thing above all else that made Christianity a conqueror in old Greece was the proof of power in the changed lives of its adherents. They did not speak great things but lived them. It was obvious to the world that something had come into the lives of the eleven. They were changed persons and charged up. Their courage was strong, and their commitment unquestionable. They marched on and on against insuperable odds. Why?

I think I have the answer. Jesus had empowered them and sent them forth under His banner. He gave them authority over unclean spirits and power to heal the sick. They held in their hands and hearts spiritual power to release and to heal, almost awesome power if misused. They also had the power of a quickened faith.

Other men have been able to teach, inspire, and guide their followers, but only Jesus had the power to impart power to His followers. He was truly a dispenser of power.

One might liken the lives of the disciples before Christ to dead batteries, which are of little value, but after their lives were recharged by Him, the disciples went forth with "dynamite" in their souls. He gave them tolerance, protection, and encouragement. He can still recharge our dead and weak spiritual batteries.

8. Frank S. Mead, *The March of Eleven Men* (New York: Grosset and Dunlap, Inc., 1931, 1932), p. 37.

Ensign of the People

"In that day there shall be a root of Jesse, which shall stand for an *ensign of the people;* to it shall the Gentiles seek: and his rest shall be glorious" (Isa. 11:10).

As an ensign, Christ is our standard bearer. He assumed that role while on the cross, and it is with this banner that as Christians we march into the world.

Daniel W. Whittle in the mid-nineteenth century penned the words to the hymn "The Banner of the Cross":

> There's a royal banner given for display
> To the soldiers of the King;
> As an ensign fair we lift it up today,
> While as ransomed ones we sing.
> Marching on, marching on,
> For Christ count everything but loss!
> And to crown him King, toil and sing
> 'Neath the banner of the cross!

My, how proudly that banner has been borne through the centuries. In less than three hundred years after Christ was nailed to the cross, an unlikely army, comprised of the maimed, the blind, and lame tortured and disfigured by Rome, saw that banner of the cross float victoriously from the capitol of Rome. One thing very soon became certain to those who dealt with such an army; Jesus represented forces vaster than the contemporary rulers could direct or command, arrest, or annihilate.

When Jesus, our Ensign, planted the banner of the cross on Golgotha's summit, it was more powerful than when Hitler raised the German swastika atop Mount Olympus, the mythical home of the ancient Greek gods. The banner of the cross stood for life while the German banner stood for death.

Someday "every knee [shall] bow, of things in heaven, and things in earth, and things under the earth; And . . . every tongue should confess that Jesus Christ is Lord, to the glory of God the Father" (Phil. 2:10-11).

Eternal Life

"We know that the Son of God is come, and hath given us an understanding, that we may know him that is true, and we are in him that is true, even in his Son Jesus Christ. This is the true God, and *eternal life*" (1 John 5:20).

There is a legend about a swan and a crane. A beautiful swan swoops down out of the sky and alights on the banks of a lake in which a crane is looking for snails. The crane asks, "Whence did you come?"

"I came from heaven."

"Where is heaven?" asks the crane.

The swan describes at length the grandeur of the eternal city only to be asked, "Are there snails in heaven?"

"Snails! Of course not," answers the swan.

"Then," the earthbound crane replies, "you can have your heaven. I want snails more than anything else."

This legend is a parable of many people. They prefer the snails of earth to the fellowship with the Eternal Life in the world to come. Christ brought life and immortality to light. When I think of Him as Eternal Life, I think of four aspects of a Christian's life relating to Him.

Life comes from Him. He is the source of life through His part in the creative acts.

Life is in Him, "For in him we live, and move, and have our being" (Acts 17:28). Apart from Him we are nothing.

Life is to be lived for Him. Living for Jesus is the supreme goal of the Christian's life. Paul, in writing to those at Philippi, said, "I count all things but loss for the excellency of the knowledge of Christ Jesus my Lord: for whom I have suffered the loss of all things, and do count them but dung, that I may win Christ" (Phil. 3:8).

Life is to be lived also with Him in the New Jerusalem, the Holy City, which John saw coming down from heaven, as a bride adorned for her husband (Rev. 21:2).

What a joy to anticipate!

101

Everybody, Only a Little Taller

"He shall grow up before him as a tender plant, and as a root out of a dry ground: he hath no form nor comeliness; and when we shall see him, there is no beauty that we should desire him" (Isa. 53:2). "For in him dwelleth *all the fulness* of the Godhead bodily" (Col. 2:9).

In January 1952 I was on the campus of Union University in Jackson, Tennessee, as guest speaker for Christian Emphasis Week. One afternoon I was meeting with an English class and saw on the classroom wall a John Hancock Insurance advertisement with a picture of Abraham Lincoln in the center. These words were at the top of the ad: "He was everybody, only a little taller."

I thought then, and I still think, that Lincoln was a great person, but no one meets that description like Jesus. He was everyone, only much taller.

Let us call the roll of some of the professions:

To artists, He is the One altogether lovely.

To architects, He is the Chief Cornerstone.

To physicians, He is the Great Physician.

To preachers, He is the Word of God.

To philosophers, He is the Wisdom of God.

To the dying, He is the Resurrection and the Life.

To geologists, He is the Rock of ages.

To farmers, He is the Lord of the harvest.

To professors, he is the Master Teacher.

To prodigals, He is the forgiving Father.

To the lost sheep, He is the Good Shepherd.

To thirsty souls, He is the Water of life.

To the hungry, He is the Bread of life.

To philanthropists, He is God's Unspeakable Gift.

Nineteen centuries after His sojourn on earth, His shadow is larger and growing larger than ever before. No one can measure His height or His influence.

102

Everlasting Father

"His name shall be called . . . The *Everlasting Father*" (Isa. 9:6).

Once I read about a foreign missionary's son who had remained in America. The lad kept a picture of his father over his desk. At Christmas one of the boy's friends asked, "What would you like most to have this Christmas?"

The young man replied without hesitation, "I would like for my father to step out of that picture."

In Christ, God did just that.

The name *Everlasting Father* or *Father of eternity* carries with it the idea of tender care and immortal life, beautifully blended. Jesus has much to do with eternity. There is a modern song which says, "He was there all the time."

As Everlasting Father, it is said of Jesus that "Before Abraham was [born], I am" (John 8:58). He is now our reigning Lord, and he is Lord of all future time. "Jesus Christ the same yesterday, and to-day, and for ever" (Heb. 13:8).

As Father of eternity he has never been a forsaking Father, nor a vindictive Father, nor a jealous Father. He has always been a forgiving Father, an ever-present Father, and a loving Father.

How wonderful it is to be associated with an Everlasting Father who is unchangeable, unflappable, and unerring. We do not have to cater to the changing whims of a stern despot, nor seek to serve a temperamental deity.

Our work is to find the Father God in Christ and serve Him with mind, body, and soul. And what we ask God to do for us, we should be willing for Him to do through us.

Dying persons need and have an undying Christ. Living persons need and have a living Christ. All of God's children need an Everlasting Father who will provide guidance, love, and peace.

Jesus is the One.

Expert

"When the multitude heard this, they were *astonished at his doctrine*" (Matt. 22:33).

A trite definition of an expert is one who knows all the answers if you ask the right questions. An expert may be more familiar with reasons why something can't be done than why it can be done.

A more accurate definition of an expert is a person who is skilled, knowledgeable, capable of giving counsel, experienced, adept, adroit, proficient, and possessed of the facility of performance. Now, who then is an expert?

Jesus knows why things can be done. He can make the problem become an opportunity. He can provide the resources, so a performance can be skilled and proficient.

Again, it has been facetiously said that an expert will give you his advice "fee-ly." Jesus gives His freely.

Why am I so adamant about Christ's being an expert? Maybe I should answer that question by asking some questions. Did He ever fail to complete successfully a task to which He set His hands? Did He ever fail for lack of knowledge? Did He ever throw up His hands and say, "That's impossible. It can't be done"? Did he ever "fumble the ball," so to speak?

His skills are many, but He is best at taking a life which has been torn by sin and making it whole again. He can take the shattered pieces of a broken home and bring again wholeness and love. Jesus is an Expert.

You don't have to look up His number in the yellow pages. Just dial it—P R A Y E R. Grace has paid His consultant's fee! Give Him a call.

Express Image

"Who being the brightness of his glory, and the *express image* of his person, and upholding all things by the word of his power, when he had by himself purged our sins, sat down on the right hand of the Majesty on high" (Heb. 1:3).

In the biological world, the gene—a small part of the chromosome—is the entity concerned with the transmission and development of hereditary characteristics. It is amazing how accurate genes are in transmitting even minute physical markings. My father had a small mole just to the right of his nose. I have one at the exact spot, and our youngest daughter had an identical one. One can only exclaim, "What accuracy!"

But, think of the spiritual world—the accuracy of God in that Christ was the express image of God. He had the divine essence stamped upon Him. He might be called the Father's "alter ego," His very image.

Christ has upon Himself the exact impress of Deity. He is the perfect representation of God's essence and this is the perfect revealer. The Greek word *charakter* means the impress made from an engraving tool. It occurs nowhere else in the New Testament. As the imprint of the die perfectly represents the original design, so in Christ there is the display for those who have eyes to see God's very essence.

Jesus said, "I and my Father are one" (John 10:30). He also said, "He that hath seen me hath seen the Father" (John 14:9). A very similar assertion is made in Colossians 1:15, "Who is the image of the invisible God."

In the world of tool and die making, it is impossible to get a perfect die or a perfect impress from the die. But in our Hebrew passage, the language is clear that Christ is the "express [perfect] image" of God. He is also the effulgence of divine glory totally related to God as rays of light are related to the sun with neither existing without the other.

Since we as Christians are "little Christs," we should bear His essence in our lives. Our striving, therefore, is to be more like Him. The striving is never over.

105

Faithful and True (Warrior)

"I saw heaven opened, and behold a white horse; and he that sat upon him was called *Faithful and True*, and in righteousness he doth judge and make war" (Rev. 19:11).

On a Confederate soldier's tombstone in Charleston, South Carolina, are these words:

The Hour of Conflict,
    The Day of Defeat,
The Years of Oppression
Brought to his courage
    No slackness
And to his Loyal Service
    No Abatement.

What a testimony to a loyal soldier, truer even in describing our Lord.

The Book of Revelation mentions three enemies of Christ and His church: the dragon, the first beast, and the false prophet (which is the second beast). You will do well to read Revelation 6:2, which also describes Jesus as a conqueror on a white horse. He is Faithful and True in avenging His people, in carrying out His purposes, and in establishing Himself and the Kingdom of righteousness.

The future fulfillment of His promises substantiates the veracity of all that had been prophesied.

All things expected and anticipated about the coming One, and the final triumph and reward were never in doubt. God's clock keeps ticking unerringly through all the turmoil and adversities of the centuries. It has never run down nor lost its accuracy.

Jesus keeps ever at His God-given task. He has never backpedaled or avoided confrontation. He never went "AWOL." He has answered every roll call and marched straight into the jaws of death in order to complete His work as a faithful and true warrior.

May we fight the good fight of loyalty and faithfulness.

Faithful and True Witness

"Unto the angel of the church of the Laodiceans write; These things saith the Amen, the *faithful and true witness*, the beginning of the creation of God" (Rev. 3:14).

Lawyers and judges want faithful and true witnesses rather than ones who oscillate, vacillate, and fluctuate. They want ones who are trustworthy, ones to be believed.

In today's reference and in Revelation 1:5, Christ is labeled as a faithful and true witness. "Faithful" and "true" in the Greek language were words which express essential faithfulness and truth very strongly.

A faithful and true witness is one who is unerring in relating all truth involved in testimony. The recounting of all events involved are always the same.

A faithful and true witness is one who is unshakable. The intensity of the questioning or the testimony given in no way shakes or upsets the witness to the extent that the response is questionable. The witness is always firm and convincing.

A faithful and true witness is one who is undaunted. The adversary or an unfavorable atmosphere does not cower the witness. There is a deep and convincing courage which shines through.

A faithful and true witness is unchangeable. An "off-again, on-again" witness is frequently more a liability than an asset. The testimony must ring true from the beginning until the end.

Jesus fulfilled all of these requirements. He spoke with authority. He spoke convincingly. He spoke consistently and with courage and calmness. He stood like the Rock of Gibraltar. There were no chinks in His armor. He was a faithful and true witness to all the promises of the Father, through all the trials and calamities of the ages, even unto death.

How stable, strong, and effective is our witness? A good question.

Fallen One

"He bearing his cross went forth into a place called the place of a skull, which is called in the Hebrew Golgotha" (John 19:17).

Alvah Hovey, in commenting upon this verse, quoted from the well-known book *Ben Hur:* "He was nearly dead. Every few steps he staggered, as if he would fall. A stained gown, badly torn, hung from his shoulders over a seamless under-tunic. His bare feet left red splotches upon the stones. An inscription on a board was tied to his neck. A crown of thorns had been crushed hard down upon his head, making cruel wounds, from which streams of blood, now dry and blackened, had run over his face and neck. The long hair, tangled in the thorns, was clotted thick. The skin where it could be seen was ghastly white. His hands were tied before him. Back somewhere in the city, he had fallen exhausted, under the transverse of his cross, which, as a condemned person, custom required him to bear to the place of execution; now a countryman carried the burden in his stead. Four soldiers went with him as a guard against the mob, who sometimes, nevertheless, broke through, and struck him with sticks, and spit upon him. Yet, no sound escaped him, neither remonstrance nor groan."[9]

What a sight to behold!

About 750 years prior to this heinous event, Isaiah prophesied, "He was despised and rejected of men; a man of sorrows, and acquainted with grief: and we hid as it were our faces from him; and we esteemed him not." Yet when He was afflicted, He "opened not his mouth" (Isa. 53:3,7).

And we quickly ask, "How could they treat Him so cruelly?" "How could He refrain from retaliation?" He was innocent, but the innocent do not always escape hurt from their follow beings. Also, our sins of omission may hurt Him as severely.

Let us examine ourselves. Is He still being hurt?

9. Alvah Hovey, *An American Commentary on the New Testament,* Vol. 3 (Philadelphia: The American Baptist Publication Society, 1881), p. 380.

108
Famous One

"At that time Herod the tetrarch heard of the *fame* of Jesus" (Matt. 14:1).

Famous names and faces are now known in public places, thanks to the television and newspapers. But there were no television and newspapers to spread the face or the facts about Jesus; however, Herod heard about Him.

The Gospels speak several times about how the fame of Jesus had been spread abroad. His reputation went before Him, and his character was of sufficient strength and purity to substantiate and extend that fame.

During His early ministry, as Jesus went about Galilee preaching and healing the sick, Matthew says, "His fame went throughout all Syria" (Matt. 4:24).

Luke tells us that when a man full of leprosy was brought to Jesus and healed by Him: "But so much the more went there a fame abroad of him" (Luke 5:15).

While at Capernaum Jesus healed the woman with an issue of blood, and He also raised Jairus's daughter from death. "And the fame hereof went abroad into all that land" (Matt. 9:26). Then at Capernaum, two blind men came to Him, and He touched their eyes, and they were healed. "But they, when they were departed, spread abroad his fame in all that country" (Matt. 9:31).

Is it any wonder that Herod the tetrarch heard of the fame of Jesus? He had good reason to hear and to be somewhat troubled. Was this man coming on as a competitor? Was He going to overthrow the "powers that be" and establish His own kingdom? Some famous persons are dangerous persons.

Let us spread His name at home and abroad. He is not a dangerous person, but a divine One!

Feeder of the Flock

"He shall feed his flock like a shepherd: he shall gather the lambs with his arm, and carry them in his bosom, and shall gently lead those that are with young" (Isa. 40:11).

Some of the happiest moments of my young life on the farm were when my dad would ask me to go up into the hayloft to toss some hay into the stalls for the horses and the cows. I liked that work because for a minute or two I could roll in the hay, and then see the pleasure that came over the cattle and horses as they reached for the hay that was tossed down. Feedings were done regularly, and the cows and horses always knew that time of the day, even coming out of the fields at the proper time.

I don't know much about sheep, but in reading I have learned that a good shepherd cares tenderly and gently for his sheep. He feeds his flock by leading them into good and green pastures. A good feeder will not overdrive the young, suckling ewes in transferring the flock from one pasture to another. Frequently, shepherds can be seen carrying the young ones in their bosoms while leading the flock to other grazing areas.

A feeder of the sheep nurtures them with love. He is not like a hunter who stalks his prey with fierceness and firmness, but a shepherd will treat his sheep in a humane way. They are sorta family.

In Ezekiel 34:14-15 there is a beautiful picture of the relationship of the feeder with his sheep, "I will feed them in a good pasture, and upon the high mountains of Israel shall their fold be: there shall they lie in a good fold, and in a fat pasture shall they feed upon the mountains of Israel. I will feed my flock, and I will cause them to lie down, saith the Lord God."

Jesus does even more for us. He provides abundant soul food for our spiritual lives and also gives us the bread of immortality. And, where is the price tag? Paid with His own precious blood.

110

Fellow of the Lord of Hosts

"Awake, O sword, against my shepherd, and against the man that is my *fellow*, saith *the Lord of hosts:* smite the shepherd, and the sheep shall be scattered: and I will turn mine hand upon the little ones" (Zech. 13:7).

Our Scripture verse for the day is a good illustration of the saying, "The good news is that the bad news is wrong." This truth can apply to the smiting of the shepherd with the sword, the scattering of the sheep, and the redemption of the "little ones" by Jehovah's hand. And that's the good news which counteracts the bad news.

There are questionable words in the verse, and those are "my fellow." There are several conjectures about them. Some think they refer to Zechariah representing all the prophets while others think the application is to Judas Maccabeus. Two other translations throw a little light, "The man who stands next to me" (RSV) and "The man who is close to me" (NIV). However, most writers and commentators think the reference is to Christ because He quoted this verse while in the Mount of Olives just after He had eaten the Passover supper with His disciples (Matt. 26:31). This was the night that He was betrayed.

Furthermore, it seems appropriate to refer to Jesus, the Person, as Jehovah's "fellow" or equal because such a usage is a familiar term in Palestine, for persons dwelling together as neighbors were known as fellows or equals.

Jesus, as the Good Shepherd, was smitten with a sword, and His sheep were scattered, but the ultimate result was the saving of the sheep by the Shepherd. In Matthew 9:36 we read, "But when he saw the the multitudes, he was moved with compassion on them, because they fainted, and were scattered abroad, as sheep having no shepherd."

The persecution of Christians in Jerusalem by Saul caused them to be scattered abroad throughout the regions of Judaea and Samaria (Acts 8:1).

But those scattered for the gospel's sake will be saved by the Shepherd, for that is where the good news proves the bad news to be wrong.

111
Finisher of Faith

"Looking unto Jesus the author and *finisher of our faith;* who for the joy that was set before him endured the cross, despising the shame, and is set down at the right hand of the throne of God" (Heb. 12:2).

It is a great trait to be one who finishes what one begins. Some persons are wonderful starters. They take off with enthusiasm and zeal but never gain their second wind. They burn out before reaching the halfway mark. Others have great staying power.

Life is like running a race. We should pace ourselves and run with patience and persistency. Just as one cannot buy up time and store it, neither can one deposit faith for future use, for the more faith is used the stronger it becomes.

Jesus set a wonderful example for us in this respect. He is the perfect example of faith. He is the perfecter of the faith, our faith, and of faith itself. He is the leader, pioneer, and completer of faith. He brought objective completion to the facts of Christian faith by his death, resurrection, and ascension. He puts Christians on the path of faith and brings them to the goal. He provides the incentive we need for sustaining faith. He is the object of joyous faith.

As leader of the whole army of faith, it is His standard that we are to follow. There were no cracks in His armor of faith. In all the trials of His earthly life, we find Him operating on faith. When He faced decisions His submission in faith was described in such terms as: "Nevertheless not as I will, but as thou wilt" (Matt. 26:39); "They shall never perish, . . . [because] My Father . . . is greater than all" (John 10:28-29); and "the gates of hell shall not prevail against it" (Matt. 16:18).

In Him also we see the faith of one who willingly submits to death with the certainty (faith) that He will rise. "Destroy this temple, and in three days I will raise it up" (John 2:19).

We should pray, "God, help us to have faith in faith and to follow our 'author and finisher of our faith.' "

112

Firstborn of Every Creature

"Who is the image of the invisible God, the *firstborn of every creature*" (Col. 1:15).

The meditations for today and the next two days deal with aspects of Christ's life and function relating to Him as firstborn or begotten (see Heb. 1:6). There is a similarity in the terms but yet a distinction.

As the Father's eternal, everlasting Son dwelling in His bosom (John 1:18), He was the Firstborn of every creature, implying preeminence over the whole creation. He was the Firstborn among many brethren (Rom. 8:29). He was the Firstborn from the dead and the firstfruits of them that sleep (Col. 1:18; Rev. 1:5).

One commentator has stated that Christ descended from heaven as the only begotten of the Father but reascended to heaven as the firstborn and the exalted Redeemer and chief creation of God.

Saint Francis of Assisi, around the beginning of the thirteenth century, penned the words to the hymn "All Creatures of Our God and King." He was the founder of the Franciscian Order of the Catholic Church. In 1202, following a serious illness in war service, Francis turned from frivolity to give consecrated attention to the poor and sick, even giving away all of his possessions. With this in mind, the words of his hymn become more meaningful.

> All creatures of our God and King,
> Lift up your voice and with us sing
> Alleluia! Alleluia!
> Thou burning sun with golden beam,
> Thou silver moon with softer gleam!
> O praise Him, O praise Him!
> Alleluia! Alleluia!

113

Firstborn (Begotten) of the Dead

"He is the head of the body, the church: who is the beginning, the *firstborn from the dead*" (Col. 1:18).
"Jesus Christ . . . is the faithful witness, and the *first begotten of the dead*" (Rev. 1:5).

Robert Lowry wrote the hymn "Low in the Grave He Lay" which we use frequently at Eastertime but not at other times. Why not?

> Low in the grave He lay, Jesus my Saviour!
> Waiting the coming day, Jesus my Lord!
> Up from the grave He arose,
> With a mighty triumph o'er His foes;
> He arose a victor from the dark domain,
> And He lives forever with His saints to reign.
> He arose! Hallelujah! Christ arose!

Jesus did arise from the grave. He became the firstborn of the dead because He was the first born to eternal life after the death which ends earthly life. Through this act He blazed the trail for everyone. He plowed new ground. He cut the pathway to glory, leading from the tomb to heaven.

The pledge and guarantee of the resurrection from the dead as firstfruits of them that sleep indicate there are other harvests. One of the great messages of Easter is that there is more beyond—more to come, more to experience, more to enjoy.

Through the centuries death had been the dark veil, the black night, and, to many, the end of it all. But with Jesus it is always evening and morning, the dawning of something else—not morning and evening, the ending of it all.

Since Christ is the firstborn of the dead, hope takes on a new meaning. Hope sees a star and hears the ruffling of wings. Death has yielded to a new life: eternal life.

O, what a glorious expectation to those who die in the Lord.

114

Firstborn Among Many Brethren

"For whom he did foreknow, he also did predestinate to be conformed to the image of his Son, that he might be the *firstborn among many brethren*" (Rom. 8:29).

Two things have had much attention during the past few years. One of these is the effort to establish a semblance of equality of all on the payroll, even though duties and responsibilities are unequal. Even in the academic community one has heard this utterance, "Just one among equals." The second is the reemergence of the round table. Some administrators and corporate officials now use a round table in the board room, suggesting the idea that no one around the table is at the head of the table. There is good and bad in both of these.

Without a doubt Jesus was the Firstborn among many brethren, but He also stood out to the extent that the Scripture says, "For whom he did foreknow, he also did predestinate to be conformed to the image of his Son, that he might be the firstborn among many brethren" (Rom. 8:29).

Foreknowledge and foreordination are tough theological concepts to deal with in a sentence or two. Both concepts carry the idea of a union of divine foreknowledge with a divine purpose. It would be impossible to decree anything, foreordain, without knowing about that thing. And since God knows all things, decreeing things is a part of the whole. We say, therefore, that foreknowledge and foreordination involve each other.

I think I am correct in saying that, in the context of our Scripture verse, the divine purpose of foreknowledge and foreordination is to stress the truth that Christ is the Firstborn among many brethren. They should seek to conform to His image so that in glory Christ will not be standing alone but with many who have shaped their lives after Him, thus showing His preeminence.

We can't know and understand everything, but, thank God, we can keep on learning and understanding.

Firstfruits of Them that Slept

"But now is Christ risen from the dead, and become the *firstfruits of them that slept*" (1 Cor. 15:20).

Jesus taught His disciples much about death: how to look at it. Death is not to be thought of as the end but the beginning; not defeat but reward; not a sad experience but a happy experience for those who die in the Lord.

But remember that He *never told His disciples how to conduct funerals, but He did tell them to anticipate resurrections.* What a difference! As the "firstfruits of them that slept," Jesus' resurrection was a harbinger of other resurrections. What He did and accomplished through His resurrection, a like experience would come to His followers. As He came forth from the grave victorious over death and the grave, so would there be other like fruit— resurrections—at the appointed time. The first ripe fruit on a tree heralds the ripening of other fruit.

Jesus always says, "Follow me." He leads the way. He never says, "You go that way, and I will go this way," but always, "Follow me." This is true both in life and in death, and even through death.

Christopher Wordsworth, an English bishop and scholar of the nineteenth century and nephew of William Wordsworth, wrote a lovely hymn entitled "Hallelujah! Christ Is Risen." The second stanza reads,

Christ is risen, Christ the firstfruits
    Of the holy harvest field,
Which will all its full abundance,
    At His glorious advent, yield;
Then the golden ears of harvest
    Will before His presence wave,
Rising in His sunshine joyous,
    From the furrows of the grave.

When He comes again, there will be a beautiful harvest field awaiting the reaper, that is, if we do our part in telling the good news of salvation. Every day can be harvest day!

First Gentleman in the World, The

"They sent messengers before his face: and they went, and entered into a village of the Samaritans, to make *ready for him*" (Luke 9:52).

If my mother said to me once, she must have said a hundred times, "Son, pretty is as pretty does," meaning, you can't act ugly if you want to be nice. She gave me sound and good advice.

Jean Lacordairé, a French Dominican orator of the first half of the nineteenth century, left us these words about Jesus: "Alone amongst all the great names, he possesses authentic genealogy which remounts from him even to the father of the human race, and that he is thus, undoubtedly, the first gentleman in the world."[10]

A gentleman is a person wellborn, courteous, kind, and refined in manners of formal and gracious courtesy. Jesus meets all of these qualifications. He respected all people as persons, not as digits in a decimal system or computer numbers. Each was a distinctive person with a precious soul.

Jesus had good manners. He was never coarse or crude in speech or action. He knew how to reach the individual and the group with skill and kindness. He did not stoop to insult or speak harshly or abrasively, except when dealing with the self-righteous scribes and Pharisees.

He took careful cognizance of the feelings, thoughts, and emotions of people. He knew when they were hurting, discouraged, and half beaten. He was sensitive of their condition and never trampled upon their spirit.

When desperation set in at the wedding feast in Cana of Galilee, Jesus, in response to a sensitive situation, was master of the moment.

Let me say to men, "It is never prudish, effeminate, or a sign of weakness to be courteous, gracious, and a proper gentleman. Keep trying!"

10. Lacordairé, Jean Baptiste, "The First Gentleman in the World," *Behold the Man*, ed. Ralph L. Woods (New York: The Macmillan Company, 1944), p. 54.

Fisherman, The Great

"Simon Peter saith unto them, I go a-fishing. They say unto him, We also go with thee. They went forth, and entered into a ship immediately; and that night they *caught nothing*. ... Then Jesus saith unto them, Children, have ye any meat? They answered him, No" (John 21:3-5).

Lloyd C. Douglas, about a quarter of a century ago, wrote a book entitled *The Big Fisherman*, a novel about Simon Peter. I imagine that Peter, like some other fishermen, was quite apt to talk about his fishing by letting the fish grow immeasurably faster between the time it was caught and the time he described it to his friends.

Jesus had to teach Simon how to fish, quite a jolt to Peter's ego. Peter told the disciples that he was going fishing. Too much had been happening in too short a time. His nerves needed relaxing. He went to his favorite "holes" but caught nothing after toiling all night. But a fisherman has eternal expectations even though experiencing perpetual disappointment.

Early in the morning Jesus came and asked them, "What did you catch?"

"Nothing."

"Then let down your net on the right side."

I can imagine Peter saying under his breath, "Baloney." But since he had caught nothing, he couldn't do worse. My goodness, he now has caught so many that they were scarcely able to draw in the nets. And everyone, save Jesus, was goggle-eyed.

Jesus then asked Peter pointed questions about Peter's love for Him with instructions to feed His sheep. In essence, Jesus was saying, "Peter, you can no longer do that which you have done in the past. You are now to become a full-time fisher of men." He had told Peter and Andrew this early in His ministry while in Capernaum (Matt. 4:19).

We have to fish to catch fish. We have to work at being fishers of men. The fields are white unto harvest.

118

Foot Washer

"After that he poureth water into a basin, and began *to wash the disciples' feet*, and to wipe them with the towel wherewith he was girded" (John 13:5).

Henry David Thoreau, the American naturalist of the previous century, spent two years of his life in simple living at Walden Pond. Later in his book *Walden* which details his life in the woods, Thoreau wrote, "Humility like darkness reveals the heavenly lights." Nothing could be more appropriate in contemplating the biblical event describing Jesus' washing of the feet of His disciples.

The incident occurred after the discussion as to which of the disciples would be greatest in the Kingdom. Jesus performed the act of foot washing and in so doing expressed His love for them, their duty relating to humble service for others to avoid separation, due to His superiority and to enhance unity. Such an act was a good discourse on humility. It was a good example in service, not necessarily an act for replication. True, it was good for their tired feet. He is always providing rest for weary feet.

On the human level, it is very hard for one of superior dignity to be impelled to lowliest submission, but there is something in true humility which exalts the heart. Humility makes one subject to God, and those in subjection to God are exalted within.

In a larger context, three passages will shed some additional light. In Luke 22:27, it is recorded that Jesus said to His disciples, "I am among you as he that serveth." Paul, in writing to those at Philippi, said, "took upon him the form of a servant" (2:7). Simon Peter uttered these words, "Be clothed with humility: for God resisteth the proud, and giveth grace to the humble" (1 Pet. 5:5).

From Him who washed His disciples' feet, we take our cue. Here we have both an example and an exhortation!

119

Forerunner

"Whither the *forerunner* is for us entered, even Jesus, made an high priest for ever after the order of Melchisedec" (Heb. 6:20).

A forerunner is a messenger sent ahead to give notice of the approach of others. A forerunner is a herald, an announcer, a harbinger of news, or what the French call an *avant coureur*.

There are two great illustrations of forerunners from secular history.

The Battle of Marathon in 490 BC was fought between the Greeks and the Persians. After the Persians retreated to their ships, Pheidippides, a champion runner, was sent to Athens to announce the good news. He ran 22 miles, and as he entered the city, exhausted, gasped out the message, "Rejoice, we conquer." Then he fell dead. Now we have the heralded Marathon runs, a total of 26 miles, 365 yards.

Paul Revere, at midnight April 18, 1775, roused the minutemen of Boston as he rode through the town crying, "The British are coming."

Both Pheidippides and Paul Revere were in the strictest sense forerunners. They gave notice of the approach of others and shared news. They did these things for others.

Christ entered heaven as our forerunner. It is His presence within the veil that emboldens us to go thither. The veil was between the holy of holies and the holy place and is considered here as heaven. We are anchored to Christ through hope and as He entered heaven, the holy of holies, He did so as our representative with us still latched to Him by the cord of hope.

Since Jesus, as our high priest, has entered the holy of holies on our behalf and since we are anchored by hope, we have been admonished by the author of Hebrews to "lay aside every weight, and the sin which doth so easily beset us" (Heb. 12:1).

Life is a race to be run, and we get our second wind through patience and hope. Keep running. Be a spiritual jogger.

Forgiving One

"Jesus saith unto him, I say not unto thee, Until seven times: but, Until seventy times seven" (Matt. 18:22).

I don't know which is harder: to forgive or to ask for forgiveness. Both are tough to handle. I guess Alexander Pope was right when he said, "To err is human, to forgive divine."

During the colonial days in Georgia, John Wesley was trying to calm Governor Oglethorpe because a servant of the governor had broken open and drunk several bottles of the governor's wine. Enraged, Oglethorpe shouted at the offender, "Sir, I never forgive." Then, very calmly, Wesley replied, "I hope, sir, you never offend."[11]

What an appropriate rebuff.

In our verse for the day Simon Peter is concerned about how many times his brother shall sin against him and he forgive him. He seeks to answer the question himself; but, Jesus won't accept the answer. Even though seven is a number of completion according to the law, "seven times" is far from being enough under grace. It is just a beginning. Peter was to try it "Until seventy times seven" (490 times), said Jesus.

I am prone to say that is too many times. Why would anyone give offense that many times? But I'm dead wrong in my approach. Forgiveness is a matter of the heart and spirit, not just a matter of deed or deeds. Vengeance and reciprocity do not belong to us, only to God. We must forgive, and forgive others we must, if we expect God to forgive us.

Since God has forgiven us of our sins, we too must be in the forgiving business. Forgiven should produce forgiveness. Without a forgiving God I would be helpless and hopeless.

In dealing with the woman taken in adultery (John 8), Jesus refused to condemn her. I think He forgave her. He is so much bigger with His forgiveness than with His condemnation. He came not to destroy but to redeem.

Right now, thank Him for His gracious and forgiving spirit.

11. Ralph Sockman, *The Higher Happiness* (New York, Nashville: Abingdon-Cokesbury Press, 1942), p. 102.

Formulator of New Laws

"Ye have heard that it hath been said, . . . But I say unto you" (Matt. 5:38-39).

The Jewish laws of the Old Testament were like a bottomless pit, never full or complete. They were like a ravenous beast devouring itself for want of more. Such laws tended more to restrict and punish than to inspire and challenge.

Jesus came not to destroy these laws, but to fulfill them and to give new laws that would reward virtue and love.

Here are a few examples:

"Ye have heard that it hath been said, An eye for an eye, and a tooth for a tooth: But I say unto you, That ye resist not evil: but whosoever shall smite thee on thy right cheek, turn to him the other also" (Matt. 5:38-39).

"And if any man will sue thee at the law, and take away thy coat, let him have thy cloak also" (Matt. 5:40). Just paying minimal dues to the law is not a good way to show appreciation for and understanding of the meaning and intent of the law.

"Whosoever shall compel thee to go a mile, go with him twain" (Matt. 5:41). Compulsion is apt to produce angry and revengeful feelings. It is like doing double duty. But willingly going beyond the call of duty diminishes the angry feelings.

"Ye have heard that it hath been said, Thou shalt love thy neighbour, and hate thine enemy. But I say unto you, Love your enemies" (Matt. 5:43-44).

Don't strike back with hate, but strike out with love.

Don't look for a loophole, but look for a latchkey.

Don't look for an excuse not to, but look for a reason why I must.

Foundation Stone

"For other *foundation* can no man lay than that is laid, which is Jesus Christ" (1 Cor. 3:11).

"It seems to me that the church is always asking for money." "The members never come to call on me unless the church needs money." "Our church is like the one in New York, the steeple of which has leaned eighteen inches toward Wall Street." Have you heard statements such as these? It may appear at times that money is the sole foundation of many churches, but is that really so?

Christ is the true foundation stone of the spiritual temple, the people of Christ are the stones, and the apostles and teachers are the builders.

Faith in Christ gives the church its very base and distinction. Christ, therefore, becomes the foundation stone which ties the structure together. The apostle Paul presented this doctrine very clearly. He put it securely in his teachings. Paul wanted no substitute. He told the Corinthian church that foundations of gold, silver, precious stones, wood, hay, and stubble would be tested by fire and were false substitutes for Christ.

Therefore, a foundation stone must be a stone that is true, solid, durable and "quarried to fit its place." There is no way for the church to be of one foundation unless Christ be the solitary foundation stone. It must be built on Him. Our well-known hymn goes:

> The church's one foundation
> Is Jesus Christ her Lord;
> She is His new creation,
> By Spirit and the Word:
> From heaven He came and sought her
> To be His holy bride,
> With His own blood He bought her,
> And for her life He died.

We can truly build a spiritual edifice on Christ. It is good to be a part of it.

Fountain for Sin

"In that day there shall be a *fountain* opened to the house of David and to the inhabitants of Jerusalem *for sin* and for uncleanness" (Zech. 13:1).

The fountain for sin is a blood-filled fountain.

> There is a fountain filled with blood
> Drawn from Immanuel's veins;
> And sinners, plunged beneath that flood,
> Lose all their guilty stains.

so wrote William Cowper years ago. And it holds true for today.

Ponce de Leon, and other Spaniards, came to America looking for the fountain of youth, a mythical fountain which would bring youth to the aged and health to the sick. He thought he had found it when he reached Florida. However, people still get old, and there is no turning back from it, and illness still strikes without favor.

During the time of Christ it was thought that the pool of Bethesda had some curative power (John 5). But this was not so. The only fountain of perpetual youth, the only fountain for the sin sick, and the only fountain for the outcast is that fountain filled with the blood of Christ.

Blood is essential to physical life, and blood is essential to spiritual life. Physical blood carries nourishment and oxygen to all parts of the body and takes away waste products for excretion. The pure blood Christ shed washes away the impurities of sin in our lives. As the blood of paschal lambs was offered to atone for sin, Christ gave His blood to atone for our sins. The blood He provided for spiritual transfusions flows freely and free.

So it is still, "Nothing but the blood of Jesus."

124

Friend of Sinners

"The Son of man came eating and drinking, and they say, Behold a man gluttonous, and a winebibber, *a friend of* publicans and *sinners*" (Matt. 11:19).

A four-year-old child was asking her father about God. "Daddy, God made the heavens and the earth, didn't He?"

"Yes, my dear."

"Then, He made the flower in that flower pot, didn't He?"

"Yes!"

"Well, that means He got His hands dirty."

Yes, God was willing to get His hands dirty to be a friend of sinners. It seems logical to say that holiness and perfection might shun impurity and imperfection. But not so with Christ.

In biblical times, sinners were somewhat outcasts of the prevailing religious culture. They were shunned, sometimes exploited for gain. There was no place for them at the tables of the rich and pious. They had few friends other than those of like ilk.

Jesus Christ came to save sinners. And, even today, there are only two kinds of persons: sinners and sinners saved by the grace of a good, loving, and redeeming Savior. He shuns them not. He wants to make them whole. That is His mission.

As a sinner, my friendship with Jesus began when He became my redeeming friend. Prior to that I knew Him only in words, not in deeds. How pleased and grateful I am that He did not remain aloof from those who needed Him. I am glad He was willing to get His hands dirty for me. I, too, should be willing to get my hands dirty in service for Him. That's one of the least things I can do.

125

Friend of Those Who Do His Will

"Ye are my friends, if ye do whatsoever I command you" (John 15:14).

Years ago an English publication offered a prize for the best definition of a friend. The winning one was, "A friend is one who comes in when the whole world has gone out."

I like another, "A friend is one who multiplies joy, divides grief, and whose honesty is inviolable."

Some have said that friends are the ones who love us regardless of our warts, our eccentricities, and our vices. To those who obeyed His commandments Christ met all three definitions. In essence He said, "I regard you and treat you as My friends, if you are obedient to Me. I will let you know of My plans, counsel, and reasons. You can be admitted into a close intimacy with Me." Only the believer can limit the extent of the intimacy through lack of obedience.

In servant relationships, love, friendship, and fellowship are nearly always missing but not so in friendship relations. We are so blessed in being able to call Christ our friend. He is a "friend that sticketh closer than a brother" (Prov. 18:24), one that is not just a fair-weather friend. A friend is one with whom we can share fragile things, one who tries to suffer alongside us.

Friends may come, and friends may go, but Christ Jesus our friend will go with us through the valley and shadow of death as we depart our earthly friends. There is no friend quite like Jesus. His commandments, therefore, are not grievous but like wings to a bird.

Maybe we need to pay Him a friendly visit today.

Fruit of Thy Womb

"She [Elizabeth] spake out with a loud voice, and said, Blessed art thou among women, and blessed is *the fruit of thy womb*" (Luke 1:42).

Christ has been designated as the "fruit" of the womb of woman and "the firstfruits" (1 Cor. 15:23).

As the fruit of the womb of woman, there was the inception, the growth, and exit from the womb as the fruit product.

The dictionary defines fruit as "any product of plant growth useful to man or animals." We are familiar with the taste of apples, peaches, pears, strawberries, apricots, and figs. They are all most palatable.

The psalmist said, "O taste and see that the Lord is good" (Ps. 34:8). Sin is bitter; it should be repulsive to our taste buds. Christ the Lord is sweet to the human soul.

On the farm where I spent my childhood we grew gooseberries. I often remarked that I did not like them because they were too sour. But Mother would put some sugar and coloring with them, and I would eat with delight. They were almost equal to cherries.

Christ puts the sweetness and color into our lives, whereby we like the spiritual fruit that He brings.

Service in the kingdom of Christ never leaves a bad taste. Our teeth are not set on edge. On the contrary, we can relish the sweet morsels of Christ in obeying His commandments.

A bountiful fruit plate awaits all who come to His festive table. The cupboard is not bare!

Galilaean King

"Then when he was come into Galilee, the Galilaeans received him, having seen all the things that he did at Jerusalem at the feast" (John 4:45).

With a little imagination and leeway, I am taking the words of the hymn by John Bakewell "Hail, Thou Once Despised Jesus" to provide my designation of Jesus as Galilaean King.

> Hail, Thou once despised Jesus!
> Hail, Thou *Galilaean King*!
> Thou didst suffer to release us;
> Thou didst free salvation bring.

Jesus had a great ministry in Galilee. It was in Galilee that He delivered the Sermon on the Mount. It was in Galilee that He spoke many of His parables and performed many of His miracles. He did most of the teaching of His disciples in and around Galilee. Truly, He functioned in Galilee as a King.

I like, and hope you will also, what Emil Brunner said in his book *Our Faith:* "There is nothing remarkable in a beggar lending a hand to a beggar. But, whoever heard of a king dismounting from his horse to take a beggar's hand? That the heavenly King, whose majesty is inconceivable, comes down to seek His unfaithful child in all his squalor, is the love of God as the gospel and only the gospel knows. And we, the beggars, should know what sort of King it is who has come down to us. God desires one thing absolutely: that we should know the greatness and seriousness of His will-to-love. Our heart is like a fortress which God wants to capture."[12]

Offer no resistance! Our Galilaean King didn't bet His life on the existence of God or on His power, but on the love of God.

12. Emil Brunner, *Our Faith* (London: SCM Press LTD, 1936), p. 23.

128

Gentle Savior

"He said unto her, Daughter, be of good comfort: thy faith hath made thee whole" (Luke 8:48).

A tearful, fearful woman who had sought the help of Jesus came trembling and falling down before Him to acknowledge that she had been the one who had touched Him from behind. Jesus gently provided for her the healing she sought. He did not scold her. He did not thunder forth at her, nor shout admonitions.

Jesus is a gentle Savior. He does not rule by terror or brute force. He does not enslave His subjects with demands of loyalty and service. It is not what He demands but what He gives. He is not a stern lawgiver but a gracious, gentle life giver.

Jesus' voice seemed to draw people to Him. It had a soothing effect, but it was not sugared or syrupy. The dear lady with the issue of blood described in our Scripture for the day cried out inwardly,

Pass me not, O gentle Saviour,
Hear my humble cry;
While on others Thou art calling,
Do not pass me by.[13]

Her cry was heard. She was not compelled to follow Him. She chose to do so of her own free will. She found Him to be gentle, kind, and loving.

It is most interesting to me that this Gentle Savior, who compels no one to follow Him, who enslaves no one to serve him, gives us the most freedom when we are the most encompassed by His love. For it is when we most completely submit to Him that He grants us the most freedom.

13. From "Pass Me Not, O Gentle Saviour" by Fanny J. Crosby (1820-1915).

Gift, Unspeakable

"Thanks be unto God for his *unspeakable gift*" (2 Cor. 9:15).

An unspeakable gift would be *some gift*. If you were given the flawless, brilliant, 500-carat diamond cut from the largest stone ever found—the *Cullinan,* weighing 3,106 metric carats from the Premier Mines in Transvall, South Africa—I doubt that you would have an unspeakable gift. Many might think so, but an unspeakable gift is something beyond the power of language to describe as to value and beauty.

Such an inexpressible, unutterable gift as an unspeakable gift would probably fall in the category of something being invisible, intangible, and such a gift could come only from God.

Let me make an attempt at defining an unspeakable gift. It would be an act of bestowing involuntarily on another something of inestimable value, the value of which would be awesome and amazing.

To further stimulate thought, how about the gift of pardon for sin? How about love "so amazing, so divine"? How about hope that "springs eternal in the human breast"? How about faith that is our title deed for "things hoped for, the evidence of things not seen"? How about the glorious promise that Christ is coming again to take us home with Him? Can you put a price tag on these unspeakable gifts? Can you measure their worth on the scales of human values?

When God gave us His Son, Jesus, born of a virgin, He gave the greatest unspeakable gift the world has ever known because He gave a part of Himself, a part of God; and you and I are on the receiving end of the gift. Wonder of wonders!

Would you be willing to exchange these unspeakable gifts which Christ, the unspeakable gift of God, brought to us through His life and death for material gifts? There is no comparison.

The Glory of Thy People Israel

"A light to lighten the Gentiles, and *the glory of thy people Israel*" (Luke 2:32).

Aged Simeon, on beholding the Christ child in the Temple, sang his "swan" song Nunc Dimittis, calling the child "the glory of thy people Israel." It was a beautiful tribute to the newborn babe. He had longed to see the bright and Morning Star of the salvation of Israel.

In using the term *glory*, Simeon captured the honor and splendor, the pride and joy, and the perfection and duty that comprise such a radiant term. It is sad that Israel did not accept the offered blessing because He who came as the way, the truth, and the life would have been for Israel their glory road, their deliverance, security, peace, and eternal victory. They could have enjoyed the glory that comes from One in whom trust, fellowship, and rejoicing are exalted.

The glorious Christ still provides glory for His followers, and, as His followers, we should have no glory comparable to that which comes from the glorious victory of the cross.

B. B. McKinney penned these beautiful words in the hymn "Glorious Is Thy Name":

> Blessed Saviour, we adore Thee,
> We Thy love and grace proclaim;
> Thou art mighty, Thou art holy,
> Glorious is Thy matchless name!

May Christ this day be the glory of His people, the new Israel, who have chosen Him as their Salvation of Israel. May this glory radiate in our faces, sound forth in our proclamations, and take up residence in our hearts.

God

"In the beginning was the Word, and the Word was with God, and the Word was *God*" (John 1:1).

Never did a hyphen mean so much as when used in saying that Jesus was God-man. It is easy to think that it is paradoxical to say He was both God and man, but He was very God and very man, the fullest expression of each. In the five following devotionals, I shall refer to some additional unique characteristics of His divinity.

Today I want to share with you five reasons why I accept Him as God and everything that God was, is, and shall be, without parallel.

First, His coming into the world in the fullness of time, in fulfillment of prophecy, and in the womb of the virgin Mary suggests deity. Dr. R. G. Lee once remarked, "Christ was in the bosom of the Father in heaven without a mother, and He was in the bosom of a mother on earth without a father."

Second, His claims such as power to forgive, to love, and to redeem, have stood the tests of the ages.

Third, the genuineness of His character, His perfection, and His holiness set Him apart and above any other person who ever lived.

Fourth, His commitment to His purpose to bring eternal life and immortality to pass could only have been the role of God.

Fifth, His conquest of death, the great equalizer of all persons, was not an attribute of His humanity, only of His Deity.

He is God. He *is* God. Both the amplification and simplification of God.

God Blessed Forever

"Christ came, who is over all, *God blessed for ever*" (Rom. 9:5).

Paul, in using this term three times in His writings (Rom. 1:25; Rom. 9:5; and 2 Cor. 11:31), utters a beautifully significant doxology to the praise of Christ. He is saying, in essence, if Christ be God at all, He must be God over all and for all time.

It was most appropriate for Paul to express this doxology, an ascription of praise to Christ whom Israel had rejected, because it was an affirmation of Christ's divinity and oneness with God. He did not want to back away from giving Christ praise and honor even in the midst of those rejecting Him.

There are times in life when we need to utter praises to Him who is our Savior and God. Life should be well interspersed with doxologies other than the Sunday morning doxology, which is a good one.

Tradition has it that Alynthus and a party of Christians sang praises to God amid the awful desolations of Pompeii, even when within the hearing of the multitude rushing hither and thither for precious life. They sang with calm assurance that their Lord was very near.

Many of the early Christian martyrs sang their doxologies of praise even when in the lions' dens, and later while being burned at the stake.

It seems very reasonable to me that if doxologies can be sung by those who face death naturally or imposed on them by others, we should permeate the chapters of our lives with doxologies of praise to Christ, "God blessed for ever."

God of the Whole Earth, The

"Thy Redeemer the Holy One of Israel; *The God of the whole earth* shall he be called" (Isa. 54:5).

There is not one foot of soil, nor one person, nor one act that is not under the domain of Christ. No section is too removed or too remote or isolated to escape His providence. There is no such thing as pigmentation priority in the relationship of the Son of God with humankind. He is not a tribal god, nor an ecclesiastical god, nor a political or military god. Red and yellow, black and white—all are precious in the good Lord's sight.

Paul, in writing to those at Philippi, said "That at the name of Jesus every knee should bow, of things in heaven, and things in earth, and things under the earth, And that every tongue should confess that Jesus Christ is Lord, to the glory of God the Father" (Phil. 2:10-11). That is pretty clear language. Its meaning is not obscure, for all means all. It is true that millions do not acknowledge Him in that capacity. They choose to ignore Him, but that does not alter the fact.

It is a good thing we do not have the choice of which God, from among many gods, that we wish to serve. Our choice is only how to honor Him, the only God of the whole earth, with reverence and acceptable service.

I am so glad He plays no favorites. I might never have been chosen. I am glad He makes no monetary demands for His salvation. It is as free as the grace of God and as the dew of the morning. It would be a sad thing indeed not to be loved by Him, but it would be a much sadder thing not to be able to love Him. It is this two-way love that really counts.

God, our Father, is at home. Give Him a call, and tell Him of your love!

God Omnipotent

"All Power is given unto me in heaven and in earth" (Matt. 28:18).

How does one measure the power of persons? Some would do it by physical strength, others by the possession of wealth, others by influence, while some would use such criteria as knowledge, skill, and energy. In each of these evaluations there are limitations.

When reference is made to Christ as God Omnipotent, the inference is that He is unlimited, unequaled in power. The powerful elements of nature such as rain causing floods, winds producing damaging tornadoes, and lightning which wreaks havoc on what it hits—all obey His voice.

The omnipotence of Christ is seen also in His ability to remove obstacles in carrying out His purpose. He has command of all possible ways and means of doing His will.

The universe is evidence of God's creative power, but it did not exhaust Him. His power is manifested on earth through His conquest of disease, death, and the things of nature. He has power in hell over demons and evil spirits. He has power in heaven.

There is no limit to His power other than that which is self-imposed. He cannot deny Himself. He does not destroy the natural laws. He will not intrude into human power to choose. These actions are, however, in accordance with His holy nature and purpose.

Nuclear power, jet power, and atomic power are powerless before Him by comparison. His power to create, and His power to redeem place Him on a solitary pedestal. We do not worship a dead Christ but a powerful, living Lord who is God all-powerful.

135

God Omnipresent

"For where two or three are gathered together in my name, *there am I* in the midst of them" (Matt. 18:20).

Our six-year-old granddaughter asked her father, "Daddy, is God everywhere?"

"Yes, God is everywhere," he answered.

"Well, that means that God can come crawling out of a box just like a roach."

That's pretty good perception, but it is not correct in that when the roach is in the box, it can be nowhere else at that time.

God, on the other hand, is everywhere equally present at one and the same time. He cannot be shut out or excluded from anything or anyplace. He can be turned off, and, if so, then what a tragedy.

At times, many of us have made the mistake of praying, "Lord, come and be with us." He doesn't need to come, for He is here. He is there, also. I think that what we are actually expressing is a desire that He would manifest His presence by sharing with us and by hearing our prayers.

It is great to know that He is with every missionary. He is with every preacher. He is with every father and mother, in every home. He fills all things, every place. But He may be ignored, neglected, or pushed aside. He heeds a call. He hears a prayer. He responds to a cry. He reacts to praise and adoration.

I can illustrate this by sharing with you the sincere prayer of grace at meals offered by an old mountaineer when, with an obvious awareness of the presence of Christ, he bowed his head and said, "Much obliged, Lord." That said it all, so personal.

God Omniscient

"Now are we sure that *thou knowest all things*" (John 16:30).

A college freshman was told during an orientation session that, when taking examinations, it would be best to write something in response to each question even though the answer was uncertain. When asked to give a certain quotation from Robert Browning which he did not know, the student wrote these words, "The roast was in the oven, browning." Quite clever, you say? But cleverness is not to be equated with knowledge.

Christ was possessed with all knowledge. He had no need to resort to cleverness. His knowledge was immediate, distinct, complete, and related to things past, present, and future.

At times it has been difficult for me to understand how to reconcile the foreknowledge which Christ has with reference to whether or not that knowledge predetermines or necessitates the occurrence of the event. Then too, at times we may stumble over the question of man's free will in light of Christ's foreknowledge. We go on to raise this question, "Is a person's will free when it is foreknown what will be done?" Knowledge is not synonymous with action.

So many times we presume upon the knowledge of God in Christ. We ask such questions as: "Does God know how many angels can stand on the point of a needle?" "Can He count the snowflakes as they fall in a snow storm?" "Does He make a daily calculation of the hairs on my head?" Nonsense! Such trivia. He is too busy with important things, and knowledge is not served by such questions.

Christ knows all He needs to know and all there is to know in order to be God omniscient.

A Governor

"Thou Bethlehem, in the land of Juda, art not the least among the princes of Juda: for out of thee shall come a *Governor*, that shall rule my people Israel" (Matt. 2:6).

During the middle 1960s, I played golf one afternoon with then-Governor Buford Ellington, of Tennessee. It was a happy experience. I noticed that the golf balls played no favorite with him. He had to look for his ball in the rough just like I had to look for mine, but he was a pretty good golfer.

Upon our return to the city, a difference did crop up. We went by a car that developed trouble. The governor asked his driver to stop, check out the situation, and radio for assistance, which arrived quickly. You see, a governor is an important person. He is the chief executive officer of the state, which is the highest position. His presence is important. What the governor says carries influence and weight, and his plans and programs are significant to the citizens of the state.

Governors are elected by the citizens by popular vote. They are responsible to the electorate. Occasionally, a governor has been impeached.

Jesus tried to be a good governor, but His people would not let Him. They opposed many of His plans and programs. They did not like His impartiality. They sought to overthrow Him. His own people did not receive Him.

Seldom has history restored a governor of one of the states of our nation who has left office in shame and disgrace. But time has shown Jesus to be a worthy governor for all people. His fame has spread far and near in spite of the fact that He was crucified by His contemporaries.

The Governor of all governors is Christ our Lord. Let us pray for His presence in the fifty governors' mansions of our nation.

Gracious One

"If so be ye have tasted that *the Lord is gracious*" (1 Pet. 2:3).

Tennessee Ernie Ford, one of America's best-loved popular singers, in advertising a flour product on television has exclaimed hundreds of times, "Goodness gracious, it's good!"

In the truest sense that could be an interpretation of our Scripture verse for the day. The apostle Peter was writing about newborn babes growing by desiring "the sincere milk of the word," and he wrote, "If so be ye have tasted that the Lord is gracious." He could have said, "Goodness gracious, it's good!" The Word of God in Christ is so good.

I think a more literal translation of the word *gracious* would be "good." Some translations say, "kindness" (Amplified New Testament) and "goodness" (Weymouth).

The psalmist wrote, "O taste and see that the Lord is good" (34:8), and Peter was reiterating that eternal truth.

A comment should be made here about the word *taste*. The meaning is more than just wetting the tongue or sipping, for sipping would not nourish. It is like trying something out for taste then being so pleased with the taste as to proceed to partake generously.

The Word of God should taste good to the believer. An occasional sipping is not adequate. Our hungry souls need to feed on the pure milk of the Word of God regularly if growth is to transpire. In this way Christ is gracious, good, kind, and compassionate in the building us up in Him.

Most of us are allergic to food for thought. Does the same apply to the Word of God, which is good soul food?

Greater than Moses

"Master, Moses said, . . . Jesus answered and said unto them, Ye do err, not knowing the scriptures, nor the power of God" (Matt. 22:24,29).

How many times have you heard a statement like this, "He is a great person, but . . .?" The inference is that there is a kink in the person's armor, one weakness, at least. Moses would fall into that category.

In comparing Jesus with Moses and showing His greatness over Moses, let me run a few comparisons first. Both were a problem at birth to the kings: Moses to Pharaoh, and Jesus to Herod. Both were lawgivers: Moses gave many of the Jewish laws, and Jesus was the Fulfiller of those laws. Both were deliverers: Moses led the children of Israel out of Egypt toward the Promised Land, and Jesus is still leading His dear children through the grave of death to an inheritance incorruptible. Moses was a man of great faith; he saw the Red Sea divide when he had enough faith to get his feet wet first. Jesus became the Author and Finisher of our faith.

But, now the difference! Moses did not get to enter the Promised Land, only to view it from Mount Nebo, because of his disobedience to God at the waters of Meribah. Jesus made it clear that His will and that of the Father were one. Whereas Moses died before entering the Promised Land, Jesus is at the right hand of the Father making intercessions for us and preparing for us a place in order to come again and take us into glory. The laws of Moses were mostly prohibitions while those of Jesus are of love and grace. Moses was a great man, but Jesus was greater—no kink in His armor. I am glad I am under grace, not under law.

The laws of Moses were guidelines while Jesus is our Guide.

140

Greater than Solomon

"Behold, a *greater than Solomon* is here" (Matt. 12:42).

Could anyone build a greater temple than was built by Solomon? It was modeled after the tabernacle of Moses. Solomon's father, David, bequeathed to him an equivalent of five billion dollars in gold, silver, and brass for the Temple. Then, too, Solomon added to this from his personal treasury. What would such a temple cost in today's money?

Could anyone be much wiser than Solomon, whose scintillating proverbs are often quoted today? There is much wisdom in these proverbs.

Could anyone be much wiser in making judgments than Solomon? He did so with impartiality and justice.

Wouldn't you agree that the temple Jesus spoke of—the temple of God that is within us—is a far more precious temple than the one built by Solomon? Solomon's temple was a house for God and not for the people while Jesus' temple of God was placed within His people. He spoke of it as being worth more than the whole world.

Wouldn't you agree that the Sermon on the Mount (Luke 6) has more distilled spiritual wisdom than all the proverbs of Solomon?

Wouldn't you agree that the wisdom shown over and over again in the judgments and decision made by Jesus far exceeded those made by Solomon?

Solomon was a wise man, a great builder, and a just judge, but Jesus built not with straw and stone but with hearts and souls.

A Greater than Solomon was Jesus because He possessed infinite knowledge, love, and truth.

Greatest Gentleman Who Ever Lived

"Jesus said, Let her alone; why trouble ye her? she hath wrought a good work on me" (Mark 14:6).

Irvin S. Cobb, a fellow Kentuckian and well-known humorist and author who died in 1944, wrote, among many things, a work entitled "Ladies and Gentlemen." Cobb spoke of Jesus as "The first true gentleman of recorded history and the greatest gentleman that ever lived."[14] And I think Mr. Cobb knew a gentleman when he met him, either personally or in the sacred pages.

Jesus was a gentleman whether at high noon or in the dark. He didn't lead a dual life, one in the light and another in the darkness. Some people do, acting differently in the dark or away from home.

Let me pose this question. Would you act differently if you had a magic ring that would make you invisible and allow you to do anything you wished without being seen and recognized? Sometimes goodness is "badness held in check" for fear of recognition.

I once read about two men at a banquet table. When the drinks were passed, one man accepted while his friend did not. The first man said, "At home, I don't drink, but when I am away from home, I do as I please." The second man said simply, "I am doing as I please now."

Think for a moment about the dark. The night has a thousand eyes. It is never dark to God. The human conscience should not be put to rest at sundown.

The night is a good time to do good things. The day is always lighter and brighter when the night has been used well—no hangovers. A gentleman is not a gentleman who isn't one in the dark.

Can we be trusted in the dark, away from home, or at a party? Jesus doesn't retire early or close His eyes when we leave home!

14. Irvin S. Cobb, "Greatest Gentleman that Ever Lived," *Behold the Man*, ed. Ralph L. Woods (New York: The Macmillan Company, 1944), p. 15.

142

Guide

"He saith unto them, Follow me, and I will make you fishers of men" (Matt. 4:19).

The pathway of life is sometimes awesome, treacherous, dark, and foreboding. We all need a good guide.

History records the names of some good ones: Columbus, Daniel Boone, Lincoln, and others. We also have roadmaps, compasses, and the AAA to help us on our way. We still have the stars. But none of man's aids or individual guides is infallible. I recall being in Munich, Germany, in the summer of 1980 with one of my tour groups. One night our guide got lost, and we had to hire a taxidriver to get us back to our hotel.

Can we look to our inheritance to guide us down the right path? No! Can we look to the mores of society? No! Can we look to education? No!

Christ is our infallible guide. He does not falter or grow weary. He does not desert the party, nor does He lose His way. He can lead us through any labyrinth of evil.

He is experienced, trained, and knowledgeable. He is a lamp unto our feet and a light unto our pathway. He has provided the best guidebook in the world—the Bible—without error.

He can take a hungry man to the Bread of life.

He can take a thirsty man to the fountain of living water.

He can find a resting place for the weary.

He can find exotic, exciting, unharvested places of service.

He can bring healing to the sick and forgiveness for sin.

He knows the way home. He won't get lost. Trust Him!

143

Habitation

"Because thou hast made the Lord, which is my refuge, even the most High, thy *habitation*" (Ps. 91:9).

Several years ago the building of bomb shelters was all the rage. The fear of nuclear war drove many to erect such shelters, and they may have been wise.

We have lightning rods on buildings and houses to ground the lightning if it strikes a building. Television stations give weather warnings in an effort to help protect persons. But tragedies still come, and disaster strikes.

Is there any real hiding place from the storms of life? Maybe no absolute one, but some places are safer than others. However, in the spiritual world, where sin lurks, there is a safe and secure hiding place, a safe habitation. Christ is our hiding place, our habitation.

In Him we can find shelter from the deadly attacks of sin. We can find security from the ravages of evil. In Him we find sustenance in a dry and thirsty land. He also provides companionship, a great therapy for that stalking monster of loneliness.

The psalmist spoke, "Thou art my hiding place; thou shalt preserve me from trouble; thou shalt compass me about with songs of deliverance" (Ps. 32:7).

Fanny J. Crosby put it beautifully:

He hideth my soul in the cleft of the rock
That shadows a dry, thirsty land;
He hideth my life in the depths of His love,
And covers me there with His hand.

He calls us out of the storms of life into His quiet safety.

What a wonderful Savior! When tempted, try Him, not drugs, alcohol, etc. His boat won't sink. His arm is not too short.

Harmless One

"For such an high priest became us, who is holy, *harmless*, undefiled, separate from sinners, and made higher than the heavens" (Heb. 7:26).

The word *harmless* in this context literally means "without evil." Jesus, as our high priest, was free of infection of evil. He received none from working with people or going in and out among them.

In performing the office of high priest He was not a victim of others' narrowness, selfishness, or degrading thoughts. Their actions served only to stir His concern, love, and sympathy. He never usurped the office of high priest.

People do infect other people. It is recorded that in 1520 one man brought smallpox to Mexico, resulting in half a million deaths. In 1348 another man landed in England, and through him the Bubonic Plague became the greatest killer Great Britain had ever known. Thomas Carlyle tells of a poor Irish widow who contracted typhus fever and infected seventeen of her neighbors, who likewise died.

Jesus never infected anyone adversely. In that respect He was harmless. He did, however, infect others with a desire for goodness and righteousness. He is still in that business. His pure, blameless, harmless life is today the most potent factor drawing men and women to a higher level of living.

Additionally, He is the greatest cure the world has ever had for those infected with sin. His pure blood was given to flush sin out of the bloodstream of any who would accept such atoning grace.

It is so good to have a Harmless High Priest. It is even better that He did not choose to isolate Himself in His purity and holiness from a sinful world. His availability, providing atonement for the believer, is God's greatest gift.

145

Head of All Principality and Power

"Ye are complete in him, which is the *head of all principality and power*" (Col. 2:10).

The hymn "All Hail the Power of Jesus' Name" has an unusual distinction in the *Baptist Hymnal.* It is repeated on three different pages with a different hymn tune: CORONATION, DIADEM, and MILES LANE. Each tune and each repetition of the hymn seem to stress a different emphasis. One stresses the fact that Christ is Lord of all, one that the crowning is of great importance while the third puts the emphasis on the Person being crowned. No other hymn has been given as much attention in the hymnal.

The compilers of the *Baptist Hymnal* were wise in giving this accentuation to Christ's name. Paul, in writing to those at Colosse, strongly accentuated the fact that Christ was "head of all principality and power" (Col. 2:10). Whether Paul was talking about Christ's being superior to all rule, authority, and government of earth or whether he was referring to Christ's superiority to all orders of heavenly being, we are not sure. Probably both, because Christ was capable and worthy in both respects.

Therefore, I say without hesitation that the hymn writer, the compilers of the *Baptist Hymnal,* and the apostle Paul were all putting Christ on the proper pedestal. They saw Him in His role as a crowned King, superior to everyone and all powers and bodies.

So let us bring forth "the royal diadem,/And crown Him Lord of all," for if He is not Lord of all, He is not Lord at all.

Head of Every Man

"I would have you know, that *the head of every man* is Christ" (1 Cor. 11:3).

In writing to those in Corinth, Paul was talking about a Christian order: Christ the head of every man, the head of the woman is the man, and the head of Christ is God. The life-style of those in Corinth at the time Paul wrote his letter to the Corinthians justified the order which he described.

There are three types of persons: those who want to rule others, those who are content to be ruled, and those who have no desire to rule. In Paul's mind only Christ was suited to be the head of everyone. It is very difficult for people to rule people. Selfishness, greed, partiality, lack of love, and inability of judgment put flaws in the armor. But not so with Christ. He is the perfect, capable master of His servants. He gave His life for them, He is preparing now for them, and He is interceding for them with His Father.

We are just apprentices in His school. We are to learn at His feet. He should orchestrate our lives. He is the headmaster.

Albert Schweitzer called Christ "an Imperious Ruler," adding, "He sets us to the tasks which He has to fulfill for our time. He commands. And to those who obey Him, whether they be wise or simple, He will reveal Himself in the toils, the conflicts, the sufferings which they shall pass through in His fellowship."[15]

That's the privilege of the head of every person and it becomes a privilege of every person.

15. Albert Schweitzer, *Contemporary Thinking About Jesus,* comp. Thomas S. Kepler (New York: Abingdon-Cokesbury Press, 1944), p. 391.

147

Head of the Church

"He is the *head* of the body, *the church*" (Col. 1:18).

When we built a new sanctuary at McLean Baptist Church in Memphis, Tennessee, in the mid-fifties, we inscribed over the door into the sanctuary the words, "Enter to worship," and on the other side of the door to be seen as the worshipers left, these words, "Depart to serve." It was our way of saying that we wanted Christ to be head of that particular body of believers.

We recognized no pope, no founding father, and no self-proclaimed messiah, no one other than Christ who loved the church and gave Himself for it. He gave the church its existence, its unity, and its government. The members of the local congregation, a local church, are to be controlled, directed, and kept alive spiritually by the one head who is Christ.

Christ had at least three purposes in becoming the head of the church. First, He did so in order to purify it, to make it acceptable, alive in Him. Second, He did so in order to preserve the church, to give it stability, permanency, even if the gates of hell should come against it. Third, He did so in order to present the church to Himself as His bride.

I ask here a very simple question. If Christ so loved the church, what should be our relationship to it? Could there be any doubt?

Bruce Barton once remarked that businesses checked on themselves frequently to be sure they were headed toward their original goals. Should not the church and her members do a similar checkup?

What do you think?

Healer

"Stretch forth thine hand. And he stretched it out: and his hand was *restored* whole as the other" (Mark 3:5).

Did you ever do an absolutely foolish thing? Well, I have and recently. There was a large cardboard box about three feet square that would not go in the trunk nor the passenger section of my car. I decided to get on top of the box, jump up and down, and crush it. I had done smaller boxes that way. I got atop it, jumped, and, when I came down, the box didn't crush. It threw me off, and I hit at an awkward angle. A hot pain flashed in my right hip. I thought the hip was broken. I hurt for days, but X-rays showed no damage other than strained muscles. What a foolish thing to have done. But the hip healed. Who did the healing?

I think Christ had a part in the healing. He created these self-healing qualities of our bodies, but He does not override our stupidity. No invention of humankind has a self-healing quality. The natural processes of healing and restoration are part of His goodwill in creation.

But He has done, and He continues to do His work of healing in addition to the usual, natural ways. He did so in the case of the man with a withered hand in the Scripture passage. He instructed the man who had exhibited strong faith to stretch forth his hand. That was painful. But the man did, and his obedience to the command of Christ brought results.

Christ is certainly a great Healer. I believe in faith healing but not the sensational, commercial kind by which people are frequently exploited. Christ can heal physical maladies; He can heal racial hurts and fractures; He can, and does, restore emotional wholeness; and He has put the shattered pieces of family life back together. Visit His clinic and take His prescription.

149

Heir of All Things

"Hath in these last days spoken unto us by his Son, whom he hath appointed *heir of all things*" (Heb. 1:2).

Some wills today are lengthy and very detailed. They contain minute designations and specifications. Frequently, there are numerous codicils. But God appointed Christ "heir of all things." A simple will it was, but it contained more than any human will. Christ inherited His father's dominion which is universal. He was given all the possessions of the owner, God, His father.

I have wondered many times if King Tut ever thought of making a will. Obviously not. He was buried in a solid gold casket. Did King Croesus ever think of making a will? As the rich king of Lydia with many gold mines, he is remembered only in these words: "rich as Croesus."

But God in Christ provided a lordship that was universal, possessions vast and unlimited, and wealth untold. We speak reverently and, rightly so, of the "unsearchable riches of Christ" (Eph. 3:8). John, while exiled on the isle of Patmos, wrote: "Worthy is the Lamb that was slain to receive power, and riches, and wisdom, and strength, and honour, and glory, and blessing" (Rev. 5:12). What a legacy! What an inheritance!

But, wait a minute. Let us not be envious or jealous. For "Eye hath not seen, nor ear heard, neither have entered into the heart of man, the things which God hath prepared for them that love him" (1 Cor. 2:9). If that isn't enough, reach for this section of the will, "To an inheritance incorruptible, and undefiled, and that fadeth not away, reserved in heaven for you" (1 Pet. 1:4). And it was the old fisherman, Peter, who penned those words.

We are faring well in the will of Christ, much better than we deserve. It is time to be grateful!

150

High Priest For Ever
After the Order of Melchisedec

"Even Jesus, made an *high priest for ever after the order of Melchisedec*" (Heb. 6:20).

Melchisedec was the king and priest at Salem, or Jerusalem, at the time of Abraham. He bestowed upon Abraham the blessings of "El" (God), and in return Abraham gave Melchisedec a tithe of all he possessed. Melchisedec was a superior type of priest.

The author of the Book of Hebrews was presenting Christ not solely as a priest after the order of Melchisedec but as one who superseded the Levitical priesthood. The author wanted to prove the claims of Christ to be called priest. It was impossible to consider Jesus as an Aaronic priest, for He was descended from the tribe of Judah and not from the tribe of Levi.

With reference to Melchisedec, Westcott helps us: "The lessons of his appearance lie in the appearance itself. Abraham marks a new departure . . . but before the fresh order is established, we have a vision of the old in its superior majesty; and this, on the eve of disappearance, gives its blessing to the new."[16]

We see, then, in Christ the new order of the priest-king. While on the cross Christ was fulfilling His priestly duties and at the same time was also King. As recipients of His redeeming love, we need both the priestly sympathy and the resources of royalty. He graciously fulfilled His priestly role royally and His royal role in a mediatorial way.

The word *forever* indicates the perpetuity of our high priest which eliminates the need of any other priest. How good for us. There is no need of concern for priestly rank or succession. He stands alone, as always.

16. James Orr, *The International Standard Bible Dictionary*, Vol. 3 (Grand Rapids: Wm. B. Eerdmans, 1949), p. 2020.

151

High Priest of Our Confession

"Wherefore, holy brethren, partakers of the heavenly calling, consider the Apostle and *High Priest of our profession* [confession], Christ Jesus" (Heb. 3:1).

We all need what we might call a "Father Confessor." There are times when we just must share with another. We want another's ears and heart. A confession is an admission, an acknowledgment, an avowal of matters pertaining to oneself. These matters need to be brought out into the open.

Many times, I have ached inwardly, needing someone to share with, to confess my burdens. Many times I have been the one hearing problems and burdens of others. Confidentiality, love, and humility are always essential in such relationships.

Christians can affirm Christ as their High Priest and feel free to "unload on Him" the hurts of the heart. Christ has given the assurance that He hears us, cares for us, and that He is willing to plead our case. He can emphathize and sympathize with us. Speak to Him regularly.

As the High Priest of our confession, He is busy making intercession for us. He does more than just listen.

It is no shame to confess one's faults. In fact, James, the brother of our Lord, urges us to "Confess your faults one to another, and pray one for another" (Jas. 5:16). Confession should flow because Christ's mercy abounds. "If we confess our sins, he is faithful and just to forgive us our sins, and to cleanse us from all unrighteousness" (1 John 1:9).

Confession is good for the soul. I know! Thank you for your forgiving spirit.

High Tower

"The Lord is my rock, and my fortress, and my deliverer; my God, my strength, in whom I will trust; my buckler, and the horn of my salvation, and my *high tower*" (Ps. 18:2).

This is a very unusual verse. In this one verse there are listed eight epithets (titles) of the Lord. The eight are:

He is my rock
　　　my fortress
　　　my deliverer
　　　my God
　　　my strength
　　　my buckler
　　　the horn of my salvation
　　　my high tower

It appears that David was contemplating on the greatness and the glory, and the power of God, his Lord, and began to enumerate some of the titles that he chose to attach to God. These titles grew out of the functions that God had provided for David.

The one for today's emphasis is "high tower." Both words need to be stressed. A tower was usually built to provide a lookout post. Vision was better at the top of the well-located tower. It was used as a fortress, a citadel. There is one on the campus of Belmont College in Nashville, Tennessee. It was used during the Civil War days as a water tower and a lookout tower for the estate owner. The word *high* in conjunction with the title David gave His Lord, High Tower, indicates that it towered into the blue of the sky. It could be seen easily. It would be a beacon to a lost shepherd or a lost sailor.

He, as our High Tower, is not a Tower of Babel but a Tower of Blessing, standing tall with outstretched arms.

Holy One

"Ye denied *the Holy One* and the Just, and desired a murderer to be granted unto you" (Acts 3:14).

For four devotionals we will be dealing with Christ as the *Holy One*, the *Holy One of God*, the *Holy Child Jesus*, and the *Holy One of Israel*. The *Holy One* is a messianic title denoting spiritual wholeness, soundness, and perfection.

It is interesting to note that most hymn books place Reginald Heber's hymn "Holy, Holy, Holy" among the first in the book. I think this is an attempt, maybe unconsciously, to acknowledge the holiness of Christ, His ethical perfection, and, in so doing, to add an extra gesture of honor.

The third stanza of that hymn conveys more fully the uniqueness of the meaning of *holy*.

> Holy, holy, holy! tho' the darkness hide Thee,
> Tho' the eye of sinful man Thy glory may not see;
> Only Thou art holy; there is none beside Thee,
> Perfect in power, in love, and purity.

It is no wonder that Heber also spoke of saints adoring Christ, the Holy One, and that cherubim and seraphim would fall down before Him. That is the effect Christ, as the epitome of holiness, has on all of lesser characters.

Who among us feels worthy to stand alongside such an One? We feel more comfortable kneeling in homage and adoration.

Isn't it still an enigma that people then desired and even now desire a murderer's presence among them rather than the Holy One? What poor choices we mortals make. And choices do determine our destiny.

Holy One of God

"Saying, Let us alone; what have we to do with thee, thou Jesus of Nazareth? art thou come to destroy us? I know thee who thou art; *the Holy One of God*" (Luke 4:34).

Impure blood cannot cleanse impure blood. One does not wash dirty clothes in dirty water with the hope of getting the clothes clean. Evil cannot cast out evil. It takes pure blood to cleanse impure blood. It takes clean water to clean clothes, and it takes holiness to drive out evil.

When Christ went into the synagogue in Capernaum on the sabbath day, He met a man with an unclean spirit who cried out to Him immediately, asking to be let alone, because He recognized Christ as the Holy One of God. The man knew that an unclean spirit could not associate with holiness. He felt that the power of holiness would destroy the evil and He was right.

I wish we knew today the power of Christ Jesus to rebuke an unclean spirit. Only His pure blood can cleanse an impure blood-stream, but somehow we just don't make haste to try the man of Galilee, the Holy One of God. But when He is tried, when He is allowed to take possession of one's life, He can give the blood transfusion necessary to purify out the impurities. I have seen Him work that way. I have some friends who have most recently had such a grand experience. Miracles have happened.

His blood bank is adequate. His skill is perfect, and He is waiting to be brought in on the case. Who is next? And no one has to stand in line and wait, or return at a more convenient time.

155

Holy Child Jesus

"For of a truth against thy *holy child Jesus,* whom thou hast anointed, both Herod, and Pontius Pilate, with the Gentiles, and the people of Israel, were gathered together" (Acts 4:27).

Some of the translations have used the word "servant" in the place of "child," and that is fine because others draw the idea further out by saying "consecrated servant."

A holy child is a dedicated, consecrated one set aside for a particular function. Our churches have children's dedication day, an expression of a desire to portray the hope that the child will grow into spiritual maturity. The act is not efficacious or vicarious, only symbolic.

Christ was set apart from the beginning as a Holy Child. Herod sought to destroy the holy child, and Pilate surrendered the holy child—grown into a holy man—to the mob for crucifixion.

I am grateful that we have the example of Christ's being set apart, dedicated, for a holy mission.

Well do I remember an event which came to me in 1937 when I felt the call of God to the gospel ministry. I wrote my mother and father to share with them. I wanted them to know my decision immediately because my childhood dream had been shaped by a yearning to become a medical doctor, a surgeon in particular. Mother wrote immediately, saying, "Son, I am not surprised at the call. It is an answer to prayer even though I never shared my prayer with you." In her heart my mother had secretly dedicated me to the service of God, and God honored her prayer.

Parents have much to do with the spiritual life of the child. Even though my parents could not support me financially while I was in college, their prayers did support me, by far the better of the two.

Holy One of Israel

"Fear not, thou worm Jacob, and ye men of Israel; I will help thee, saith the Lord, and thy redeemer, *the Holy One of Israel*" (Isa. 41:14).

Isaiah, in his use of the term *Holy One of Israel* was somewhat like the minister who, in talking about the blind man, said, "Brethren, he was blind; he couldn't see. He was deprived of sight, and both of his eyes were out."

Such repetition is what we frequently call "redundancy."

On the other hand, such repetition can be most effective. Isaiah used the title "Holy One of Israel" twenty-five times in his book. He was speaking to Israel. He was speaking to them about God. He was trying to tell them that God wanted to be their God and that God had shown Himself as their God in many ways.

Israel was special to God, and Isaiah was trying to get Israel to recognize God as being special to them. It was Isaiah's favorite designation of the Almighty in God's covenant relationship to Israel.

The prophet emphatically exhorted Israel to remember the help that God had provided for them. He had brought down Egypt, Ethiopia, Babylon, and Chaldea. He had become both Deliverer and Redeemer. The record should have been clear to Israel.

May I ask if the record is clear to us: How has God blessed us individually? How has He blessed our nation? And, how has He made provisions for our deliverance from sin? If the record is clear, the subsequent action also should be clear. If gratitude doesn't abound and bring spiritual commitment and growth, then what will? We know we are to have no other god before Thee, but we are so glad we can have Thee.

Hope of Israel

"For this cause therefore have I called for you, to see you, and to speak with you: because that for *the hope of Israel* I am bound with this chain" (Acts 28:20).

We are all creatures of hope. Pope said, "Hope springs eternal in the human breast." Hope is the "eyes of faith" directed toward the future. It is desire accompanied with expectation.

There is a humorous story making the rounds of a man caught in flood waters. He was asked to go out of the water with a friend but refused, saying his hope and trust were in the Lord. The water continued to rise, and a coast guard cutter offered assistance, but the refusal was the same as previously. Then a helicopter pilot flew over and, seeing the water was up to his neck, said to the drowning man, "I will throw you a rope. Climb up."

"No, my hope and trust are in the Lord." Our victim died and questioned the Lord about letting him drown.

The reply was, "I sent you a friend, the coast guard, and a helicopter. You refused each."

Without being too facetious, I think that Israel's hope in the coming Messiah may have been a little too particular and narrow. The promises of the Coming One, the Hope of Israel, were anchors of hope to hold the soul fast, but when the Desire of all nations came, He was rejected by them. To those who then and even now accept him and his plan for the ages, they have a better hope, rooted and grounded in Christ's resurrection.

Our hope today is our faith directed toward the future, His coming again. So hope and faith go on and on, until they become *fait accompli.*

Horn of Salvation

"[God] hath raised up an *horn of salvation* for us in the house of his servant David" (Luke 1:69).

Whenever the word *horn* is used in the Old Testament, it stands for strength and victory. Certain animals have horns which are used for protective purposes—weapons of offence. The horn as a musical instrument is one of the key instruments used in proclaiming or announcing victory. The blowing of car horns is usually done to denote victory.

The term *horn of salvation* is also a metaphor used in classical writing. In referring to Christ as the "horn of salvation," Zacharias, the father of John the Baptist, was shadowing forth the strength and conquering might that Christ would assert in the deliverance of His people.

We as Christians have the opportunity to blow the horn, sound the trumpet, because of victory through Christ. It is a privilege to tell this good news. We are no longer torn by the horns of a dilemma of doubt and defeat, but we have the golden responsibility to sound forth the glorious news that the "horn of salvation" has come, bringing strength and victory.

We are not orphans of apes left to fend for ourselves in a sinful world without a beneficent "horn of salvation." We are the recipients of Christ's power, love, salvation, and eternal triumph: truly a cornucopia—a horn of plenty.

Let us join the parade of disciples behind the banner of the cross, held high because of our Horn of Salvation. In this way we can demonstrate our faith and invite our friends to come with us.

Hosanna

"Blessed be the kingdom of our father David, that cometh in the name of the Lord: *Hosanna* in the highest" (Mark 11:10).

As Americans we are well known because of all kinds of parades: ticker-tape parades for returning heroes, victory-day parades, athletic-event parades (Rose Bowl, Sugar Bowl, etc.), and Easter parades. A parade is a group demonstration or a ceremonial march to call some important event to mind or to introduce a new idea or person.

Christ's triumphal entry into Jerusalem was an expression of Him as King and of things to come. In one sense, it was a victory-day parade. The participants shouted, "Hosanna in the highest."

"Hosanna" is the Greek transliteration of the Hebrew, meaning "save now, pray," and it is used six times in the Gospels as an acclamation of praise. Some go on to say it is equivalent to saying, "Salvation unto God." It is, however, more an ejaculation of praise or welcome in this case than a supplication for salvation. Both meanings are a part of the fuller picture.

The Jewish people had a Hosanna Day which they observed as the seventh day of the Feast of the Tabernacles. It was a joyous day of celebration.

Would there be anything wrong with Christians having a hosanna day occasionally as a part of praise and worship? I think not. I am for it. It would do us much good, and the world needs to see and hear such a demonstration. It could be the most meaningful of all our parades, following the Grand Marshal, Hosanna. What a mighty army!

160

I AM

"Jesus said unto them, Verily, verily, I say unto you, Before Abraham was, *I am*" (John 8:58).

I have heard many self-introductions at various gatherings, and so have you. Never have I heard even one person stand and say, "I am," and then be seated.

When Jesus repeatedly announced to the world that He was "I am," in some cases adding words of enlargement or distinctive service He was to perform, none were ethnic related. All were spiritually or messianic related. Never was there any hint of braggadocio nor an ego trip. To me, He seemed to be making a special announcement to a special audience, the whole world, and He did so conscious of brevity and relevancy. Not only was He the great "I Am," but He spoke of Himself as the I am of the Bread of life, the Water of life, the resurrection and the life, the way and the truth and the life, etc.

In calling Himself "I am," he was bringing out a truth about Himself similar to how God identified Himself to Moses as given in Exodus 3:14. In response to Moses' inquiry of God as to what Moses should tell the children of Israel when they asked: "What is his name?" God said to Moses, "I AM THAT I AM." In other words, "I am the God of the past, the present, and the future, and will be all that is necessary for Me to be your one and only God."

It was a brief self-introduction that Christ gave of Himself, but it was not brief in meaning and significance. I am getting closer to the time when I will hear Him say, " 'I Am' is your escort to your home over there. Take Me by the hand, and we will cross Jordan together."

Neither I nor any Christian will have to go it alone. And what a super feeling that thought brings.

161

Image Breaker—Image Maker

"I say unto thee, That thou art *Peter,* and upon *this rock* I will build my church; and the gates of hell shall not prevail against it" (Matt. 16:18).

A rather well-known evangelist attracted much attention during the past few years by leading a wealthy individual to destroy some priceless jade characters by the thought that possession of such objects was image worship.

There is a legend that one morning Abraham, whose father, Terah, was a manufacturer of idols, was asked by his father, "Who, during the night, destroyed some of the idols in the warehouse?"

Abraham's response was, "The large one in the corner did it in a moment of fury."

"Why, son, that big idol could not come down from his pedestal."

"Since that is true, then why do people worship idols if they have no power?" replied Abraham.

Christ never spent time either breaking or leading others to destroy their idols or graven images even though they had no place in His teachings and worship. He did, however, become an image breaker and an image maker in the lives of others. He caused the old image of the big fisherman, Peter, to be broken, and in its place He gave him a new image, Peter, the rock. He caused the old image of Saul to be replaced by the new image of Paul. And, most important of all, He shattered many false images of God as law and vengeance and gave the world an image of God as love and mercy.

I hope He is destroying my old image and giving me a new one under His Spirit. That would be a welcomed face-lifting.

162

Image of God

"Who is the *image of* the invisible *God,* the firstborn of every creature" (Col. 1:15).

About fifty years ago there was a popular song entitled "If I Had a Talking Picture of You," and, if my memory is correct, it went something like this:

> I would play it every time I felt blue,
> I would give ten shows a day
> And a midnight matinee,
> If I had a talking picture of you.

Christ, while on earth, was a walking, talking picture of God, a perfect image of Him. In all of the relationships of His being with other persons He is the likeness, image, and the representation of God.

Christ as the eternally preexistent Word, the humanly manifested Son and the living, reigning Lord, at all times and on every occasion was the image of God.

Paul, writing to the Colossian Christians, was refuting, trying to throw off, their doctrinal heresy by declaring null and void the practice of ascetic ceremonialism and belief in angelic meditation. He taught that access to God was in and through Christ, the perfect image and fullness of God.

It never becomes trite to say that if one wishes to know what God is like, look at Jesus, try to understand Jesus and to be more like Him.

The more we come to know Jesus, the more we know about God, and we find the access door open. A standing invitation has been given. The next move is our move. He expects, however, to hear from us within the context of time. It's too bad to be too late!

Immanuel

"Behold, a virgin shall conceive, and bear a son, and shall call his name *Immanuel*" (Isa. 7:14).

The word *Immanuel* is the Hebrew word for "God with us," and the Greek word meaning the same thing is "Emmanuel." (See Matt. 1:23.) The term *emmanuel* appeared also in the Septuagint (the Greek translation of the Old Testament). It is sad that neither the Jews nor the Greeks accepted Christ when He came as God with us.

The promise in Isaiah 7:14 was a sign that God gave Ahaz. The house of David at that time was beset by enemies, and its reigning representative was weak in faith. The promise was to shore up faith.

There was a longing too in the hearts of the Egyptians and the Babylonians for a divinely born savior. Recent discoveries have substantiated this fact.

There is an old Latin hymn written by John Neale in 1851 entitled "Veni Emmanuel," which translated means "O come Emmanuel," and picks up the yearnings and expectations of hearts in exile.

> O come, O come, Emmanuel,
> And ransom captive Israel,
> That mourns in lonely exile here,
> Until the Son of God appear.
> Rejoice! Rejoice! Emmanuel
> Shall come to thee, O Israel!

So whether you wish to call Christ "Immanuel" or "Emmanuel," it doesn't matter. The thing that matters most is whether or not our recognition and homage is given to Christ as God with us. It is not a onetime act, but a daily devotional act.

164

Immortal

"Now unto the King eternal, *immortal*, invisible, the only wise God, be honour and glory for ever and ever" (1 Tim. 1:17).

Walter Chalmers Smith wrote, during the mid-nineteenth century, his beautiful hymn "Immortal, Invisible," the first stanza of which reads:

Immortal, invisible God only wise,
In light inaccessible hid from our eyes,
Most blessed, most glorious, the Ancient of Days,
Almighty, victorious, Thy great name we praise.

Christ as the Immortal One was eternal, enduring, undecaying, and incomparable. Paul was giving to his son in the ministry, Timothy, a statement in the form of a doxology which seemingly was intended directly against the Essenes who invested their immediate agents with divine powers of creation. In Paul's mind Christ was the great and only Potentate, who as the Immortal One was exempt from the liability to die and exempt from oblivion.

May I raise a few questions here. Is death a liability? Is it paying the debt to nature? Is death the end of our mortality, thrusting us into permanent oblivion?

My answer to these questions is a direct no in each case. Death to the Christian is not a liability. It is an inheritance. It is not paying the debt to nature. It is casting off the restraints of nature. Death for the Christian is not the means whereby we are cast into oblivion and outer darkness. It is the means whereby we are translated into the land that is fairer than day. Death only wounds to cure. We fall, only to rise.

165

Invisible

"Now unto the King eternal, immortal, *invisible*" (1 Tim. 1:17).

Do we have to see to believe? If so, then is seeing believing? If that be the case we will never believe in God for God is invisible. "No man hath seen God at any time; the only begotten Son, which is in the bosom of the Father, he hath declared him" (John 1:18).

But, thank God, His Son made a clear and concise declaration of who God is and what God is like. We don't have to see God; we can know Him in Christ.

The last stanza of the hymn referred to in the previous page picks up the proclamation of the Immortal, Invisible One.

Great Father of glory, pure Father of light,
Thine angels adore Thee, all veiling their sight;
All praise we would render; O help us to see
'Tis only the splendor of light hideth Thee!

I have no problem with an invisible God. In fact, I think I adore Him more strongly and more genuinely than I would a visible one. A visible God would have to be subject to the constraints of physical concepts. He would lose majesty, awe, and incomparability.

With Christ having declared God, I have neither wish nor craving to see God while I am in the flesh. My day will come, and when it does come I just want to be somewhere working for my Lord, singing this beautiful doxology which Paul gave to Timothy.

The eternal, heavenly clock ticks on with unerring pace, and we keep getting closer home.

Impostor?

"By what authority doest thou these things? and who gave thee this authority to do these things?" (Mark 11:28).

The chief priests and the scribes thought Jesus was a put-on, a make-believe, an imposter, passing himself off as someone else as many worldly imposters have done.

My Aunt Mary found this out the hard and costly way. A well-dressed man knocked on her door and posed as a friend with an important bit of knowledge. She was advised to go to the bank and draw out some of her hard-earned money in order to shift it into another safer and more dependable bank. She followed the advice and trusted the imposter who absconded with her money. It's an old con game, conning a dime a dozen as a longlost brother, a friend of a friend, or as agents of mercy.

Most of you, my readers, have never tried to pose as someone else in order to fleece another. But in an even more serious way we may be "flimflam" imposters. We can try to pose as good and kind persons when inwardly we hate and are haughty and arrogant. We can pose as loving and compassionate while at the same time we are selfish and greedy, jealous and envious of others. We may pose as honest and upright while failing to give God the tithe and refusing to accept stewardship obligations.

Christ may have appeared to darkened eyes as an imposter. He may have shocked those who were unable to read His motives and were ignorant of His omniscience. But He was the most genuinely real person who ever walked the paths of life. He was void of sham and make-believe.

Am I real?

The Incarnate One

"But made himself of no reputation, and took upon him the form of a servant, and was *made in the likeness of men*" (Phil. 2:7).

When we speak of Christ as "the Incarnate One," we are referring to His coming from the state of glory to the state of humiliation. This He did without compulsion. It was voluntary.

I think Dr. E. Y. Mullins has the finest seven statements about the incarnation that can be found:

1. It was a divine self-emptying. The New Testament repeatedly states the fact.

2. It was a divine self-emptying for redemptive ends, under the form of human personality.

3. The self-emptying of God in Christ reveals the infinite mobility of divine love. It is described by the word *grace*.

4. The self-emptying of Christ, the eternal Son, carries with it great consequence for our salvation and spiritual destiny.

5. The self-emptying of Christ was not a putting off absolutely of divine attributes. It meant the retention of divine qualities and powers but under restraints and limitations of a human life.

6. It is impossible to grasp the process by which this self-emptying took place.

7. Finally, the self-emptying of Christ was the answer to the human search for God.[17]

In Jesus Christ, God and humanity become one. Humanity finds itself ideally and forever in Him.

17. Mullins, E. Y., *The Christian Religion in Its Doctrinal Expression* (Nashville: Baptist Sunday School Board, 1917), pp. 182-87.

168

In Him All the Fullness of the Godhead Bodily

"For *in him* dwelleth *all the fulness of the Godhead bodily*" (Col. 2:9).

I am not a grammarian to the extent that I should question something that has long been accepted, but I do question how, if something is full, can it be fuller or fullest? But, grammatically, *fuller* and *fullest* are correct. In practice that is not so. When my tea cup is full, it is full. When my gas tank is full, it is full.

Saying that in Christ "dwelleth all the fulness of the Godhead bodily" is comparable to saying that no more of the Godhead could be added either during His earthly life or during His present exaltation. In other words, Christ possessed the fullness of Deity, and fullness means full, and full means having within its limits all it can contain.

Paul used here strong and striking language. He was saying that at no time was Christ more or less God, but that at all times He was fully God.

Christ came in the fullness of time with the fullness of Deity in order that His followers might know the love of Christ "which passeth knowledge, that ye might be filled with all the fulness of God" (Eph. 3:19).

Christ, therefore, in sharing His fullness of the Godhead with His followers has no less, but His followers gain much.

What a beautiful sharing plan, ample, amicable, available and accessible, filled with all love, peace and joy. There is no fine print to destroy the advantages promised the recipients.

Innocent (Faultless) One

"Then said Pilate to the chief priests and to the people, I *find no fault in this man*" (Luke 23:4).

Cicero, a Roman statesman and philosopher who lived a century before Christ, said, "We should never persecute the innocent." As paradoxical as it seems, it was Cicero's Roman government that crucified the innocent One even after the official representative of the Roman government stated that he found no fault in Christ. Truisms and realities are frequently far apart.

An innocent person is one free of guilt, of sin. There is an absence of disloyalty to God. It includes both freedom from condemnation and freedom from the guilt of sin producing the condemnation.

We, as individuals, lost our innocence in the fall of humanity and through our sins. We can regain it only through the innocent One, slain for our sins of omission and commission. We cannot claim ignorance of the laws or commandments because ignorance is not innocence but sin.

The innocent do suffer with the guilty. The rain does fall on the just and the unjust. Many times the innocent suffer far more than the guilty. In the case of the guilty, mercy and grace seemed to be sought for the offender while with the innocent the punishment is inflicted more severely in order to cover up any vestige of innocence. That's why the death on the cross was so infamous: He was innocent.

The faultless One took upon Himself our faults so that we might stand before God with our faults forgiven, covered by the blood of the Lamb.

Intercessor, Interceder

"Seeing he ever liveth *to make intercession* for them" (Heb. 7:25).

An intercessor is one who mediates on behalf of another. An intercessor pleads the case of the client or friend before a jury or judge.

Intercession was a vital part of the role of Moses on behalf of the children of Israel. He uttered to God vivid, passionate prayers, wrung from his devout soul. Samuel also uttered many intercessory prayers on behalf of his people.

In Christ, however, we find intercession rising to its highest level. He taught His followers to use intercessory prayer. He did Himself, frequently.

Christ, as our High Priest, interceded on our behalf. In John 17 we find His high priestly prayer for His friends and followers. Read that chapter and notice the urgency of His priestly role.

His intercessory prayers for His disciples—for Peter in particular—and for all of His disciples present and to come portray Him as the Great Interceder.

His appearance on our behalf before God is a great intercessory act. His defense against the sentence of the law is another intercessory act as He offered Himself as surety from the condemnation of the law. Then, too, He gives our prayers more acceptability at the throne of grace.

He charges no fees. He represents us because of love, grace, and mercy. He knows what law and justice demand, but He knows the heart of the Judge.

171

Interpreter

"Nicodemus answered and said unto him, *How can these things be?*" [Interpret for me, please] (John 3:9).

Several years ago I was speaking to the administration and deans of the Seinan Gakiun University in Japan. I was asked about donor support of Belmont College. I replied that a certain donor had given us several millions of dollars and added, "That isn't chicken feed." They sat up very quizzically. "Chicken feed? We don't understand." Right there and then, I had to take the role of an interpreter and explain the meaning of some of our American "slanguage."

Time and time again, Jesus was asked the meaning of His statements. Many times He sought to explain them by relating parables. On the other hand, He had the marvelous capacity to express Himself in simple, clear language.

The nice thing about having Christ as our interpreter is that He not only knows all the answers, but He can actually understand where we are coming from. He knows our limitations. He knows our motives, and He can plumb the depths of our knowledge.

He interpreted the Law and the prophets by using them as foundations. He interpreted the Ten Commandments as the foundation for the fatherhood of God and the brotherhood of man, a bulwark against the theory that one god is as good as another, and that might makes right.

He interpreted goodness not as a theory but as a way of living. He taught that sacrifice was the giving of self. He believed that the law was made for people and not people for the law. His interpretations were accurate and errorless. He could see the heart of the matter and bring it to the heart of His listener.

Jahweh, Jah, Jehovah, Etc.

"And God [Elohim] said to Moses, I AM THAT I AM [*Jahweh*]" (Ex. 3:14).

The name *Jehovah* stems from the verb *to be,* and means "I am, I was, and I will." Jehovah then is the great "I Am." It is used over 6,800 times in the Old Testament and shows Jehovah as the One who will become what is necessary for Him to become to be the one God.

Jah, a short form, is used fifty times in the Old Testament and is always translated "Lord." We see this used in our word *Hallelujah,* which means "Praise ye the Lord" and is found twenty-five times in the Psalms. It is seen also in the name *Eli-jah,* "God of Jehovah," and other names such as Zechari*ah,* Zephani*ah,* etc.

Other usages of the word are:

Jehovah-Sabaoth, "The Lord of Hosts" (Gen. 32:2); "Bless ye the Lord, all ye his hosts" (Ps. 103:21).

Jehovah-rapha, "The Lord that Healeth" (Ex. 15:25); "He [Jehovah-rapha] healeth the broken in heart" (Ps. 147:3).

Jehovah-Shalom, "The Lord Sends Peace" (Judg. 6:24).

Jehovah-Jireh, "The Lord will provide" (Gen. 22:14).

Jehovah-Nissi, "The Lord, my Banner" (Ex. 17:15; Rom. 8:37).

Jehovah-Shammah, "The Lord is there" (Ezek. 48:35; see John 14:3).

Jehovah-rohi, "The Lord is my Shepherd" (Ps. 23:1; see Isa. 53:6).

Let us join with the heavenly host mentioned in Revelation 4:8 and acclaim Jehovah as "Holy, holy, holy, Lord God Almighty, which was, and is, and is to come."

He is worthy of all our accolades.

Jeremias

"Some say that thou art John the Baptist: some, Elias; and others, *Jeremias,* or one of the prophets" (Matt. 16:14).

Why Jeremias? There were many prophets significant in the life of Israel.

I can give several reasons which seem valid.

Jeremias was venerated by the Jews at the time of Jesus. The Jews fondly hoped that Jeremias might return and restore the ark, the tabernacle, and the altar of incense. In the book *The Apocrypha,* a compilation of fourteen books which were revered by the Jews, one of the books, 2 Maccabees 2:1-8, states that records tell of Jeremias taking the ark, etc., to a cave for safety. The doctrine of metempsychosis, transmigration, or the passing of the soul from one body into another was accepted among the Jews, and therefore it seemed logical that the soul of Jeremias might be reincarnated in Christ.

Jeremias was known as the weeping prophet. He wept over the sins of his people. Jesus wept over Jerusalem: "When he was come near, he beheld the city, and wept over it" (Luke 19:41). He also wept in Bethany over the death of Lazarus (John 11:35).

As Israel was God's instrument in Jeremias's day, so spiritual Israel is God's instrument today.

Jeremias was a prophet of individualism which is one of Christianity's chief cornerstones. So the similarities could go on and on.

Indeed, Jeremias was not a bad guess. It was an advance in thinking to liken Christ to one of the spiritual, teaching prophets.

However, the question still is: Whom do you say that I am?

Jesus

"She shall bring forth a son, and thou shalt call his name *JESUS:* for he shall save his people from their sins" (Matt. 1:21).

You will notice I have capitalized the letters in the name *JESUS.* I think that precious name which we have been talking about so much deserves that attention. His mother, Mary, was commanded by the angel to call Him by that name, Jesus. It is His personal name and used throughout the Gospels and Acts, but generally in the Epistles it appears in combination with Christ: JESUS CHRIST.

The name *Jesus* is equivalent to the Alexandrine Greek *Joshua.* Throughout Hebrew literature it may appear as Joshua, Jehoshua, Jeshua, or Jeshu. But the main thought is that of deliverance: salvation.

Like Joshua who led Israel into the Promised Land, Jesus is the leader of His people, the new Israel, to God.

Philip Doddridge wrote, during the middle of the eighteenth century, a lovely hymn tribute to the name *Jesus* under the title "Jesus! I Love Thy Charming Name."

> Jesus! I love thy charming name,
> 'Tis music to mine ear;
> Fain would I sound it out so loud,
> That earth and heav'n should hear.

Couple that tribute to the one by John Newton of the same period entitled "How Sweet the Name of Jesus":

> How sweet the name of Jesus sounds
> In a believer's ear!
> It soothes his sorrows, heals his wounds,
> And drives away his fear.

JESUS!

Jesus Christ Our Savior

"Which he shed on us abundantly through *Jesus Christ our Saviour*" (Titus 3:6).

There is nothing in the world of outdoor sports quite like the way bird dogs will back each other when sniffing a covey of quail. I have seen two dogs freeze instantly when the lead dog found the covey. There was no motion; they backed each other as if they were stone statues.

When Paul said to Titus, "Mine own son after the common faith" (Titus 1:4), referring to Jesus as "the Lord Jesus Christ our Saviour," it was all there. The names hung together, and the context indicated a working of the Trinity in unison and togetherness, like hunting dogs.

Our salvation has its source in the love of God for people. It comes to us through Jesus Christ, our Savior, who died for our sins. It is made complete and effectual in the soul by the washing of regeneration and the renewing of the Holy Spirit—the three-in-one action.

Even though the emphasis thus far has been on the name of "Jesus Christ our Saviour," I feel that some accent should be placed on the word *our*. This personalizes the whole truth for us. He is our Savior. He comes to us. He died for us. He dwells within us. It is a "me-and-thee" proposition.

The personal closeness of the Savior to His redeemed is one of Christianity's greatest assets. He is not a far-away despot off on an exciting hunt. He is always near. He is approachable. He is accessible. Could we ask for more?

He wants to bless us. He waits to bless us. He watches our every thought and action in order to respond to our requests. Let us ask for more and love Him more.

John the Baptist

"[Herod] said unto his servants, This is *John the Baptist;* he is risen from the dead; and therefore mighty works do shew forth themselves in him" (Matt. 14:2).

Two of the most difficult things to explain that have occurred in the history of the human race are: What brought about the Golden Age of Greece? Historians don't know. They just know it happened.

The second, how could Jesus' contemporaries account for his life and deeds? They were stumped. No historical cause will account for genius and Deity.

When Jesus' contemporaries were asked about Him, they gave diverse answers. Herod Antipas, the weak, cruel, vociferous tyrant, had superstitious fear in his gilded palace, for he had beheaded John the Baptist. Herod thought he might be seeing John's ghost or that John had risen from the dead or that Christ was animated by the spirit of John the Baptist. It was not easy for Herod to get John off of his mind, much less explain who Jesus was. He was on the horns of a dilemma. His fears haunted him. Reality stared Herod in the face, and the public was reacting favorably to Christ. So Herod blurted out a quick, irresponsible answer.

There were some similarities between Jesus and John, who were cousins. John preached repentance of sins and so did Jesus. John was possessed with a holy courage, and Jesus, though meek and lowly, was without fear. Both lived lives of simplicity.

But a greater than John the Baptist had come, One inexplicable and incomprehensible to many. One thing we do know for sure: we can call Him our Lord and Master.

Judge (Righteous Judge)

"Henceforth there is laid up for me a crown of righteousness, which the Lord, *the righteous judge,* shall give me at that day" (2 Tim. 4:8).

It is quite possible that the apostle Paul in speaking to Timothy, his son in the ministry, was contrasting the difference between Christ, the righteous Judge, and Nero, an unrighteous earthly judge-king.

Nero acted like an animal that had tasted blood. He plunged into every type of vice and profligacy. For six days Rome burned, but Nero showed himself unmoved by the disaster, playing upon his fiddle and reciting verses about the burning of Troy. He was even accused of starting the fire. He did fear the wrath of the people and laid the blame upon the Christians. He fed them to lions, watching from his royal box as they were slaughtered. There Nero also received his warriors who had fought good fights and awarded them their crowns.

Paul had fought a good fight. He had won the race. He had reached his goal—all because of God's grace. Paul knew his reward would be forthcoming, a reward of righteousness. It was laid up for him, kept in a safe, secure place to be awarded him by the righteous Judge. The prize was reward enough for the hardships endured.

Additionally, Paul stressed the fact that a similar crown of righteousness was in store for all that look for, plan for, and love Christ's appearing.

Life is a battle, a race to be run, a crown to be won, and a goal to be sought. The righteous Judge is at the finish line.

Judge of the Quick and the Dead

"He commanded us to preach unto the people, and to testify that it is he which was ordained of God to be *the Judge of quick and dead*" (Acts 10:42).

A judge is a very powerful person. He holds the destiny of lives in his hands. He is one with knowledge to decide the merits of a case and to pronounce sentence or settlement.

Jesus was appointed of God to be the Judge of the quick and the dead. He will act in that capacity with reference to all who shall be on earth at the time of His final appearance and of all who have lived previously and have died.

Some say that the "quick and dead" refers to the righteous and the wicked. Of that I am not sure, but Christ will judge the living and the dead, the righteous and the wicked, and make a final decision as to the inheritance of all.

In life, people have been guilty of trying to bribe judges. They have sought special favors from the judge. Some have succeeded while others have been apprehended and prosecuted.

Our Judge of the quick and the dead cannot be bribed. He gives no special favors. He is fair, just, and knowledgeable.

The record of our life and deeds will be errorless before Him because, as the black minister said, "My Lord, He knows all I do, He hears all I say. He's just a'writin' all the time."

But I had rather have Jesus than any judge that ever sat on a judicial bench. I can expect fairness, justice, love, and mercy. Isn't that enough!

Just Man, A

"Have thou nothing to do with that *just man*" (Matt. 27:19).

Our Scripture reference for the day comes from the context of Jesus' appearance before Pilate. Pilate's wife, Claudia, had a dream and sent word to her husband that he should have nothing to do with Jesus, a "just man." This reference is found in the Gospel of Matthew only.

It is interesting to note that this woman, wife of a heathen governor, is the only one who pleaded for Christ. She pleaded with her husband to deliver the Just Man, the Innocent One. She spoke up for Jesus. Some noncanonical accounts say she later became a Christian.

As men, we make much of our courage and fairness, but, as is so frequently true, we have to take a back seat to the women. Their perspectivity exceeds ours. They can read situations with insight while we have only sight. Claudia is to be commended while her husband is to be censured. Why didn't Pilate listen to her? He knew she was right. Where was his courage? Did the crowd back him off?

It's a pitiful procedure that Pilate followed. He forsook his role as leader and tossed the decision to the crowd, an angry mob. He should have known what their decision would be, and, in asking them, he was virtually agreeing with their mood and temper.

A Just Man, the Innocent One, is falsely condemned and turned over to a bloodthirsty crowd by a weak-kneed governor who spurned the wise counsel of his wife. Justice was thwarted, and evil blossomed.

Will we stand up this day for Jesus?

Just One

"Ye denied the Holy One and the *Just*, and desired a murderer to be granted unto you" (Acts 3:14).

The trading, bartering, and exchanging of one thing for another is usually predicated on value judgment.

I recall while in grammar school taking my lunch of two biscuits with country ham and a piece of mom's cake in a tin box. I would meet a friend of mine at noon under a big shade tree and swap my lunch with him for a can of Vienna sausage and two store-bought cookies. I wanted what I didn't usually have at home. It hurts me even now to think of that deal. It was a bad deal for me then, and it would be a worse one now.

The disciples, Peter and John, were in Jerusalem at the Temple. They had healed a lame man in the name of Jesus of Nazareth. Then, going out on Solomon's Porch of the Temple, Peter began to answer the people thus: "You delivered Christ to Pilate. Christ was the Holy, Just One, but you were willing to trade him off for a murderer, Barabbas. What a swap out!"

He added, "Did you do it through ignorance as did your rulers? You must repent, therefore, and be converted."

Aren't we guilty of trying to wash away too many things with ignorance? Ignorance is not a valid excuse. We still ply that trade, and we still trade the Just One off, at least for a period of time. Where was reason when the choice was made between a murderer and the Just One, and the murderer was chosen to be given freedom?

Are we better at making choices today? I wonder!

Keeper of the Keys of Hell and Death

"I am he that liveth, and was dead; and, behold, *I* am alive for evermore, Amen; and *have the keys of hell and of death*" (Rev. 1:18).

Failure to have the right keys in my pocket has caused me much inconvenience. I have locked myself out of our house, my office, and the car. I have not always found an easy way to enter the house, the office, and the car without keys. Keys unlock and close doors and are needed for both purposes.

Jesus told Simon Peter that he would give him the keys to the Kingdom of heaven (Matt. 16:19). This did not mean that Peter had final or exclusive rights of the keys. They were later given also to the church. Peter knew the way of admission into the Kingdom. His confession showed that. He was an agent of the gospel with keys that, if used, would provide admission into the Kingdom for those who would accept the message of redemption.

In the passage in the Book of Revelation, Jesus is stressing the fact that He is the possessor of both the keys to death and Hades and controls the entrance to both: acceptance or rejection of Him determines His stance.

He was saying in both cases: "I have the keys. I can open the doors of salvation, death, and Hades. I can close the doors. All is a privilege and responsibility of mine."

Here is an anonymous poem I ran across:

Hail to the prince of life and death
  Who holds the keys of death and hell
The spacious world unseen is His
  And sovereign power becomes Him well.

Remember that He, too, holds the keys to heaven's gate in the city of God, the New Jerusalem.

King of Glory

"When the Son of man shall come *in his glory*, and all the holy angels with him, then shall he sit *upon the throne of his glory*" (Matt. 25:31).

Put the word *king* with *glory*, and you have the summum bonum of a tribute to the kingly aspects of Christ's role and rule.

He will be exalted above the heavens. He is at the right hand of the Father. He accomplished His mission without a kingly robe. He had no crown but a crown of thorns and a crown of righteousness. He had no castle on a high hill overlooking a lazy stream: He had no place to lay His head. He had no retinue of servants to wash His tired feet at the close of the day—no one to fan away the heat.

But there now resides upon His head many diadems: "His eyes were as a flame of fire, and on his head were many crowns" (Rev. 19:12).

The story is often told that one day Queen Victoria, in the year of her coronation, attended a public performance of Handel's oratorio, *The Messiah*. She was told that the audience would rise when the Hallelujah Chorus was sung but that it was her royal privilege to remain seated. When the chorus began, the audience rose. There seemed to be a temporary struggle in the mind of the queen, but when the choir came to the inspiring passage, "King of kings and Lord of lords," she could remain seated no longer. She rose to her feet and stood in the royal box as a silent tribute to the King of kings, the King of glory.

Can we do any less?

King of Israel

"Nathanael answered and saith unto him, Rabbi, thou art the Son of God; thou art the *King of Israel*" (John 1:49).

The children of Israel were described in the Old Testament as God's chosen people. They were at first designated as the people of the Northern Kingdom, with Judah being considered the Southern Kingdom. But Israel was a nation, a people, who wanted a king. In actuality, they really did not know what they wanted, even after getting kings.

The words of Ralph Waldo Emerson from his "Boston Hymn" seem most appropriate here:

> God said, I am tired of kings
> I suffer them no more;
> Up to my ear the morning brings,
> The outrage of the poor.

If only they could have perceived Jesus to be King of Israel as did Nathanael, things would have been very different.

The response of Nathanael was evoked by the recognition given Nathanael by Jesus when He saw Nathanael coming to Him, "Behold an Israelite indeed, in whom is no guile!" (John 1:47). Having been thus saluted by Jesus, the faithful subject recognized his King and saluted Him: King of Israel, the king's relationship to the chosen people.

Jesus commended Nathanael for His recognition and faith and assured Nathanael that he would see greater things. Proper recognition and service to the King has its progression of rewards.

King of the Jews

"Ye have a custom, that I should release unto you one at the passover: will ye therefore that I release unto you *the King of the Jews?*" (John 18:39).

The obvious answer should have been yes. But it was a resounding no. The king was too good to live. They wanted release given to Barabbas, a robber, who was too bad to live. Hasty, emotional decision-making has, at times, very strange quirks.

The Jews were a devoutly religious people who should have very much wanted good to prevail and crime to be punished.

John Dryden, a distinguished English poet of the seventeenth century, wrote in *Absalom and Achitophel:*

The Jews, a headstrong, moody, murmuring race,
As ever tried th' extent and stretch of grace;
God's pamper'd people, whom,
    debauch'd with ease
No king could govern, nor no God could please.

The harshness of Dryden may be excessive, but with reference to our focal point today, he was close to being just right.

Then Pilate, in response to the crowd, had Jesus scourged, and the soldiers placed a crown of thorns on His head, a purple robe on His shoulders, and said, "Hail, King of the Jews" (John 19:3).

A trilingual inscription was nailed to the cross over the head of Jesus. The words *King of the Jews* were written in three languages: Greek, the language of the street; Hebrew, the language of religion; and, Latin, the language of the law.

Our King, Jesus, was King of all three and is still!

King of Kings

"Which in his times he shall shew, who is the blessed and only Potentate, the *King of kings*, and Lord of lords" (1 Tim. 6:15).

Call the roll of the greatest kings of all times: King James, King Richard, the lionhearted, and Queen Victoria of England; Ferdinand and Isabella of the Golden Era of Spain; King Louis XIV of France; Maximilian I, the greatest of the early Hapsburg rulers of Germany; Catherine the Great of Russia; Ch-ien-lung of China; ad infinitum.

Then, call the roll of the conquerors: Alexander the Great, Julius Caesar, Hannibal, Napoleon, Genghis Khan, Kaiser Wilhelm, Hitler, ad infinitum.

Now, who out of this list would you select a king of kings? Certainly not any one of them! Not one of them could touch the hem of the garment of the lowly Nazarene who became King of kings. He was every inch a king.

Why do we place so much emphasis on such a kingship? First, there will come a time when every knee shall bow, and every tongue shall confess Him. No other king ever gained such prominence.

Second, He shall reign forever and forever. Death came to all other kings. Their dynasties were broken. Their royal lines were shattered. Their subjects scattered and almost forgotten.

What about the world's greatest conquerors? Some wept because there were no more worlds to conquer, but there was still the inner world of the human soul which they never conquered. But our King of kings is still striding across the centuries changing stagnant swamps into fragrant rose gardens. He is still winning the hearts of people. I vote for King Jesus.

King of Saints

"Just and true are thy ways, thou *King of saints*" (Rev. 15:3).

Did you ever stop to think that you are probably a saint? True, neither you nor I have been canonized; nor will we ever be from the standpoint of being approved and venerated because of our virtues on the authority of an ecclesiastical body.

A saint is one not primarily because of moral attainment, goodness, or strength of character but because one has a relationship of consecration and service to God. Saints are God's people, believers who have been redeemed and enlisted in God's service.

Jesus is their King, their Leader. He is King, not because of earthly conquest or special prowess but because He has conquered their hearts. They march behind Him under His flag, the banner of the cross. Homage is paid Him by His subjects.

Another translation of the words "King of saints" is "King of the ages." This is helpful. The King of saints will be their King forever and forever. He will never be toppled from His throne. He is there to stay. His saints will live on with Him in glory.

Aristotle once remarked that a man is not a king unless he is sufficient to himself and excels his subjects in all good things; therefore, he will not look to his own interest but to those of his subjects.

I think Aristotle would give Jesus an $A+$ both as King of saints and as King of the ages.

King of Sion (Zion)

"Tell ye the daughter of *Sion* [Zion], Behold, thy *King* cometh unto thee, meek, and sitting upon an ass" (Matt. 21:5).

Zion was the name of the citadel of the Jebusites in the city of Jerusalem, and both the citadel and the Jebusites were conquered by David. It later became the hill of the Temple. It was true then, and basically true now, that castles, fortresses, and temples were placed, if possible, on hills.

In designating Jesus as King of Zion (or Sion), one is saying that He is King of the fortress, the palace, and the temple. In this way He becomes far more personal. We find our strength (fortress) in Him. We share our palace (home) with Him. We worship Him on the holy hill (the temple).

Martin Luther, the great reformer, wrote a very stirring hymn, "A Mighty Fortress Is Our God," which to me says that the King of Zion shall always possess the holy hill.

> A mighty fortress is our God,
> A bulwark never failing;
> Our helper He, amid the flood
> Of mortal ills prevailing:
> For still our ancient foe
> Doth seek to work us woe;
> His craft and power are great,
> And, armed with cruel hate,
> On earth is not his equal.
> Did we in our own strength confide,
> Our striving would be losing;
> Were not the right Man on our side,
> The Man of God's own choosing:
> Dost ask who that may be?
> Christ Jesus, it is He;
> Lord Sabaoth, His name,
> From age to age the same,
> And He must win the battle.

He is still King of Zion. Hallelujah!

Lamb

"With the precious blood of Christ, as of a lamb without blemish and without spot" (1 Pet. 1:19).

Christ is likened to a lamb because lambs are meek, gentle, defenseless, and unsophisticated. They were used as sacrifices in worship. The word *lamb,* referring to Christ, is used twenty-seven times in the Book of Revelation.

In parentheses here, we give graduates, upon graduation, a diploma, frequently called a sheepskin, denoting work accomplished, sacrifices made.

In the story of Abraham offering up Isaac, Isaac was spared, and a ram (lamb) which was caught in a thicket was offered up instead of Isaac as a burnt offering. Through this act God was disapproving human sacrifice and allowing the sacrifice of a lamb to be the prototype of the ransom sacrifice of His Son.

John in Revelation 5:12 speaks of the Lamb being worthy to receive "power, and riches, and wisdom, and strength, and honour, and glory, and blessing."

Matthew 18:12 talks about a man with a hundred sheep who has one of the sheep to go astray and raises the question: Would not the man be willing to leave the ninety-nine and go after the lost one? Such is a parable of Christ the Lamb coming to save the lost sheep of the house of Israel.

Elizabeth Clephane in the last century wrote her well-known hymn "The Ninety and Nine" in which she tells of the perils, hazards, and persistence the shepherd went through to bring a straying lamb safely home.

Jesus was called "Lamb" because He bore suffering with patience; He was sacrificed for sin by the shedding of His blood.

Rejoice, for the Shepherd (Lamb) has brought back the lost lamb.

Lamb of God

"The next day John seeth Jesus coming unto him, and saith, Behold the *Lamb of God* which taketh away the sin of the world" (John 1:29).

The title "Lamb of God" was bestowed especially by John the Baptist. It is generally understood to refer to the fifty-third chapter of Isaiah, prophetic of the Coming One who was wounded for our transgression and bruised for our iniquities. Such an one was also oppressed and afflicted but in gentleness and meekness He opened not His mouth.

It is appropriate to refer to the important place of lambs in daily sacrifices, both morning and evening. As lambs were provided for sacrifices, God provided—gave—His Son. Christ was our expiatory sacrifice. In Him was to be fulfilled in a perfect manner the whole idea and office of sacrifice by blood.

There are two nineteenth century hymns which express this thought beautifully:

The third stanza of "Jesus Paid It All" by Elvina Hall:

> For nothing good have I
> Whereby Thy grace to claim;
> I'll wash my garments white
> In the blood of Calv'ry's Lamb.

and "Just As I Am" by Charlotte Elliott:

> Just as I am, without one plea,
> But that Thy blood was shed for me,
> And that Thou bidd'st me come to Thee,
> O Lamb of God, I come! I come!

If you have never come to the Lamb of God or have strayed from Him, will you now come to Him? He made the sacrifice with His own blood shed on the cross, and He waits with outstretched arms to receive all sinners.

Lawgiver

"There is one *lawgiver,* who is able to save and to destroy" (Jas. 4:12).

Some of the ancient manuscripts add the word *judge* after the word *lawgiver.* Laws have no efficacy unless administered by a judge or court, so Jesus was both Lawgiver and Judge, able both to save and to destroy.

Moses was the principal lawgiver of the Old Testament Jews. God gave Moses the Ten Commandments on Mount Sinai, and many other of his laws are recorded in the Pentateuch, the first five books of the Bible.

Some scholars find three codes of laws in the Old Testament: The covenant code in Exodus, chapters 20—23; the priestly code, which is found in Leviticus and Numbers; and the Deuteronomic code, a transition between the covenant code and the priestly code. All of these provided the Israelites with cumbersome laws.

Christ did not destroy these codes of laws. He interpreted them as a lawyer and gave new laws which stressed more inwardness than outwardness. He paid his respect to the laws of nature, gravitation, the seasons, and the laws of the harvest. He instituted the new law of love: love God with all your heart and your neighbor as yourself. He taught the law of sowing and reaping. He gave the laws of discipleship which state that a disciple is to forsake all in following Him. The disciples are to count the cost and, having put their hands to the task, they are not to look back.

Jesus cautions His followers to refrain from judging others, from speaking evil of others, and from playing the role of a censor, a judge. As His disciples we are to obey His laws!

Leader and Commander

"Behold, I have given him for a witness to the people, a *leader and commander* to the people" (Isa. 55:4).

It is frequently true that a commander is not a leader, and a leader is not a commander. Commanders may have the ability to shout commands, but they may show up poorly as leaders. Leaders may have all the qualities of discovering the pathway but be incapable of giving directions to their followers. Christ was both a superleader and a chief commander. He could give orders, and He could show others the way.

Years ago, I ran across a story about a peculiar happening at the palace of the czar of Russia. For several centuries a guard had been stationed at a certain spot on the imperial grounds. No one knew just why, but the commander of the palace guards always saw to it that the guard was there. An inquisitive soul sought to find why. He learned that nearly two centuries earlier the czar's wife had a very fine and favorite rosebush that she treasured greatly. She asked that a guard be stationed there to prevent it from being stomped by visitors. The rosebush had died long before, but the command had not been canceled. The command stayed in place, but somewhere, somehow, the leader of the guards had not sought to find out why the guard remained.

No such frivolous commands ever came from Christ. He gives us instructions and keeps them updated. He bids us to follow Him as "the way, the truth, and the life" (John 14:6).

If Dante in his *Purgatorio* was correct when he said, "Evil leadership is the cause which has made the world sinful," then I can say without reservation that the good leadership of Christ has brought the world redemption from sin.

Liberator

"He hath anointed me . . . to preach deliverance to the captives, . . . *to set at liberty* them that are bruised" (Luke 4:18).

The speaker at the Kiwanis Club meeting was an official of the local Salvation Army. He told of the thirty-three years he had spent in prison in Texas and of the day he was unexpectedly set free. The emotion was still in his voice, and tears came to his eyes. Freedom for a slave, a prisoner, or a demon-possessed person is a gratifying and emotional time.

Christ came into the world as a liberating force. He came to set the slaves of the law free. For centuries, legalism had bound people's minds and actions. Regimentation was a significant part of the system. But Jesus broke the bonds of the law and allowed people to choose, reason, love, and voluntarily go the second mile.

He came to free persons from the sins of the flesh. His teachings added a different dimension to the use of the body, passion, and desire. The human body became the temple of God.

Jesus came to free His believers from the cords of death, the last enemy. Death no longer was to be feared. He conquered it by breaking asunder its bonds as He arose from the grave at the appointed time. Acclaimed liberators of all humankind such as Bolivar of Peru, O'Connell of Ireland, and Garibaldi of Italy as well as extreme rebels and desperate revolutionaries remained slaves of death. To each of them death was inevitable, unconquerable.

Freedom of the mind, the body, and the soul are in Christ. We can be delivered. He is the great Liberator as much as He is our great Savior.

Life

"*I am* the resurrection, and *the life*" (John 11:25). "*I am* the way, the truth, and *the life*" (John 14:6).

My "father in the ministry," the late Norman W. Cox, told me of reciting in class one day while a student in New Testament at The Southern Baptist Theological Seminary. He was asked to give something of the early life of Paul. He began quoting from his professor's book: "Very little is known about the early life of Paul." His professor, Dr. A. T. Robertson, shot back, "Well, he had a mother and father, didn't he?"

"Yes, Dr. Robertson. I have never thought of him as being a spontaneous generation."

The truth is that life always comes from life. It is never spontaneous. When Jesus spoke of Himself as "the resurrection and the life" and "the way, the truth, and the life," He was saying that the Christian's life here and the blessed life in God depend upon Him. He is the Source, the fountainhead of spiritual life. Righteousness, peace, and joy come from the Holy Spirit.

Jesus is both the resurrection—the One who raises again—and the life—the One who makes alive again.

He is the way, for without Him we could not find our way through the valley and shadow of death to the Father's house. He is the truth, for without Him we would be totally ignorant of and blind to those truths which make us free. He is the life, for without Him death would still have its clamps tightly fastened around us.

He once lived in glory. He once came to live among us. He now lives for us again in glory, and He will come again in glory for us. What a life in Christ!

194

Life (Eternal)

An old black minister in stressing the truth of perseverance of the saints and eternal life in Christ gave this illustration.

"Brethren and sisters, my eternal life is like this. Take a ham, put it in a meatbox, put that meatbox in the meathouse and put a lock on that meathouse door. Now, I am like the ham. My life is in Christ; Christ and God are one, and my redemption has been locked and sealed by the Holy Spirit. Now, no devil has an arm strong enough or an ax sharp enough to break that lock, get in the meathouse, and take that ham out of the meatbox." He was so right.

Jesus Christ is the Author of an immortality of blessedness. He told us to accept the truth, "Because I live, ye shall live also" (John 14:19).

The certainty and safety of our lives is in Him. He provides the endless continuation of our lives. He "hath brought life and immortality to light through the gospel" (2 Tim. 1:10).

The fifteenth chapter of 1 Corinthians is an eloquent statement of Christ as our life:

"For as in Adam all die, even so in Christ shall all be made alive" (v. 22); "As we have borne the image of the earthy, we shall also bear the image of the heavenly" (v. 49); and "this corruptible must put on incorruption, and this mortal must put on immortality" (v. 53).

He is our certainty, our security, and our safety. He is not a loser. We can rest our case in Him and with Him. Nothing will be lost.

195

Lifter Up of My Head

"Thou, O Lord, art a shield for me; my glory, and the *lifter up of mine head*" (Ps. 3:3).

King David had fled from his son Absalom. This had produced a depressed feeling in him as father. Then, too, all was not well otherwise in David's kingdom. As we so often say, "His head was hanging low." He was very despondent, dejected, and downcast.

I guess David felt like he was in a situation which a song writer of recent vintage has described in these words: "Hang down your head, Tom Dooley, poor boy, you're bound to die." On the surface, David had a good reason to feel that way. And many of us have at times have shared such dejection.

But—and that word makes a startling transition—in Christ the picture can be very different. Human beings are creatures created with an upward look, and they have been promised that they will never be left alone.

In contrast to the song about Tom Dooley another song, "You'll Never Walk Alone," says, "Hold your head up high. You'll never walk alone." The reason is that Christ is truly the "lifter up of my head."

There is no greater power for the production of a positive mental attitude than to have confidence in Christ who never leaves nor forsakes. Many times, in His gentleness and love, He comes to lift us from the miry clay and set our feet upon a rock (Ps. 40:2).

It behooves us as followers of Christ to stand tall, to look up with heads held high, not with conceit but with confidence in Him who can help us become more than conquerors.

196

Light

"He was not that *Light*, but was sent to bear witness of that *Light*" (John 1:8).

When Jesus came it was like the dawn of the divine daybreak. It was the morning of immortal day. For He who said in the beginning, "Let there be light," and provided that light for the physical world did not withhold the spiritual Light from a sinful world in darkness.

When Jesus was coming out of Jericho with His disciples and a great number of people, He saw Bartimaeus, a blind man, sitting by the roadside, begging. When the blind man asked that he might receive his sight, Jesus responded by saying, "Go thy way; thy faith hath made thee whole. And immediately he received his sight, and followed Jesus in the way" (Mark 10:52).

And, just as the faith of the blind man brought the restoration of his natural sight, so faith in Jesus Christ as the "Light" brings spiritual light to those in darkness.

Louis Benson, around the turn of the present century, wrote a hymn which he entitled "The Light of God is Falling."

> The light of God is falling,
> Upon life's common way;
> The Master's voice still calling,
> "Come, walk with Me today."
> No duty can seem lowly
> To him who lives with Thee,
> And all of life grows holy,
> O Christ of Galilee!

When a light is turned on in a dark room, the darkness is immediately dispelled. We ask, "Where did the darkness go, and how did it vanish so quickly?" The answer is that it was overcome completely by the light, and so it happens in a life which is darkened by sin. Jesus, the Light, performs the miracle.

A Light to Lighten the Gentiles

"A light to lighten the Gentiles, and the glory of thy people Israel" (Luke 2:32).

Our Scripture points to the Christ child as the Light of the world and sees Him as a Light also to lighten the Gentiles as well as the Israelites. This indicated the universal scope of Christ's redemptive ministry. In other words, Jesus came to bring salvation to the Gentiles, to provide for them a light out of darkness. He became to them as a lighthouse pointing the way home.

Classic writers tell of a lighthouse erected about 300 BC on the island of Pharos. Known as Pharos of Alexandria, it was famed as one of the seven wonders of the ancient world. Christ, as a Light to the Gentiles, is a lighthouse that is the wonder of all wonders.

There is another analogy which we might make here. The fiery pillar of fire was used to guide the children of Israel during their dark wilderness days, and Christ is now the bright Light to lead not only the Israelites but the Gentiles out of the wilderness of sin.

Additional help and inspiration can be found by reading Ephesians 5:14 and 2 Corinthians 4:4. These references, and other references regarding Christ as a Light to the Gentiles, provide a very distinct statement of His purpose to extend the benefits of salvation, generally to all and particularly to each one.

Should we not reciprocate His concern for the Gentiles today by seeking the salvation of the Jews? Think about this.

Are we not to be a lighthouse to show people the way to Christ? The light should never go out: "some poor sailor may be tempest tossed."

The Jews may be waiting today for us to share with them. Let us do so both in word and in deed. We are His messengers.

Light of Men

"In him was life; and the the life was the *light of men*" (John 1:4).

All true knowledge of God which humanity has ever gained has come from Christ. Through Him persons have been able to see and know God.

Light and truth are used interchangeably. To see is to know, and to know is to see. Here again a title of Christ suggests the universality of His purpose.

Even though He came as the Light of men everywhere and at all times, when He came, He was twice rejected. "The world knew him not," and, "He came unto his own, and his own received him not" (John 1:10-11). What a sad commentary!

Through the centuries people in all places have sought a light to follow. Some have quickly aligned themselves unconditionally behind intellectual lights, military luminaries, or the lights of power, but these were false, temporary lights. Darkness may have a thousand lights which men may follow, but truth—light—has but one, the Light of men, Christ Jesus. So it is with the heart, it has but one, the Light of love.

We may live in an enlightened age with scientific discoveries and advances opening up new fields of knowledge, but we still need Christ to guide our fast-moving steps on earth and through space. It still gets dark in the human soul, and that darkness cannot be dispelled without that true Light which lightens every person.

The Light of the world is Jesus. Turn Him on!

Light, which has been called the queen of colors, entices us with its varied shades and shadows while darkness causes the colors to vanish. Christ as the Light of men draws us to attention by the colors of His gracious soul of love, mercy, and grace.

Spirituality in Christ is not black and white; it is full color.

Light, True

"That was the *true Light*, which lighteth every man that cometh into the world" (John 1:9).

Rudyard Kipling in his first novel, *The Light That Failed*, written in 1890, penned these words, "Blind men are ever under the orders of those who can see . . . Dick was dead in the death of the blind."[18]

Dick's condition was but a parable of all those in the darkness of sin who have not the true Light. Christ was the true Light, self-revealing and God-revealing. His purpose in coming into the world was that everyone who believed in Him would pass out of spiritual darkness into spiritual light. As the true Light, He was in opposition to false, imperfect lights and likewise in opposition to ceremonial types.

It was in and through Christ that divine truth was offered to the souls of all persons. As the eternal, divine Word of God, His divine nature was manifested in three aspects: life, love, and light—all were inseparable, and all constituted the glory which the disciples beheld in Him.

It is so good to have in Christ the Light that never fails, the Light that can lead onward and upward, cutting through the thick darkness of despair, gloom, and defeat.

The words of Cardinal Newman's poem "Lead, Kindly Light," which he wrote in the past century, are so beautifully expressive:

> Lead, kindly Light! amid th' encircling gloom,
> Lead Thou me on;
> The night is dark, and I am far from home,
> Lead Thou me on;
> Keep Thou my feet; I do not ask to see
> The distant scene; one step enough for me.

18. Rudyard Kipling, *The Light that Failed* (New York: Grosset and Dunlap, Inc., 1890), p. 161.

Light of the World

"Then spake Jesus again unto them, saying, I am the *light of the world:* he that followeth me shall not walk in darkness, but shall have the light of life" (John 8:12).

Jesus uttered this statement just after His encounter with the scribes and Pharisees who had brought to Him the woman taken in adultery. He pricked their consciences and did not condemn the woman nor condone her sin, but He forgave her. Here again it was a case of the Light of the world dispersing the darkness of sin.

In saying that He was the Light of the World, He was making it very clear that the light was not to the Jews only. Just as the sun's light is diffused to the entire world, so is His light to every nation and race. As the sun's light exhibits power, so does His light exhibit power and glory. As the sun's light is a blessing to the world— Would you like to live in total darkness?—so is Christ's light a blessing spiritually.

In the spiritual world, light and darkness coexist while in the physical world one follows the other—the day, the night. However, when Jesus came darkness could neither apprehend nor overcome it.

Philip Bliss, a century ago, placed these words in his hymn "The Light of the World Is Jesus":

The whole world was lost in the darkness of sin,
The Light of the world is Jesus;
Like sunshine at noonday His glory shown in,
The Light of the World is Jesus.

It has been said that the Persians worshiped the rising sun. We should worship daily the risen Christ as the Light of the world, the risen Son.

The Lily of the Valley

"I am the rose of Sharon, and *the lily of the valley*" (Song of Sol. 2:1).

Charles W. Fry, midway in the nineteenth century, wrote a beautiful hymn which captured my fancy as a young lad. Whenever I heard anyone sing "The Lily of the Valley," it brought to my mind the concept of purity and beauty from the white lily. I thought of Christ in a similar vein.

I have found a friend in Jesus,
He's everything to me,
He's the fairest of ten thousand to my soul;
The Lily of the Valley, in Him alone I see
All I need to cleanse and make me fully whole.
In sorrow He's my comfort, in trouble He's my
    stay;
He tells me every care on Him to roll.

Some expository writers suggest that the reference in the Song of Solomon to the "lily of the valleys" is a reference to an abundant herbage that grew in the rich fertile valleys which was not like a white lily. Whatever the truth, to me Christ is the "Lily of the Valley." He is purity, beauty, and sweetness. He is also the resurrection lily of Easter.

So I pick up some more of the words of that fascinating hymn:

Then sweeping up to glory to see His blessed
    face,
Where rivers of delight shall ever roll:
He's the Lily of the Valley,
    the Bright and Morning Star,
He's the fairest of ten thousand to my soul.

Those words are not only music to my ears but music to my soul.

The Lion of Judah

"One of the elders saith unto me, Weep not: behold, the *Lion of the tribe of Juda*" (Rev. 5:5).

It seems paradoxical to try to think of Jesus as the "Lion of Judah" and the "Lamb of God," but maybe not.

I recall seeing recently a television special about the lion, the king of the forest. The strength, boldness, and courage of the animal were outstanding. He was truly the king of the forest, a force to be feared and avoided.

Jesus, because of His strength, boldness, and courage, can be rightly called the "Lion of Judah." He has those kingly qualities. As the Lion—King—of the tribe of Judah, he is also the paschal Lamb—Savior—of every tribe and nation. In this respect, the Lion and the Lamb do lie down together, for His redemptive love can tame the ferocious nature of sin.

One of the elders told John, the author of the Book of Revelation, that the Lion of the tribe of Judah has overcome and has been made worthy to open the sealed book. As John stopped weeping and looked to see the lion, he beheld instead a Lamb. Here, a lion quickly became a lamb. There must be some symbolism in this. The lion represents absolute and unparalleled strength while the lamb represents absolute and untainted goodness. So the Lion-Lamb Son of God is the One worthy and capable of producing strength and goodness for weak and sinful persons. He has the power to break the shackles of sin, and He has the goodness and righteousness to bring about salvation.

May the "Lion of the tribe of Judah" make us lionhearted followers.

Logos

"In the beginning was the Word, and the Word was with God, and *the Word was God.* The same was in the beginning with God" (John 1:1-2).

The apostle John used the term *logos* meaning "word" six times as a designation of the divine preexistence of the person of Christ. His central purpose was to start with the person, Christ.

He makes four affirmations about Christ as the logos, the Word:
1. "In the beginning was the Word";
2. "The Word was with God";
3. "The Word was God";
4. "The Word was made flesh, and dwelt among us" (John 1:1-14). He was saying that all that God is, the Logos is. The Logos and the Father are one.

Classical Greek used the term to signify "reason," also, "word." In the New Testament the term *logos* generally implies "word," yet every word implies thought. Thought is the conception of truth while word is its expression. So divine wisdom was especially manifested in Jesus Christ. He was both thought and word: conception and expression. All of both!

William How wrote, during the middle of the nineteenth century, an expressive hymn entitled "O Word of God Incarnate":

O Word of God Incarnate,
O Wisdom from on high,
O Truth unchanged, unchanging,
  O Light of our dark sky:
We praise Thee for the radiance
  That from the hallowed page,
A lantern to our footsteps,
  Shines on from age to age.

Let us think Jesus! Let us talk Jesus!

204

Lord

"For unto you is born this day in the city of David a Saviour, which is Christ the *Lord*" (Luke 2:11).

The term Lord appears more times in the names and titles which I am using in this book than any other word. It is used in twelve different titles. This is significant and very significant that the title "Lord" was announced to the shepherds by an angel.

The title "lord" signifies a relationship with others, not just a high position where one with authority, leadership, and headship "lords it over others." Shepherds understood quickly and easily the position of one in authority.

In bringing the news to the shepherds, the angel referred to the Coming One as "Christ the Lord," meaning that He would be an Anointed Lord: one chosen and set aside for a very special purpose.

The word *lord* is easy to say and almost overworked in general conversation, but it is difficult to submit totally to the one Lord who has power over us. It is hard for a person with the power of choice and freedom of will to say, "My Lord and my God."

Frances Havergal's hymn "Lord, Speak to Me, that I May Speak" to a great extent captured the full meaning of the word *Lord*. I like the fourth stanza best of all:

Oh, use me, Lord, use even me,
Just as Thou wilt, and when, and where;
Until Thy blessed face I see,
Thy rest, Thy joy, Thy glory share.

May I suggest that we try to keep our minds and hearts open and receptive as we think about the many aspects of Jesus as Lord. There are eleven to go!

Lord of All

"There is no difference between the Jew and the Greek: for the same *Lord over all* is rich unto all that call upon him" (Rom. 10:12).

Peter, in preaching in the house of Cornelius at Caesarea, was very emphatic that "God is no respecter of persons" (Acts 10:34). He found no ethnic priority in Christ's plan of redemption.

A poem by Oliver Wendell Holmes, "Lord of All Being, Throned Afar," has been set to music, and the fourth stanza comes through quite strongly about all being equal:

Grant us thy truth to make us free,
And kindling hearts that burn for thee,
Till all thy living altars claim
One holy light, one heav'nly flame.

Paul, in writing to those at Rome, expressed his heart's desire for Israel's salvation but then stressed the "whosoever" which included all alike (Rom. 10:13).

Divine justice and integrity which allowed Christ to go to the cross do not permit two plans of salvation. If there were two plans, one might repudiate or cancel out the other; one might be easier than the other.

The chosen of God today are those who have chosen Christ! That's it! These are the spiritual Israel of God.

Lord of the Dead and the Living

"For to this end Christ both died, and rose, and revived, that he might be Lord both of the dead and living" (Rom. 14:9).

Paul Tillich, in his book *The Shaking of the Foundations*, tells of a witness who appeared in the Nuremberg war-crime trials who had lived for a time in a Jewish graveyard in Poland. During that time the witness wrote poetry and one of the poems was a description of a birth. An eighty-year-old gravedigger assisted in the birth, and when the baby uttered his first cry, the old man prayed, "Great God, hast Thou finally sent the Messiah to us? Who else than the Messiah himself can be born in a grave?"[19]

The grave wherein our Messiah lay is where we had our birth to eternal life. It was the place of His final triumph.

Christ was the Lord of the dead in that He was not bound to spend eternity there. He broke out of the tomb and became alive again to live forevermore. The power and majesty of His lordship is manifested here again. He followed the natural processes of life and death, but in the tomb He began His divine trek back to whence He had come. He came into the world a living person. He went from earth a risen Lord in order to open the doors of death for those who in faith followed in His train.

New life would not be new life if it did not come forth from the complete end of the old life. It is no half-and-half deal: one half of a new life grafted on to one half of the old life. Christ makes all things new, and that is just the way it works out in Him. Old things are passed away, for He makes all things new.

19. Paul Tillich, *The Shaking of the Foundations* (New York: Charles Scribners' Sons, 1948), p. 165.

Lord God Almighty

"Great and marvellous are thy works, *Lord God Almighty;* just and true are thy ways, thou King of saints" (Rev. 15:3).

These words of John in the Book of Revelation hark back to the time of Moses when he led the children of Israel through the Red Sea. The children of Israel had experienced a miraculous deliverance from the Egyptians. They had crossed the Red Sea on dry land while the Egyptians, who were in pursuit, were immediately drowned.

In acknowledgment of God's deliverance, Moses and the children of Israel sang to the praises of God Almighty, their Deliverer. Now John sees a day coming when the saints will experience such a wonderful deliverance, and they too will sing praises to the Lord God Almighty. That term *Lord God Almighty* encompasses three strong titles: Lord, powerful; God, ruler; and Almighty, the all-powerful One.

Henry Van Dyke wrote similar words about the place of the Lord God Almighty in the life of our nation. They were put to music by Walter Wilkinson. Here are the words:

O Lord our God, Thy mighty hand
Hath made our country free;
From all her broad and happy land
May worship rise to Thee;
Fulfill the promise of her youth,
Her liberty defend;
By law and order, love and truth,
America befriend!

This is a good prayer and a wonderful admonition. America is you. America is me. Now what?

Let us pray for our president and our nation!

Lord of the Harvest

"Pray ye therefore the *Lord of the harvest*, that he will send forth labourers into his harvest" (Matt. 9:38).

Governor Bradford of New England in 1621, during the earliest days of our nation, issued his first proclamation:

'Tis meet that we render praises
Because of His yield of grain,
'Tis meet that the Lord of the Harvest
Be thanked for the sun and the rain.

He knew that God is the "Lord of the harvest" and that from Him all blessings come. That is still true.

But, also, in another sense and way, He is "Lord of the harvest." Jesus, in speaking to His disciples, referred to fields being white unto harvest (John 4:35), and the harvest being truly plenteous (Matt. 9:37). He was thinking of those persons who had no saving knowledge of His redemptive power. He did not want them to perish and be like wheat that is not reaped. His call to them, therefore, is His call to us: Who will go into the fields and glean for Me?

The first stanza of the hymn "Lord, Lay Some Soul upon My Heart" is anonymous as to its author, while stanzas 2 and 3 were written by Mack Weaver and B. B. McKinney. The first stanza sounds the call:

Lord, lay some soul upon my heart,
And love that soul through me;
And may I bravely do my part
To win that soul for Thee.

I couldn't say it any better. That stanza stabs me. It is like a special delivery from the "Lord of the harvest."

209

Lord from Heaven

"The first man is of the earth, earthy: the second man is the *Lord from heaven*" (1 Cor. 15:47).

In this passage Paul is contrasting the first Adam and the second Adam. Adam, as the first man, was created from the dust of the earth—earthy. His eternal pilgrimage is heavenward. The second Adam, Christ, came from heaven to earth to assist in the pilgrimage, for man is "just a poor wayfaring pilgrim."

Christ holds the place as "Lord from heaven" by virtue of having been there before He came to earth, and by virtue of returning there from earth.

The cry of the human soul is:

> I've wandered far away from God,
> Now I'm coming home;
> The paths of sin too long I've trod,
> Lord, I'm coming home.
>
> ....
>
> My soul is sick, my heart is sore,
> Now I'm coming home;
> My strength renew, my hope restore,
> Lord, I'm coming home.

Won't it be wonderful to be greeted at the river of death by the "Lord from heaven" as He waits to welcome us into the land where we never grow old! The air will be pure, the storms of life will be over, and the tender outstretched hand will be marred with a scar, but soft and warm.

Such an occasion bars description. It will be a day of rejoicing, a day of beginning all over again. I can't imagine just how wonderful a host the "Lord of heaven" will be. I must go on preparing for what He is preparing for me.

Lord of Hosts

"As for our redeemer, the *Lord of hosts* is his name, the Holy One of Israel" (Isa. 47:4).

Arthur C. Benson's hymn "O Lord of Hosts who Didst Up-raise" sets the stage quite well for our consideration just here.

> O Lord of Hosts who didst up-raise,
> Strong captains to defend the right,
> In darker years and sterner days,
> Thou armedst Israel for the fight,
> Thou madest Joshua true and strong,
> And David framed the battle song.

Thus the title "O Lord of Hosts" means just what it says. Christ is the Lord of all created things: all laws, all commandments, all groups of persons, and all plans. He has dominion over all things.

Rudyard Kipling recognized these truths when, on the occasions of Queen Victoria's Diamond Jubilee in 1897, he penned his famous poem "Recessional." Many people came to England with troops and navies to celebrate. Kipling, however, as much as he rejoiced in Britian's greatness, viewed the occasion with conflict of heart. He trembled at England's pride, and the burden of his poem is a strong plea that his country will not stand on its own merit but seek the leadership of the "Lord of hosts."

I have thought time and time again how appropriate Kipling's views and attitudes are for us. We wallow in pride. We think we are a superpower, rather self-contained. We bark and growl like the king of the forest.

But who is the lord of our hosts? Is it the "Lord of hosts"?

211

Lord Jesus

"They stoned Stephen, calling upon God, and saying, *Lord Jesus*, receive my spirit" (Acts 7:59).

Dr. Luke, in writing The Acts of the Apostles, has recorded for us how the early Christians frequently used the name: "Lord Jesus." There is an interesting progression of that usage in the Book of Acts.

Peter preached at Pentecost about the Lord Jesus, and many souls were saved (Acts 2). Their sins were washed away.

James Nicholson's hymn "Whiter than Snow" reiterates that truth:

> Lord Jesus, I long to be perfectly whole;
> I want Thee forever to live in my soul;
> Break down ev'ry idol, cast out ev'ry foe:
> Now wash me, and I shall be whiter than snow.

When Stephen was stoned and his witnesses laid their clothes at the feet of a young man named Saul, Stephen called upon God saying, "Lord Jesus, receive my spirit" (Acts 7:59).

Peter and John preached at Jerusalem shortly thereafter, and many were baptized in the name of the Lord Jesus (Acts 8:16).

Then Saul, the persecutor, become Paul, the persecuted, who preached to the Jews and Greeks at Ephesus, and the name of the Lord Jesus was magnified (Acts 19:17).

Later Paul exclaimed while in Caesarea at Philip's house, "For I am ready not to be bound only, but also to die at Jerusalem for the name of the Lord Jesus" (Acts 21:13).

When we serve the Lord Jesus, we should be willing to go with Him from salvation even unto death. It could be a hard journey.

Lord Jesus Christ

"Grace be to you and peace from God the Father, and from our *Lord Jesus Christ*" (Gal. 1:3).

These words were the familiar salutation which Paul wrote to those at Galatia, Philippi, and Ephesus. The words *the Lord Jesus Christ* do not appear in many ancient manuscripts in the salutation to those at Colosse, a slight deviation.

It seems to me that Paul was trying to cover all bases in the wording of his salutation. It was like saying a friend's entire name —John Henry Thomas Jones—when speaking of him even to those who know him. There is a strong element of emphasis inferred which some find almost distasteful, but why? Not so with Paul. He wanted the full impact of Jesus' name felt by his readers.

Peter and John also employed the same wording.

God's favor and God's peace come to us through our Lord Jesus Christ. What a triumvirate of titles grouped for effect. Lord Jesus Christ!

The title was used even by our Lord and most frequently by His apostles as an indication of the warm and precious relationship and fellowship of service which existed among them and which is available for us also. It portrays His full participation with us in all areas of life.

The question for us is: Are we fully submissive and deeply grateful to the Lord Jesus Christ for His mercy in redemption, His grace in abundant living, and His guidance each day, or, are we rather placing our allegiance in a system, a denomination, or a church?

It's a toughie.

Lord Our Righteousness, The

"In his days Judah shall be saved, and Israel shall dwell safely; and this is his name whereby he shall be called, *The Lord our Righteousness*" (Jer. 23:6).

This Jeremiah passage was a prediction of the restoration of Israel but the name Lord our Righteousness belongs to the Lord Jesus Christ. It is appropriate only for Him.

Christ makes us righteous in God's esteem, for we cannot be righteous in ourselves. Salvation through Christ and righteousness in Him are linked. It would be unjust and unholy if God delivered a person from sin while that person continued the practice of sin. Salvation is both an instantaneous act of adoption into the family of God and a continuous act of growing in righteousness.

Christ as "Lord our Righteousness" has a threefold connotation. Righteousness can be conferred only by Him, for our righteousness is as dirty rags. Righteousness is to be the rule of His people. Grace and righteousness in Christ have replaced the law and duty of Judaism. Righteousness, when embodied and shared, will save God's people from the error of their ways.

He is our righteousness as, daily and habitually, we trust Him. We do this by keeping in touch with Him through prayer and His Word. By sharing with Him and by laboring with Him, we partake of His righteousness. When we look to Him for counsel and guidance and rely on Him for succor and support, then His righteousness flows into our lives.

May our prayer ever be: "Lead me, Lord; lead me in Thy righteousness. I am a poor wayfaring pilgrim, likely to go astray if I go it alone. So, precious Lord, take my hand; lead me on."

Lord of the Sabbath

"For the Son of man is *Lord even of the sabbath day*" (Matt. 12:8).

They called Jesus a breaker of the sabbath. They got very angry with Him because He didn't "toe the mark." Why didn't they call Him instead a sabbath maker?

Jewish laws regarding the sabbath were so minute and cumbersome as to make rest on that day impossible. How could one find rest trying to stay in line with all the laws of the day? The sabbath was also intended to be a day of delight. Special dress was worn, and special food was prepared to be eaten on that day. The rabbinic sabbath laws were truly incongruous.

Jesus took the initiative as Lord of the Sabbath. He healed a man on the sabbath, and to the Jews that made Him a sabbath breaker. Will you notice what Jesus asked the troubled souls who were worried about the laws: Is it right to do good or to do harm on the sabbath? That was an unanswerable question. And it is so hard to forgive another when given an unanswerable argument by that person.

Certainly, it was lawful to do on the sabbath that which would save a life or prevent death. And that is where Jesus had them. He made the sabbath into a holier day by using it for useful, holy purposes.

We need a holy day. It has been said that even animals and machines need one day of rest out of seven. Since Jesus, whom we serve, is Lord of the sabbath, we should serve Him in and through the sabbath which is Sunday, the Christian's day of rest and worship. We need such a day!

A French journalist and statesman of the early nineteenth century wrote: "Without a sabbath, no worship; without worship, no religion; and, without religion, no permanent freedom."

Lord of Lords

"Which in his times he shall shew, who is the blessed and only Potentate, the King of kings, and *Lord of lords*" (1 Tim. 6:15).

And so we come to the last title with the name "Lord" in it. How fitting and proper that it should be "Lord of lords." This is an expression of His sovereign authority. It places Him at the top of the list, as always, number one. Even the proudest and mightiest must acknowledge that fact.

The marvel of the ages is the way the kingdom of Christ goes on conquering and to conquer. Napoleon found this out. So have other warlords. They had their days, and death made them all equal. Napoleon once remarked, while in exile, "Tell me, Betrand, how do you account for the great abyss between my misery and the eternal reign of Jesus? I am forgotten: so it is with Caesar and Alexander. Our exploits are given to pupils in school who sit in judgment upon us; but behold the destiny of Christ! His kingdom extends over the whole earth; and there are millions who would die for him."[20]

The answer is obvious: He is Lord of lords—King of kings.

The lords and admirals, the commanders and the captains, all line up in defeat while our lowly Nazarene stands as Lord of lords. His victory came not on the battlefields of the plains nor on the surface of the seas but in the hearts of lowly, totally surrendered people who love Him dearly.

The Lord of lords is living still, mightier than ever. Are we on His side?

20. *The Treasury of the Christian Faith,* ed. Stanley Stuber and Thomas Clark (New York: Association Press, 1949), p. 806.

Man

"For there is one God, and one mediator between God and men, the *man* Christ Jesus" (1 Tim. 2:5).

Jesus Christ a man. Yes! Jesus Christ, the man. Yes! Other translations have "himself man, Christ Jesus," but "man Christ Jesus" is the better and possibly correct translation. In His humanity Christ represented all people and humanity in Him was exalted to true manhood. He took the nature of man in order to be mediator for all who bear that nature.

The Gnostics of Jesus' day thought angels were likewise mediators. Some have included saints with angels as mediators, but both are to be excluded from that role as the man Christ Jesus performed and performs that function. As mediator in human flesh, He has set before every person the glorious possibility of salvation in Him and eternal life with Him. To accomplish this mission, He gave Himself as a ransom for all.

He taught the world how to pronounce and accent the word *man*, the meaning of man, the possibilities in man, the freedom of man, and a correct philosophy for man: one God centered, which does not take but which gives.

Dean Wicks, formerly of Princeton University, tells of entering his home one day to be greeted with strange music, like the cackling of fiends in hell. He couldn't figure it out until, stepping over to the record player, he noticed that the record of a Beethoven sonata was being played from a newly drilled hole one-half inch from the original hole in the record. He saw the culprit move behind the sofa, his twelve-year-old lad. The record was the same, but the music wasn't the same.

Human lives as taught by Christ must be God centered. As mediator He is trying to tell us that truth! Human life doesn't function as efficiently if one-half inch off being God centered.

Man Approved of God

"Ye men of Israel, hear these words; Jesus of Nazareth, a *man approved of God* among you by miracles and wonders and signs" (Acts 2:22).

Peter stood on the day of Pentecost and preached with much power because he was talking about One whom he knew was approved of God. Doubtless there were others named Jesus, but Peter did not want any confusion as to which one was certified, approved, and accredited by God. This was important to Peter.

He stated the fact which substantiated this claim by telling his hearers that God's fullest sanction was on all Christ did through the miracles, mighty works, and wonders which He performed.

In essence God was saying through His approval of Christ's deeds and words, "I'll vouch for Him. He is for real. Don't fear to trust Him." This was an appropriate affirmation because Jesus in men's eyes had been poor, rejected, and scorned. He did not curry the favor of the religious sects.

Another real proof of Christ's approbation by God came from the energy and the power that went out from Him. Miracles may seem easy; yet, miracles were a sign of God's power flowing through Christ, and Peter was inferring that God would not work through a false agent.

I often wonder how far away His "Well done, thou good and faithful servant" may be from me, and possibly from you. Do we merit divine approbation? My credentials aren't impressive. How about yours? We do have an Advocate who is approved of God. His credentials are impressive, and He is not haughty or arrogant but meek and lowly and, therefore, approachable and dependable. He has been divinely certified; His certification never expires, and thus needs no renewal. Stay with Him.

218

Man of Prayer

"When he had sent the multitudes away, he went up into a mountain apart to *pray*" (Matt. 14:23).

Dr. W. O. Carver, former professor of missions of The Southern Baptist Theological Seminary in Louisville, Kentucky, taught his students that Jesus was the Supreme Man of prayer. He was! Twenty-three times in the Gospels there are references that He prayed.

Of all the verbs used to denote Jesus' manifold activities such as do, tell, ask, follow, go, and abide, none is used more than "pray." It is always used with unusual significance and real beauty.

Jesus prayed regularly, frequently, fervently, particularly, publicly, secretly, silently, as well as audibly. He prayed for Himself and His mission. He prayed for and with His disciples. He prayed for Jerusalem and for the world.

Sometimes He prayed all night and with such fervor as to "sweat as it were great drops of blood" (Luke 22:44). He was then and is now the Great Intercessor, the Advocate, praying for the perfection of all believers.

If Christ felt the need and worth of prayer, what about weak, lowly, incapable persons like us? He knew the potential of prayer. It was not just a crisis tool or a crutch. It was a vital part of His everyday experiences.

One thing rather haunts me when I think about prayer: Will I stand at the judgment bar of God wishing I had used the glorious privilege of prayer more? I can do something now about that. I must! Must you?

Prayer is the best tax-free bond I know. The dividends are good, and there is no tax in the asking. And God, to whom Christ prayed so frequently, is never more than a prayer away.

Man of No Reputation

"But made himself of *no reputation*, and took upon him the form of a servant, and was made in the likeness of men" (Phil. 2:7).

It is not easy to get excited about one of no reputation. That kind of a person we usually try to avoid. We much prefer credentials, such as: from an "FFV" family, graduate of a prestigious finishing school, and now employed by one of the top 500 firms. That's not all bad, but it is far from being all good.

Christ Jesus, our Lord, emptied Himself of divine glory, made Himself of no reputation, renounced His glorious prerogatives and came down to us through the womb of a lowly virgin who was married to a carpenter of Nazareth. He did it Himself, voluntarily. He was not forced or coerced. He did it joyously, too.

It might have been somewhat difficult to put off the form of God and take upon Himself the form of man with a disgraceful death at the hand of men in the distant future. But He was not to be deterred.

As a man of no reputation, He served so valiantly that through Him persons of no reputation become worthy to share an inheritance incorruptible that fadeth not away. His servanthood was exemplary.

Seemingly, God could not totally restrain Himself from speaking on Christ's behalf, and twice during Christ's servant ministry on earth, God broke His heavenly silence. At the transfiguration (Matt. 17:5) and at Christ's baptism (Matt. 3:17), God spoke through a voice out of the clouds, "This is my beloved Son, in whom I am well pleased."

Unselfishness, obedience, and servanthood are often overlooked, but they merit commendation and are great traits in building a reputation.

Man of the Right Hand of God

"If ye then be risen with Christ, seek those things which are above, where Christ sitteth on the *right hand of God*" (Col. 3:1).

I don't think it is sacrilegious to say that Jesus was also God's right-hand man, like Friday was to Robinson Crusoe in Daniel Defoe's book. He did the perfect will of his Father, and thus was given the place at the right of God.

The place at the right hand of God was a place of honor which Christ had won through His service on earth. It was a special place of recognition and reward.

After the ascension from earth, Christ took His place at the right hand of the Father. It was not a retirement location for Him. He is still actively involved in Kingdom enterprises. He is preparing a place for us. He is planning to come again. He is our Intercessor. Quite a busy schedule, don't you think?

At the right hand of God is truly where the action is. We should keep Him busy with our prayers which we make to the Father in His name. The record of our lives is being recorded for future use. He furnishes the supply of forgiveness and mercy.

When we all get to heaven, He will share the glory and the honor of that position. In fact, the roll call will be made there. I wonder: "When thro' wonderful grace by my Saviour I stand, Will there be any stars in my crown?"

My prayer today is: "Lord, let me be Your right-hand man—a Friday. Let me always be accessible for action, quick to respond to Your wishes, and effective in serving You.

"Help me to realize that I am still a slave, but thank You, Lord God, I have a new Master in Christ, the Man of the right hand of God. May I never forget that I cannot serve two masters, and if I serve not one master, I will likely have to serve many."

Man, Second

"The first man is of the earth, earthy: the *second man* is the Lord from heaven" (1 Cor. 15:47).

I don't recall ever meeting a man who thought second place would be better than first place. The second man—Christ Jesus—was better than the first.

The first man, Adam, was of the earth, earthy—an original: sinful and selfish, yet he was the top of God's creation. He was the father of the race.

The Second Man, Christ Jesus, was from heaven—an original: sinless, sacrificing, and redeeming. He was perfect and came to lift the fallen race, the sons of the first man, Adam.

As the Second Man, Christ is our Model. He sets the example and is worthy of emulation. He provides the means whereby we might model ourselves after Him. He shows us the manner whereby we might bear the heavenly image. All of this is possible through the cooperation of divine providence and grace.

We really hit pay dirt when we stop to realize that as we bear the image of the first man by having a body, soul, and mind, we shall also bear the image of the Second Man. He has made it possible for each one of us to share celestial joys with Him. He quickens us for glorious immortality.

And it seems logical and reasonable that our life, the second one, patterned after the Second Man will be far more desirable than our first life patterned after the first man. It just gets better all the time, and the second is not second best! For such glorious immortality makes it possible for those who live in the Lord, the Second Man, never to see each other for the last time.

Man of Sorrows

"He is despised and rejected of men; *a man of sorrows*" (Isa. 53:3).

Christ was no crybaby. He did know the feeling of tears trickling down his cheeks. He wept when Lazarus lay dead (John 11:35). He did weep as He looked over the city of Jerusalem (Luke 19:41). Then, too, the author of the Book of Hebrews speaks of Him as our high priest who could be touched with the feeling of our infirmities (Heb. 4:15). But His weeping and crying were not signs of weakness.

Sorrow is more than tears. It is grief, sorrow, and lament that produce empathy, sympathy, and sharing. Christ was burdened with our infirmities. He saw our carelessness, selfishness, and weakness. He knew our frailties. He hurts when we hurt.

He saw the profanation of sacred privileges and talents. He saw jealousy rampant and legalism enslaving people. He was a man of sorrows, burdened with the griefs and sins of the world. He did not approve of professional mourners. His grief was personal, not professional. He did not measure the depth of sorrow by the loudness of the mourners. Neither did He "cow tow" to a wailing wall. He could weep in silence and in secret.

A religion that produces no tears is usually a cold religion. Now, I am not one who succumbs to tearjerkers, but I do think that duties, privileges, disappointments, and burdens should, at times at least, produce an emotional reaction, possibly tears!

Tears have a way of softening and reviving the spirit as well as providing moisture for a parched soul.

Sorrows and tears come to us without an invitation, but we can, with the help of the Man of sorrows, dispel the gloom and shorten their duration.

Man (Superhuman)

"We have found him, of whom Moses in the law, and the prophets, did write" (John 1:45). (Read Luke 4:18.)

Jesus was superhuman because for centuries before His birth He was heralded by the prophets. Thousands longed for His appearance and arrival.

He was superhuman in His arrival and during His thirty-three years on earth. He was born of a virgin to the music of the heavenly choir, and during three years of ministry, He performed over thirty-five miracles.

He was, and is, superhuman because millennia after His death and departure from earth His blessings increasingly abound.

His superhuman qualities stand forth in the manner of His service and deeds. He never had to repeat an action. He did things right in the first place.

He does not need monuments and libraries in His name. His place of abode on earth today is in the hearts of people. That is an appropriate temple for our superhuman.

Superhuman strength combines the physical and spiritual with power from above. His strength was in His meekness, humility, kindness, and gentleness, not in the size of His biceps, the expansion of His chest, or the breadth of His shoulders. His superhuman traits are hard to acquire, but He is a good coach. Enroll in His class!

Master

"A certain scribe came, and said unto him, *Master*, I will follow thee whithersoever thou goest" (Matt. 8:19).

Both you and I need a master. There is no slavery comparable to the slavery of masterlessness. For then we become slaves to our instincts, passions, and that old master, *ego*.

A master is one who is in a more favored or superior position. Masters have authority over those under their control. As their master one has a right to expect obedience and loyalty. Also, a master is one generally considered capable of handling the problems or the situations. Jesus fills all such roles superbly.

Sin enslaves. The Master, Christ Jesus, frees us from sin and frees us for service.

One of the most beautiful and meaningful poems in this respect is "The Touch of the Master's Hand" written by Myra Brooks Welch. In the early part of the poem, the poet describes an old violin being auctioned off. The initial bidding was very low until a master violinist dusted it and began to play beautiful music. Then the bidding went very high. In the last stanza, the poet likens a life in sin as being auctioned cheap to a thoughtless crowd until it, too, is touched by the Master's hand:

> But the Master comes, and the foolish crowd
> Never can quite understand,
> The worth of a soul and the change that is wrought
> By the touch of the Master's hand.

And after that our prayer should be, "O Master, let me walk with Thee," and feel Thy touch of assistance and encouragement. I need to be dusted off, tuned up, and placed in Your hands. I'm worthless otherwise.

Good Master

"When he was gone forth into the way, there came one running, and kneeled to him, and asked him, *Good Master*, what shall I do that I may inherit eternal life?" (Mark 10:17).

To soft-soap has been glibly defined as "99.44 percent lie." Was the term *good master* a bit of apple polishing, even close to soft soaping? Such a term was not customarily used in those days in addressing rabbis and teachers.

Good master is a term that could show appreciation, affection, and competence. The young man who came running to Jesus must have thought of Jesus as a good person, one able to teach him concerning the good that he would gladly do. Something at least had influenced him to that extent. We will not doubt the young man's sincerity but just wonder as to why he broke custom so sharply.

Jesus told the young man that none was good but God. Jesus was not denying His own divinity, but He wanted the young man to think not of goodness in general but in terms of perfect goodness. Jesus then repeated six of the Ten Commandments to the young man who replied that he had kept them from his youth up. Jesus drilled deeper. Any good master would want to get to the heart of the matter. "Go thy way, sell whatsoever thou hast, and give to the poor" (Mark 10:21), said Jesus, but the young man was sad because he had great possessions. His riches lessened the young man's desire for eternal life.

Maybe there was a little "soft soap" in the remark, but soft soap doesn't soften the necessity for full obedience in seeking eternal life. Action counts!

The vocal affirmation of the young man was a courteous gesture, but it was not enough. More was needed, and that more touched where it hurt most—his possessions—which seemed to possess Him. Would to God that His possessions could have become an obsession for the true riches of life.

Master Workman

"I must *work* the works of him that sent me, while it is day: the night cometh, when no man can work" (John 9:4).

My dad would frequently say, "Son, we work first, then play comes after our work is finished." We had a work clock which we followed: sunup 'til sundown or daylight until dark.

I really think Jesus followed a similar clock. He spoke of twelve hours to a day. He considered a workday at least twelve hours. His day was from dawn at Bethlehem to evening on the Mount of Olives.

What would He have done with leisuretime if he had worked only forty hours a week? Would He have been a sports enthusiast? He thought of work as a sacred trust and a part of His Father's business. He felt a compulsion to work. He felt the constraints of time, working while it is day for the night cometh.

Work is a wonderful part of any life. I feel that there is an obligation to work to earn a livelihood, to share with others and to honor God. Work should be done diligently. A worker should be dependable. Work should be done acceptably and not sloppily. And, most of all, it should be done joyously. It is good to sing or whistle while working.

The example which Jesus set as the Master Workman is an example which, if followed, will provide achievement and pleasure.

Annie Coghill wrote a hymn, "Work, for the Night Is Coming," in which she urges us all to "Work thro' the morning hours; . . . while the dew is sparkling, . . . when the day grows brighter, . . . in the glowing sun" and until the night comes. Jesus would concur with her, I think.

Mediator

"There is one God, and one *mediator* between God and men, the man Christ Jesus" (1 Tim. 2:5).

A mediator is one who tries to reconcile two parties of divergent views. A mediator tries to settle disputes and to calm troubled waters. Living as we do today in a very litigious society, such mediation frequently takes the form of plea bargaining and attempts to settle claims out of court.

Christ, as mediator, brought humanity and God together. Sin had pushed the two far apart. Let me illustrate. Every mile put on a car is registered in the speedometer. A cassette tape records words spoken into it. Therefore, every act and every word of every person are registered and recorded with God and will make an appearance at the judgment bar.

God will not turn the speedometer back. He will not erase nor destroy the tape. There is incriminating evidence against us. Persons are helpless in and of themselves to nullify the wrong or destroy its effect. In Christ we have a greater power who will mediate the case. We could not ask for more. Aren't you and I fortunate to be able to call for the services of one so competent?

Philip Bliss, of a former century, wrote the words and music to the hymn "Free from the Law, O Happy Condition":

Free from the law, O happy condition,
Jesus hath bled, and there is remission;
Cursed by the law and bruised by the fall,
Grace hath redeemed us once for all.

The one Mediator, Christ Jesus, did it all.

Merciful High Priest

"Wherefore in all things it behoved him to be made like unto his brethren, that he might be a *merciful* and faithful *high priest*" (Heb. 2:17).

Portia, in Shakespeare's *Merchant of Venice* (Act 4, Scene 1), in arguing the case for Antonio, pleads for mercy:

> The quality of mercy is not strained,
> It droppeth as the gentle rain from heaven
> Upon the place beneath: it is twice blessed;
> It blesseth him that gives and him that takes.

Portia wanted Shylock to exercise compassion, but compassion is not always forthcoming in human relationships.

Our Savior is a merciful high priest. He illustrated that quality in the parable of the prodigal son, which might also be called a parable of mercy. The characteristics of divine mercy, as shown in this parable, are:

A longing for the return of the son.

A warm welcome awaits the son.

Forgiveness without penalty is extended.

A joyous celebration transpires when the son returns home.

Jesus is merciful and long-suffering toward the sinner. However, His mercy will not protect sin, but He anxiously awaits to pardon it. This is loving forbearance. He, also, extends merciful, loving-kindness toward the forgiven saints. The moment self is thrown on God, God envelops the individual in His mercy.

Remember the Beatitude which says, "Blessed are the merciful: for they shall obtain mercy" (Matt. 5:7).

It's worth a try! See if it doesn't work. It may not be easy, but don't back away. Mercy frequently begets mercy.

Messenger

"Behold, I will send *my messenger*, and he shall prepare the way" (Mal. 3:1).

A messenger is a bearer or harbinger of news, hopefully, good news. But during the recent wars, many a family received a messenger who bore this news, "We are sorry to inform you . . ." I like much more what Dwight L. Moody said when asked, "What is the news today?" He replied, "The same news which is old news, new news, and good news. Christ died to save sinners."[21]

Jesus was the world's greatest bearer of covenant news between God and humanity. That news consisted mainly of four items:

The power of sin had been broken.

The grave has lost its terror: there is more beyond.

You will not be left comfortless: the Holy Spirit will guide you into all truth.

Redeeming grace is free.

Now that we have received this news from the eternal Messenger of the covenant, we must pass it on.

I come back to Mr. Moody and give you what he said in his famous sermon: "Good News." He imagined Jesus talking to Simon Peter after the resurrection, and in response to Peter's question about what plans Jesus has made, Jesus said to Peter, "Go, seek out that poor soldier who drove the spear into my side; tell him that there is a nearer way to my heart. Tell him that I forgive him freely, and tell him I will make him a soldier of the cross and my banner over him shall be love."[22]

What news! And good, current news, for us! What a difference such news is from the majority of that which appears in our daily papers, for instead of sin, sorrow, and death, it is news of peace, joy, and hope.

21. Dwight L. Moody, *The World's Greatest Sermons*, ed. S. E. Frost, Jr. (New York: Garden City Publishing Company, 1943), p. 184.

22. Ibid.

230

Messiah

"He first findeth his own brother Simon, and saith unto him, We have found the *Messias*" (John 1:41).

The story is told that when Thomas Carlyle was old and ill, the students of Edinburgh University sent a delegation to him for a commencement message. "Tell them to consult the Eternal Oracles, not inaudible, or ever to become so," shouted the aged seer, "and to disregard almost entirely the world's temporary noises and menacings and deliriums." What wise advice!

The Messiah came, and His word endures. His eternal oracles are still relevant. When the early disciples recognized Jesus as the Messiah, the Anointed One, they immediately wanted to introduce Him to their friends. This recognition of Him came after they had spent a day with Him. It is difficult to be with Jesus and not recognize His divinity.

The incarnation of Jesus was full and complete at the time of His birth, but there was a progressive unfolding of the consciousness of the incarnation in Him which came to its apex on the cross. A similar unfolding of this consciousness took place in the lives of his disciples. They did not have the years of testimony about him as we have today.

Priscilla J. Owens, in the last century, made it quite clear in her hymn what we as Christians are to do relative to our acceptance of Jesus as the Messiah:

> We have heard the joyful sound:
> Jesus saves! Jesus saves!
> Spread the tidings all around:
> Jesus saves! Jesus saves!

And that news must be shared with every land. It is a command performance!

231
Minister

"Even as the Son of man came not to be ministered unto, but to *minister*, and to give his life a ransom for many" (Matt. 20:28).

During my early years in the ministry in East Kentucky, I was asked to preach the annual associational sermon. The associational moderator, a layman, introduced me, "Dr. Gabhart, if I had my 'druthers' I would take a long needle and give each preacher a shot of fire. We need ministers on fire."

Right he was, but I didn't want to let that remark go unchallenged, so I replied, "Mr. Tom, you are right. Ministers should be aflame with the torch of truth. But Mr. Spurgeon, the English prince of preachers, once said, 'Though you start a fire in the pulpit, you must get kindling wood out of the pew to keep it going.' " It's a two-way deal: the minister and the laypersons.

A minister, a pastor, or a preacher—by whatever name you wish to call that person—is primarily a servant. A minister is called of God to serve. Jesus taught that. Service was an object of His life, not an accident. He sought to minister to His day by proclaiming spiritual truths, teaching His disciples, enlisting recruits in God's service, visiting the sick, feeding the hungry, ad infinitum. An overwhelming task! The minister of God is always cognizant of the difference between good and evil.

Charles Wesley wrote:

> Ye servants of God, your Master proclaim,
> And publish abroad His wonderful name;
> The name all-victorious of Jesus extol;
> His kingdom is glorious, He rules over all.

It is a high honor to be a God-called minister and a high honor to minister in any way in Christ's name!

Minister of the Circumcision

"Now I say that Jesus Christ was a *minister of the circumcision* for the truth of God, to confirm the promises made unto the fathers" (Rom. 15:8).

Paul told friends in Rome that Christ was a minister first to the circumcision, those Israelites who practiced circumcision. Christ came from that background. His first purpose was to fulfill and confirm the divine promises of the Old Testament to the fathers. His success was not good. They turned Him down and turned Him away.

They didn't like the Nazarene's newfangled ideas of brotherly love. They loved their traditions more, and even though their laws at times were tedious and tiring, they clung to these laws with unabated breath. In that respect they were a bit like the lad with the toothache. "Oh, mom, it hurts so badly when I bite down on it."

"Well, son, don't bite down on it."

"Aw, shucks, mom, I kinda like to."

There is another reason why Christ's success wasn't phenomenal: He had come back home. He was from Nazareth; Joseph's son, they said, and no doubt His schooling was not first-class in their opinion. "A prophet is not without honour, save in his own country" (Matt. 13:57).

One of our state's leading politicians and a candidate for governor said that he went back home recently, and a longtime friend said to him, "Ned Ray, just remember that when you die the number of people at your funeral will be determined by whether it rains or not."

I have wondered many times what the world, and especially Palestine, would be like today if the Jews had accepted Jesus.

Minister of the Sanctuary

"A *minister of the sanctuary*, and of the true tabernacle, which the Lord pitched, and not man" (Heb. 8:2).

Jesus is the only minister to function as minister of the sanctuary. Our passage for today refers to His ministry in heaven, the holiest of the holy places.

The Hebrews regarded the high priestly function with awe. Their priests stood and trembled within the veil of the tabernacle. Jesus did not hesitate to enter within the veil, for the throne is the heavenly counterpart of the ark of the covenant of the earthly tabernacle.

Having offered Himself as a sacrifice at Calvary, He had to appear at the sanctuary of God. Since He was not a high priest after the order of Aaron, He could not go for this purpose to the Temple of Jerusalem, so in order to be the priest of all He had to seek another temple.

Jesus descended so that He could reascend, so He reascended to heaven, the true tabernacle, and carries on His ministry there in the sanctuary of heaven.

He descended in order to minister to His own and to all people, and then in order to maintain His complete and full priestly ministry He continued it in heaven. Now He is the one mediating priest of His church. He is no longer a sacrificing priest. The great transaction in that respect was done on the cross. Symbolically, He bled and died in the outer court and represents us at the heavenly sanctuary.

He seems to be always there: inside, outside, and on all sides. His presence, availability, and willingness to function as our minister of the sanctuary bodes for us heavenly blessings untold. Gramercy!

Miracle Worker

"This beginning of *miracles did Jesus* in Cana of Galilee" (John 2:11).

They nearly kept Him busy performing miracles. In His brief earthly ministry, there are recorded thirty-five occasions when He worked miracles, and no doubt there were scores more. Should the record of these miracles be read one after the other, the reading would be classified "fantastic."

His first recorded miracle, the turning of the water into wine at the wedding feast of Cana in Galilee, introduces us to an interesting and uplifting side of His life. Three significant truths come from His performance at Cana.

First, in performing the miracle, Jesus signaled a revealing of His divine power and mission. It was like a trumpet call to come and see and hear.

Second, He showed His sympathy with humanity in a time of need. It was embarrassing for the host to run short of wine at such an auspicious occasion. Jesus came to quicken, exalt, and bring abundant life. He was not a killjoy. I am sure He could laugh and jest.

Third, He did something for enjoyment as well as sustenance. He went the second mile. He provided more than the necessities of life. He did not object to a few luxuries of life, if not carried to excess to where there was waste.

His miracles were never for Himself, always for others. There is a good lesson here.

For if we spend much time looking up to admire our halo, we are very likely to get stiff necked or to get a pain in the neck. And we just might become a pain in the neck to others.

Missing Son

"Son, why hast thou dealt with us? behold, thy father and I have sought thee sorrowing" (Luke 2:48).

Many times, while being disciplined by my mother, I would hear her say, "Son, this hurts me as much as it does you." I could never understand that and wondered why then did she do it to me. I now know. Discipline is a part of growing up.

One day a famous local columnist put these words in his column: "A twelve-year-old boy had run away from home. The dispatcher informed an officer, giving him the address of the runaway's parents. About a half hour later the officer called back this report, 'That twelve-year-old runaway has returned home and is being chastised right now.' "

I wonder if Mary felt like my mother when she gently chastised Jesus for getting separated from them while in Jerusalem, causing her and Joseph much concern and delay in getting back to Nazareth.

Do you sense the strong feeling in Mary's words? "My child, why did you treat us so? Just see how your father and I, in agony of mind, have been searching for you!" (Williams, Luke 2:48).

Jesus responded politely but with a tone of surprise. "Why is it that you were searching for me? Did you not know that I must be in my Father's house?"

Luke went on to tell us that his parents didn't understand what he was talking about. This one observation on Luke's part tells us only a little about Jesus' relationship to his parents during the teen years, yet it speaks volumes. There are many times when parents find it difficult to understand teenagers. And there are many times when parents have to chastise their children for some behavior.

Jesus grew up as a normal lad, facing life's problems, but He went through them as the Son of God. Children need discipline. They deserve to have it. I have profited from it.

236

Morning Star

"I am the root and the offspring of David, and the bright and *morning star*" (Rev. 22:16).

I may be "all wet" theologically, but I am willing to identify that star which the three kings of the Orient saw as the bright and Morning Star. It was His Star.

The morning star is called the "bright star." Its coming calls to mind the night which has gone before and suggests that something is coming out of the darkness. It heralds the dawn of a new day which is nearby. It is the symbol of promise and hope. Christ as the morning star fulfilled all these requirements.

He broke forth from a dark world to herald the dawn of a new day. He came to give substance to the promises of the centuries, and with His coming hope sprang eternal in the human breast.

And now to our song which talks of the star seen by the three kings of the Orient, "We Three Kings of Orient Are," written by John H. Hopkins:

> We three kings of Orient are,
> Bearing gifts we traverse afar
> Field and fountain, moor and mountain,
> Following yonder star.
>
> O star of wonder, star of night,
> Star with royal beauty bright,
> Westward leading, still proceeding,
> Guide us to thy perfect light.

Who else could do this but Christ, our Morning Star? This Star keeps coming up in the heavens each morning. It is there to guide throughout the sunlit hours as well as throughout the dark hours, for its brightness and glory never fade. As long as it shines, hope and assurance will never die—and the Star will never die.

237

Nazarene

"He came and dwelt in a city called Nazareth: that it might be fulfilled which was spoken by the prophets, He shall be called a *Nazarene*" (Matt. 2:23).

Dr. Ellis Fuller, while president of The Southern Baptist Theological Seminary, spoke to us students in chapel one day. "While in Nazareth recently, I said to myself, 'Oh, Lord, wasn't there some better place for Jesus to grow up rather than in this city?' A thought came quickly to my mind: 'He tarried here only an interlude, from eternity to eternity. It really was not His home.'"

Nazareth was not a town of high reputation. At least, Nathanael didn't think so. It was not named in the Old Testament. Today it stands on a hill between the Sea of Galilee and the Mediterranean Sea at Haifa with about 7,000 inhabitants.

It is supposed that Jesus attended school at the synagogue.

He and His disciples were called "Nazarenes." There is a rather thriving denomination in America called the Nazarenes. The Moslems still refer to Christians as *Nasara*, a slight modification of Nazarene.

Had Jesus been born and reared in Jerusalem, Athens, Alexandria, or Rome, some might have tried to link Him to some great movement in the city in His early days, but He took the title of "Nazarene" and made something out of it.

He preached His first sermon in Nazareth. His listeners asked: "Is not this Joseph's son?" (Luke 4:22). This was an expression of wonderment, for a carpenter's son seemed to outdo their expectations of Him. However, such wonder soon gave way to wrath, for they rose up and thrust Him out of their city—a terrible way to treat a native son!

Is there any difference today?

245

Nephew of Mary's Sister

"Now there stood by the cross of Jesus his mother, and *his mother's sister*, Mary the wife of Cleophas, and Mary Magdalene" (John 19:25).

We have enjoyed our nephews. We have been closer to some than others due to age and proximity of residence.

One of our nephews was always wanting to be involved in anything athletic. Once after returning from summer camp he was talking to my wife, Helen, and said, "Aunt Helen, I won second place in a race at camp."

She congratulated him and then asked, "How many were in the race?" This she shouldn't have done.

"Two."

That nephew today is a very fine family man and businessman, holding a notable position with one of America's largest corporations.

There is just something special about nephews and nieces. They are close to their relatives, very close. Our daughters have enjoyed so much our nieces and nephews—their cousins.

I wonder how Jesus, as the nephew of His mother's sister, enjoyed His cousins. We are not sure which one was His aunt: Salome, the wife of Zebedee, the mother of James and John; or, Mary the wife of Cleophas who might have been the Cleophas who met Jesus on the Emmaus Road (Luke 24:18).

What did His aunt think of Him? Was He a family person? The family is important, and nephews, aunts, and uncles are an important part of the larger family. I would guess His aunts liked Him very much.

May our family ties grow stronger in Christ.

Obedient Child

"He went down with them, and came to Nazareth, and was *subject* [obedient] unto them" (Luke 2:51).

Someone remarked, "Who says our children aren't obedient? They will buy any toy advertised on TV."

Were you ever disobedient to your parents? I was, and remember one time quite well. I was told most emphatically not to go swimming on a Sunday afternoon in the old muddy pond on the far side of our farm. A friend came over to see me, and the call of the pond overcame us. But the punishment followed. I had disobeyed my father outright.

It is said that Christ was the only child who knew more than His parents, yet He obeyed them: habitually and continuously, with thirty years of His life covered in the words, He "was subject unto them." He understood the relationship between child and parent. He sought to honor His father and mother. He saw no reason to spurn their admonitions.

The first law that God ever gave to man was a law of obedience in the Garden of Eden. It follows that the child's first lesson should be obedience.

The hymn by John H. Sammis, "When We Walk with the Lord," points out that the way to be happy in Jesus is to trust and obey. The third stanza says:

> But we never can prove/The delights of His love
> Until all on the altar we lay;
> For the favor He shows,/And the joy He bestows
> Are for them who will trust and obey.

Obedience should stem from love not from law. The heart should be satisfied with loving obedience. There is something lacking when fear is the source of obedience. Let love rule.

240

The One Shepherd

"Them also I must bring, and they shall hear my voice; and there shall be one fold, and *one shepherd*" (John 10:16). (See Isa. 40:11.)

There is something meaningful in Jesus' referring to Himself as a "shepherd," and part of the meaning comes from the nature of sheep and the relationship of the sheep to the shepherd. It is more appropriate to call Him a shepherd, a herder of sheep, than to call Him a cowboy, a herder of cattle.

Sheep are among the most useful of all animals to people. The wool is used for clothing, the flesh and milk for food, and the skin provides useful leather. Here, in the academic world, we refer to a diploma as a "sheepskin."

Sheep are dependent upon men. They are shy, defenseless creatures. They have to be led to their food. They do not possess the instinct of other animals in finding their way home, and they need to be taken for water once a day. One unusual distinctive feature about sheep is that they know their master's voice. Even if two or three shepherds are calling their herds at the same time, sheep do not mistake their master's voice.

The hymn, "Saviour, Like a Shepherd Lead Us," ascribed to Dorothy A. Thrupp, describes the shepherd beautifully:

> Saviour, like a shepherd lead us,
> Much we need Thy tender care;
> In Thy pleasant pastures feed us,
> For our use Thy folds prepare.

The Shepherd will defend us from sin, seek us when we go astray, and hear us when we pray. How we do need Him!

One with the Father

"I and my Father are one" (John 10:30).

Christ claimed that He and the Father were one. He made this claim in connection with His response to the Jews at the Feast of Dedication while walking in the Temple in Solomon's porch. The Jews had asked Him, "How long dost thou make us to doubt [be in suspense]?" (John 10:24). He said to them that He had told them, and they had not believed but added that His sheep hear His voice and come to Him, and they are secure in Him. Neither did this answer satisfy them, for they sought again to take Him.

His response provides for us the wonderful doctrine of the security of the believers, that blessed life which believers enjoy now and which will be preserved for them because they are in the hands of God and the Good Shepherd. While they are in the hands of the Good Shepherd, no one will ever be able to take them from Him. That security is provided through the oneness of Christ with His Father. This union makes the Shepherd's power absolute. It never fails. Therefore, all of the actions and promises of Christ are inseparable from the Father. His sheep are approved by the Father, His care of the sheep, also, and His desires for His flock.

Since the believer is secure because "I and my Father are one," the believer should recognize personal responsibility to the Shepherd. There should never be abuse, misuse, or perversion of this holy relationship and security—the hope of eternal life. We should try to live a life of prayer, commitment, submission, and faith to Christ according to His word.

It is very hard for any of us to fathom the full meaning of the perseverance of the saints—believers. We may not be able to explain it; neither can we explain it away. Security is not in self but in Christ. We can hold on and, therefore, hold out.

Optimist

"In the world ye shall have tribulation: *but be of good cheer; I have overcome the world*" (John 16:33).

Jesus was every inch an optimist. His was not a sentimental, shallow, or stupid optimism. He was not like the optimist who jumped from the top of the twenty-story building shouting, as he passed each floor, "I'm all right so far."

Christ's optimism came to Him because He kept His face to the sunshine of life and thereby lost the shadows. He had no eye strain because He looked on the bright side, not the dark side of life.

It is amazing to us that He, who saw all things, heard all things, and knew all things, could be so cheerful. His cheerfulness did not come from "pumping Himself up with ego motivation." He knew there would be hard places, but He saw the problems as opportunities. He knew that people would fall, yet it was not the fall but how high the bounce was that counted.

His optimism has been attributed to several facts. He had confidence in God. He never doubted God. He had confidence in persons. He could see their possibilities and capabilities. He had confidence in the laws of life that behind the clouds the sun was still shining. He had confidence in Himself. He knew that He was on a unique mission, and He knew that He was willing to match it with total submission, and the eventual outcome was good.

We can truly say in Him, "The best is yet to be. Get excited about tomorrow."

Optimism in Christ is the real thing. It is not a shallow, hollow "whistling in the dark." It is founded on the promises of God, bought with the blood of His Son, and backed up with the only true resurrection from the grave.

243

Our Captain

"If any man will come after me, let him deny himself, and take up his cross, and *follow me*" (Matt. 16:24).

Only a captain could give such orders as "Follow me." Only the head of the troops or the captain of the team could so command.

The word *our* is the important emphasis of our title for today. It is a possessive plural of the personal pronoun *I*. When associated with another word, the element of closeness or oneness is inferred either from the standpoint of fellowship or ownership.

William Henley, a cripple, wrote the poem "Invictus" as an expression of his courage and determination, but Henley may have gone too far with his words:

It matters not how strait the gate,
How charged with punishment the scroll,
I am the master of my fate;
I am the captain of my soul.

And he wrote that verse after having written in the previous stanza,

Beyond this place of wrath and tears
Looms but the Horror of the shade.

I wish that Henley could have thrown a bit more of himself upon "our Captain" who has removed the horror of the shade and would have been able to decrease the punishment of the scroll.

For whenever we take our own lives completely in our hands, without the help of "our Captain," trouble is sure to come. It may come even with our Helper, but our Helper will share with us. He's capable. He's good!

Our Pilot

"He arose, and rebuked the wind, and said unto the sea, *Peace, be still*. And the wind ceased, and there was a great calm" (Mark 4:39).

He piloted the ship that day not from the pilot's wheel or with an oar but with His power over the elements of nature.

A pilot needs to know His boat. He needs to know the currents of the sea. He must know where the shallows are, and the rocks aren't. He must have charted the path across, so He can dock his boat at the proper pier. Those are a pilot's responsibility.

Tennyson, in his poem "Crossing the Bar," expressed a desire to see his pilot, which he spelled with a capital *P*, when he had come to the end of the way.

> For tho' from out our bourne of Time and Place
>   The flood may bear me far,
> I hope to see my Pilot face to face
>   When I have crossed the bar.

The truth in Edward Hopper's song of the nineteenth century could have been to Tennyson somewhat reassuring:

> Jesus, Saviour, pilot me,/Over life's tempestuous sea;
> Unknown waves before me roll,
> Hiding rock and treach'rous shoal;
> Chart and compass came from Thee:
> Jesus, Saviour, pilot me.

The hymn writer goes on to ask for words from his Pilot as he nears the shore with the roar of breakers in his ears. The words the hymn writer feels he will hear are, "Fear not, I will pilot thee." Such words will come from our Pilot who brings comfort and reassurance.

Overseer

"He saith unto him, Yea, Lord; thou knowest that I love thee. He saith unto him, *Feed my lambs*" (John 21:15).

Jesus told Simon Peter to look after his sheep. The inference here is that since Jesus was going away, He wanted Peter to take His place and become an overseer of the flock.

An overseer is one who superintends, looks after, watches over, cares for a group of people.

One of my hobbies is conducting tours overseas. I have done that on eight occasions, and I leave in a week with a group of thirty-three. I have served in the capacity of tour director, an overseer of the group—handling arrangements, looking after details for the group, keeping check on the luggage, etc.

One day, while in Milan, Italy, we were to leave the hotel at eight o'clock in the morning. One law of the Medes and the Persians is that all party members must be on time. Our bus was due to leave for the train station to go to Venice. A grandmother and her grand-daughter were not there at departure time. For the good of the group, I left word with the head porter to send the two by cab to the station. They arrived just in the nick of time.

An overseer has to make judgments. An overseer must act for the good of the group, the sheep. One cannot be dilatory or negligent. Christ set us an example. He looked after the ninety-nine, and the *one* also! He did not neglect those in the fold, nor did He spend His time solely in the fold. He heard the call of the lost. Do we?

Pacifist

"I say unto you, That ye resist not evil: but whosoever shall smite thee on thy right cheek, *turn to him the other also*" (Matt. 5:39).

Oh, it's hard to turn the other cheek. The survival of the fittest is the basic law of nature. We must defend ourselves, must we not?

It is said that the Jews were addicted to seeking revenge. Their laws allowed them that freedom. But there are others who feel that we should follow the practice of nonviolent resistance, become conscientious objectors. Gandhi illustrated this basic practice in his life. So did the Anabaptists of Germany, the Mennonites of Holland, and the Quakers of our nation.

I am inclined to agree with the one who said, "Thank God for the pacifist, but thank God not everyone is a pacifist." There is a happy and safe middle ground to which I cling. Duty sometimes demands punishment.

The ultimate application of this principle which Jesus stressed in the Sermon on the Mount is that we are to seek reconciliation without delay. We are to be slow to speak and slow to anger. We are not to be revengeful. It is far better to bear the wrong gracefully and to seek peace lovingly. It is sinful to resent another in a passionate and hateful spirit. Striking back instantly does nothing more than to prolong and accentuate the situation.

Let us try to have a peaceful attitude in our daily routines. When there is tension, sharp words spoken, jealousy in evidence, and the occasion or individual "gets on our nerves," let us show no bitterness, no hatred, no upsetness. A soft, kind, and loving answer will help to turn away wrath. (The whole question of war and military retaliation is too complex to deal with here.) May we seek peace with our friends and foes alike in all person-to-person relationships: a pacific way.

Passover, Our

"For even Christ *our passover* is sacrificed for us" (1 Cor. 5:7).

The word *passover* is used to indicate the passing over of the death angel of the homes of the Israelites in Egypt with blood over their doorposts. It set the Israelites apart from the Egyptians. The blood on the lintels and the posts was a sign that marked the Israelites as the Lord's obedient people. Jews continue to observe a Feast of the Passover to commemorate that act of deliverance from death.

When Jesus is referred to as "our passover" and when at the Last Supper He instructed His disciples to partake in remembrance of Him, he was voicing a strange exercise of authority. He was saying, "Forget the past, the Passover; think about me, the new Passover." Was that the height of presumption? The Passover was important to the Jewish nation. It was a religious feast commemorating the birthday of the nation. In saying, "Forget it; remember me," Jesus asked His hearers to understand that Judaism with its laws, rites, and rituals all pointed onward to Him. He treated the Ten Commandments in similar manner.

In the Christian dispensation, the passover is a spiritual festival which began with the slain Lamb of God. It is also a spiritual fellowship suggesting to all believers that life should be consecrated to God and spent in grateful remembrance of God's deliverance from sin through His mercy and grace.

As the Jews were to rid themselves of any unleavened bread at the Passover, so should we rid ourselves of sin—unleaven—as we partake and participate in all the meaning implied in our Christian festival.

Peace

"For he is *our peace*, who hath made both one, and hath broken down the middle wall of partition between us" (Eph. 2:14).

There is an old quip which goes, "It seems that perfect peace can be found only in a cemetery." A clever respondent retorted, "Well, one other way to find peace is to look for it in the dictionary."

I am not trying to be funny or cute but merely suggesting that personal peace is difficult to come by.

In our Scripture reference for this day, the position of the words *for he* makes them emphatic. It is He—Christ and no other—that makes peace possible.

The Hebrew language uses the term *peace* in a rather trivial manner. It is in common usage as a greeting: "Peace," or, "Peace be unto thee." Personal peace is far deeper and wider.

Peace comes when conflict is absent, when the individual is free to do, to go, and to speak. It respects the rights of others. There is tranquillity rather than tenseness. There is a lack of dissension and an absence of enmity.

The wonderful hymn by Peter Bilhorn, "Sweet Peace, the Gift of God's Love," puts the emphasis where it belongs.

> There comes to my heart one sweet strain,
> A glad and a joyous refrain;
> I sing it again and again,
> Sweet peace, the gift of God's love.

So there is peace outside the cemetery. Peace can be found other than in the dictionary. Abiding in Jesus, staying close to His side, is how and where peace can be found. He is our Peace.

Let us strive to be peaceful and loving in our relationships.

Peacemaker

"Thinkest thou that I cannot now pray to my Father, and he shall presently give me more than twelve legions of angels?" (Matt. 26:53).

It is interesting to me, to say the least, that I almost wrote the word *pacemaker* for "peacemaker." And on second thought, that could well have been a good Freudian slip. For if we let the love of Christ pace our hearts, there will be peace.

A peacemaker is one who attempts to reconcile two parties or positions.

I recall the story of Mary Slessor, who went to the Calabar Coast of Africa when there were still cannibal tribes plying their trade and practicing the hellish ritual of pushing newborn twins into earthenware jars to be eaten by hyenas and the insects of the jungles. She marveled at the Power that protected her from blood-crazed drunken savages. To the chief who said that a woman's word could not break up a tribal war, she said, "You forget the woman's God."[23] And the little, Scotch factory girl demonstrated to them the power of a life full of faith in God whose Son came to bring peace.

We still need for nations to be gathered around a conference table with the Prince of peace. It seems that perpetual peace is as difficult as perpetual motion.

A soft answer still turns away wrath. Love is more formidable than hate. Reconciliation is possible through repentance. Christ is still reconciling man with God, man with man, and wants to break down the middle wall of partition. He loves his role of peacemaker. He came to fulfill that assignment. Let us give him freedom to do his work.

23. Walter C. Erdman, *Sources of Power in Famous Lives* (Nashville: Cokesbury Press, 1936), p. 134.

Perfect Man

"But was in all points tempted like as we are, *yet without sin*" (Heb. 4:15).

Perfection is not an achievement people can attain; it is a goal toward which they should strive. There is a relevance even with impossible ideals which we should not turn away from.

Our Bible plainly teaches that there are none righteous, that is, perfect (Rom. 3:10). Such a statement makes it very clear that we do not have any friend who is perfect save our Friend, Jesus.

A perfect person would be one fully developed, lacking nothing, in whom there is complete excellence.

Jesus as a perfect man was *faultless*. After much questioning, Pilate said that he could find no fault in Him. Jesus did not have an Achilles' heel—a vulnerable spot.

He was *flawless*. Many times, items for sale are reduced in price due to a tiny, almost unobservable, flaw. But not so with Christ. The most powerful magnifying glass could not find a flaw. There were no flaws in His character. All the spiritual elements were properly woven into His life. There were no weak spots, no broken threads.

He was *fadeless*. He never lost His freshness of appearance, color, or brilliance. Priceless pictures painted years ago still maintain some of their brilliance although most of them have faded somewhat, but His brilliance has brightened with the years.

He admonished us to go on growing toward full-grownness . . . maturity (Matt. 5:48).

He is ready to help us.

Philanthropist

"Labour not for the meat which perisheth, but for that meat which endureth unto everlasting life, which the *Son of man shall give unto you*" (John 6:27).

The twentieth century has been a century in which philanthropic giving has flourished. Having been president for twenty-three years of a private, church-related college, I know, firsthand, the importance of generous people.

The late Texas oilman Hugh Roy Cullen was considered an oddball because he enjoyed giving money away. It is estimated that he gave over $160 million to worthy causes before his death in 1957. When asked by a reporter why he did not save it for a rainy day or pass it on to his children, he replied, "My wife and I are selfish. We want to see our money spent during our lifetime, so we may derive great pleasure from it." And there are many more like him.

Jesus enjoyed enduring the cross that we might benefit—reap the results—of His death. He gave His all. What more can one give?

He is giving His time now making intercession for us. He is pleading our case, assisting us in achieving through His Kingdom.

There are no endowed chairs at any institution in His name as a result of His contribution to the institution. There are no buildings on any college campus bearing His name. He set up no trust funds. But, wait a minute. He has been the cause of many endowed chairs. Many buildings—churches—bear His name. Scores of spiritual trust funds are backed with His shed blood. What a giver! What a philanthropist!

Physician

"But when Jesus heard that, he said unto them, They that be whole need not a *physician*, but they that are sick" (Matt. 9:12).

I wanted to be a doctor. I yearned for that career. As a teenager I was so engrossed in medical terminology that once, while substituting in a one-room—eight grades—schoolhouse for my sister, I asked a girl to spell "coma," and she replied that it was not in the spelling lesson. She said, "Miss Elizabeth pronounces that 'comma.'" She was right, for I saw only what I was thinking, not what I was seeing.

Physicians today perform operations that fifty years ago were unthinkable. One of our leading magazines, *The Economist*, in the July 14, 1984, edition stated that for the first time since Christ, human beings, having unlocked the power to annihilate every living person already born, are now learning ways to meddle with the unborn, even producing test-tube babies. So the miracles keep coming on and on.

But, great as the miracles of modern medicine seem to be, there is no physician who can put a broken heart back together. "All the kings' horses and all the kings' men [physicians] can't put Humpty Dumpty together again."

Thank God there is a Balm in Gilead. There is a Physician who can do it all. For all those beaten in spirit, broken in heart, and bowed beneath the pain of hatred and scorn, He can put all the pieces back in proper, healthy order.

A wag remarked that a hypochondriac is one who wants very badly to be buried next to his physician. In that respect I am a hypochondriac. I want to be buried in faith and repentance with Christ, the Risen One, in order to experience the perfect life to come with Him throughout all eternity.

Pierced One

"One of the soldiers with a spear *pierced his side*, and forthwith came there out blood and water" (John 19:34).

The script for the Passion Play, which has been produced in Oberammergau, Germany, at ten-year intervals since 1634, has Faustus, one of the soldiers, saying, "To be sure he is dead I will pierce his heart with my spear."

And Mary Magdalene says, "Dear Mother, this thrust has pierced your heart, also."

Why would soldiers pierce one already dead? It was a cruel act, even though painless to the already dead one. They were soldiers, rough and cruel, who wanted to make sure that their victim was dead. To some degree their honor was at stake. But the piercing of the side added humiliation to the Son of God. It was an overkill, a trait of human nature.

There is a prophetic reference in Zechariah 12:10 to the piercing of the side.

An unusual thing occurred when Jesus' side was pierced. Medical science has indicated that blood would not normally flow from a pierced dead body. But the flow of blood and water was symbolic of sacrifice (blood) and life (water).

I really think the piercing of His side hurt humankind more than it hurt or humiliated Him. It showed a spirit of disrespect for human life, even in death. It pointed to our cruel patterns of action when another is at our mercy.

Do we still pierce His heart? I wonder. I am afraid that we do. There is probably more agony with Him, His heart hurts more, when we spurn His overtures of love and grace. He hurts when we profane His name.

Dare we do an overkill? I hope not.

Place of Hiding from the Wind

"A man shall be as an *hiding place from the wind*, and a covert from the tempest" (Isa. 32:2).

No one but Jesus could be the Man to all persons as predicted in this verse of Isaiah. He is truly our hiding place.

Wind is a current or movement of air. It is invisible, yet it can be felt. Its activities are many, both harmful and helpful to humans. The chill factor of wind in cold weather can drop the temperature significantly—by as much as 30 to 40 degrees. The speed of its movement can produce hurricanes, tornadoes, cyclones, all destructive. I was in windstorms on three occasions. Unusual things were done: once a piece of glass was blown through a church pew. (The sirocco winds are hot, dust-laden winds of the Orient.) Ships are tossed to and fro by the winds. I have seen cattle huddle together or seek shelter from the wind. A good breeze in the summertime is reviving.

Human beings face not only the natural winds of the atmosphere, but they also face the winds of human nature. There are the winds of affliction and adversity. There are the winds of the wrath of God, scorching and burning. The winds of the breath of hatred of our enemies threaten us.

A hiding place is desperately needed. There is a quiet, safe place in Christ. We can hide in Him from the storms of life.

In the hymn "Higher Ground," Johnson Oatman expresses this very human desire to attain a secure plateau:

I'm pressing on the upward way,
New heights I'm gaining every day;
Still praying as I onward bound,
"Lord, plant my feet on higher ground."

May we continue to press on. There is still room in His shelter.

Poet, True

"Jesus said unto him, *Foxes* have holes, and *birds of the air* have nests; but the Son of man hath not where to lay his head" (Luke 9:58).

As far as we know Jesus never wrote a poem, either as a teenager or as a mature man. He was, however, a great poet. He made possible this verse by Edna St. Vincent Millay:

God, I can push the grass apart
And lay my finger on thy heart.

He has caused more poems to be written, Himself being the central figure, than any other person or subject. Poetry should instruct, inspire, and please. He does all of that!

Poetry plays upon the heartstrings. It deals with things that might be. Is not this the special area of Jesus' ministry?

Jesus had a loving communion with the life of the fields and animals as seen in our verse for the day. He was sensitive to the hurts of people, and He understood the longing of the human soul.

He Himself was what I choose to call: "Poetry in motion in human form." He moved majestically. He spoke with truth and love and understanding. He showed love for all, and especially was He tender and considerate of little ones. He saw the beautiful in nature.

Whatever poetic nature or talents lie within us, we seem to call all of that into action when we try to express our love and commitment to Him, the true Poet.

I am convinced that He was truly a great poet. I wish He had written some verses for us, but He writes His verses on the minds and in the hearts of His followers. Keep on writing, dear Lord.

Policeman

"And would not suffer that any man should carry any vessel through the temple" (Mark 11:16).

Christ not only drove the money changers out of the temple, he stood guard for awhile, disallowing anyone from taking a vessel through the Temple.

We should realize that policemen are helpful, not to be shunned. I have seen them at museums protecting valuable objects of art. Jesus was protecting the Temple from desecration. This is the only time a reference is made to Jesus' doing something, then standing by to prevent further response.

About fifteen years ago I was in Baltimore, Maryland, with my wife. We were trying to locate 217 Chancery Road, the address of a donor of the college. We got in the general area through the help of some of the nice citizens but somehow couldn't find our street. I saw a parked squad car, pulled in behind it, and went up to the policeman who was seated under the wheel. His reply was, "Well, follow me, and I will take you to Chancery Road. It is easier to take you there than to tell you." Thanks to the kind policeman we arrived on time with an escort. Our host saw our arrival out of his window. The policeman had routed us properly.

He had been most helpful to us. He had kept us from taking the wrong course, getting further lost in a strange place.

Christ leads the way, the proper way, and He may reroute our lives from the common paths, but the new route will be the better route. His stance that day in the Temple is a stance needed for today. God's house is not to be little grand central station but a place of prayer and worship. Let us enter it to worship and help maintain a worshipful atmosphere.

We can help resolve the problem of misuse of God's house rather than being a part of the problem. His house should be one of prayer and worship.

Portrait of God

"Have I been so long time with you, and yet hast thou not known me, Philip? *he that hath seen me hath seen the Father*" (John 14:9).

There was a bit of pathos and disappointment in this question which Jesus posed to Philip. He and His disciples had been together a long time. He had taught them as well as Philip. They had seen Him perform miracles, two attributes of the Father. Yet Philip had failed to benefit therefrom. Others, also, no doubt.

Jesus then asked, "Why seek to see what you have already seen and now see, but somehow don't see? You can't understand Me until you see the Father in me."

Of course, there was no oil portrait of the Father, but Christ was the visible representation of the Father. His mind, will, moral glory and grace, abhorence of sin, and will to redeem the lost meshed perfectly with that of the Father.

There has been and ever will be in the human heart, though sinful the heart might be, a longing to see God. Today we say, "If I could only see Him, hear His voice and feel His tender embrace." We want to put the human touches of our being upon Him.

It was true then and is true now that acquaintance with Jesus doesn't remove ignorance. We may frequent God's house regularly and fail to see God. We may follow His footsteps across the pages of history and yet fail to identify them as His.

The more we know of Jesus, the more we know of God. They are alike; one manifests the other.

"Hang today in our hearts, O God, a portrait of Thyself, painted with the hue and colors that we know in Thy Son."

Potentate

"Which in his times he shall shew, who is the blessed and only *Potentate*" (1 Tim. 6:15).

A potentate is one who possesses great power, who can rule with independent right and absolute authority. Has there ever been one of earth? No! Only Jesus. I shall mention, however, for comparison, three who tried.

King Tutankhamen of Egypt tried to leave his mark by the elegance of his throne and the richness which attended his funeral. Howard Carter, in 1922, unearthed part of his tomb. King Tut was buried in three coffins, one of solid gold surrounded by precious jewels. Jesus was buried in a borrowed tomb.

Louis XIV, called the Grand Monarch, the "Sun King," reigned seventy-two years—the longest in French history and possibly the world to date. He built the renowned Palace of Versailles. Jesus lived to the age of thirty-three with only three years of public service. He had not where to lay His head.

Ivan IV, called "Ivan the Terrible," was the first ruler of Russia to take the title of Czar. He did much for his country, cruel as he was. In his later years, he became violent and fierce. He accidentally killed his son and in repentance became a monk shortly before he died. God gave His son who did not withdraw from the world but walked among the poor, the downtrodden and the sinful.

The only kingdom Jesus sought to expand was the kingdom of God within the hearts of His followers. He built no palace to be remembered by. He extended no physical boundary lines. He is building heavenly mansions for us and extending the horizons of our souls.

What a loving and gracious Potentate!

259

The Potter

"Hath not *the potter* power over the clay, of the same lump to make one vessel unto honour, and another unto dishonor?" (Rom. 9:21).

A potter is one who is devoted to making earthen vessels, usually from commonplace, inexpensive clay. That is, clay which is commonplace and inexpensive until the skilled hand of the potter makes it into a thing of beauty.

A potter has power over the clay. It is nothing in his hands, only something as it comes out of his hands. He can mold, shape, design, and beautify the clay vessel.

As chemical and clay human beings, we are worth probably on today's market around $7.50, while after being fashioned by the hands and heart of Christ, as His workmanship with His monogram stamped upon us, we are worth then more than money could pay for.

It is never the intention of a potter to make useless vessels just for the fun of destroying them. He makes vessels to sell and to satisfy his desires and purposes.

Jesus, therefore, as the potter, made it possible for us of clay to be made into His likeness filled with glory.

How about humming with me right now,

> Have Thine own way, Lord!/Have Thine own way!
> Thou art the potter,/I am the clay;
> Mold me and make me,/After Thy will,
> While I am waiting,/Yielded and still.

In Christ we are the real thing. His monogram is upon us. We belong to Jesus. He has made us, remade us, and now waits for us to join Him in the land that is fairer than day. The anticipation is almost uncontrollable.

Power and Wisdom of God

"Unto them which are called, both Jews and Greeks, *Christ the power of God, and the wisdom of God*" (1 Cor. 1:24).

I have referred to Christ as the "power of God" under the devotional subject: "Potentate." Let us now focus on Him as the "wisdom of God."

The three Wise Men who appeared at his birth probably were not the wisest of all time—just of a school of scholars from the East. The three wise ones which history speaks of are: Socrates, Plato, and Aristotle of ancient Greece. For a person to be wise, that person must acquire knowledge, use good judgment, think rationally, and search diligently for truth.

Socrates has been called by Plato as the wisest of them all. In his school, Socrates used the method called the "Socratic method" which sought for truth by asking questions, by inquiring whence, how, where, and to what extent.

Plato was a thinker and a scientist. To him knowledge was the path to the good life, and truth was the real world, not the world of things of the senses.

Aristotle, the tutor of Alexander the Great, was a pupil at Plato's Academy. He stressed the world of change, of becoming, a transition from the potentiality to the actuality.

Now compare Christ. No one could ask more penetrating questions. He went straight to the human heart. He taught that the good life comes from loving, sharing, and serving. He challenged His hearers on the occasion of His Sermon on the Mount to go on growing, maturing, toward perfection. He was the wisdom of God, the source of truth, and the answer to many of our questions.

261

Pray-er (One Who Prayed)

"It came to pass, that, as *he was praying* in a certain place, when he ceased, one of his disciples said unto him, Lord, teach us to pray, as John also taught his disciples" (Luke 11:1).

Does it seem strange that Jesus felt the need of prayer? Well, He did feel that need and set for us an example in matters of prayer. He taught us how to pray, when to pray, and to persist in prayer. He taught that prayer was more than just asking for something. It is an exercise in self-examination. He prayed for Himself, for others, and for the world.

He prayed a prayer of gratitude. He prayed for strength. He prayed for the forgiveness of His adversaries.

He told us to pray in His name. He also urged His followers to consider the "whatsoever" aspect of prayer. Whatsoever includes: no matter what, anything, or everything, and now and forever. Take your Bible and read right now John 14:12-14; 15:7,16; and 16:23-26. Dwell on the idea of "whatsoever"—limitless, comprehensive, and inclusive.

Continue to think of the "whatsoevers" of prayer as a blank check or checks with Jesus' name signed at the bottom and with the amount left vacant for each of us to fill in. He has backed His promises with His own blood.

I doubt that we as Christians treat anything as carelessly and as indifferently as we do our prayer life, considering the fact that Jesus taught us to regard it with solemnity and anticipation. He didn't promise us the world through prayer, but He would enjoy a call, and the rates are still the same. The source of His blessings is inexhaustible, and He wants to share with us.

Preacher

"Because he hath anointed me to *preach the gospel* to the poor" (Luke 4:18).

Call the roll of the great preachers of the century:

John Chrysostom, often called "the Homer of orators," spoke eloquently in his sermon, "Excessive Grief at the Death of Friends."

Saint Augustine's sermons showed a sublime genius, ardent love of truth, invincible patience, and sincere piety as illustrated in his sermon, "The Recovering of Sight to the Blind."

Jonathan Edwards's sermon "Sinners in the Hands of an Angry God" given in Connecticut, July 8, 1741, gave a powerful impulse to the great revival then in progress in New England.

Charles Haddon Spurgeon's sermons were evangelistic, full of vitality, and very influential upon England as seen in the sermon entitled "Everybody's Sermon."

Dwight L. Moody, with Ira Sankey, traveled over the English-speaking world, pointing people to Christ. His sermon "Good News" appealed to his hearers to accept the Christian way of life. He had magnetic, persuasive powers.

John Henry Jowett who, during his day was recognized as a leader of Christian thought on both sides of the Atlantic, delivered one of his great sermons, "The Love that Honors Christ," on October 15, 1915, at the Fifth Avenue Presbyterian Church in New York City.

Billy Graham, today's strong, clarion voice calling our world to accept Christ as Saviour and Lord, has his niche in the world of great preachers.

Put them all together. Look at the Sermon on the Mount, and what conclusion do you draw? Christ is the greatest!

Precious Cornerstone

"The stone which the builders disallowed, the same is made the *head of the corner*" (1 Pet. 2:7).

A cornerstone is probably the most important stone in a building. It relates to the other stones in a significant way. So important are cornerstones that today we have ceremonies in the laying of cornerstones. Many times a box is placed in the cornerstone containing dates, records, memorabilia, and important documents.

But referring to Christ as Peter did as the "chief corner stone" carries an additional connotation. Peter strongly emphasized the fact that we are built up a spiritual house upon this cornerstone. He went on to say that we have become a "peculiar people" (1 Pet. 2:9). Paul also used the term *peculiar people* in writing to Titus (2:14).

The redeemed in Christ are peculiar. They are different—special. They are on a good foundation, the chief cornerstone, and by virtue of that fact they can:

Be cheerful when it is difficult to be cheerful,

Push on when it would be more pleasant to stand still,

Keep silent when they want to talk,

Be agreeable when it would be easier to be disagreeable,

Be loving and gracious when they might have been sour or cynical.

Such spiritual houses built upon the Chief Cornerstone will endure the rains, the floods, and the winds of life. The Cornerstone upon which our lives as Christians are built has been hewn out of the Rock of ages and will endure the assaults of the ages. It is an impregnable stone.

264

Precocious Youth

"All that heard him were astonished at his *understanding and answers*" (Luke 2:47).

I am told that precocious children are sometimes difficult to live with and hard to handle. Their alert minds keep asking for more, and their skills are beyond normal usage and understanding.

The word *precocious* means flowering or fruiting early, before usual time, exceptionally early in development.

The world has had quite a few "child wonders."

George Frederick Handel, composer of *The Messiah*, made his debut as a performer at the age of twelve in Berlin.

Clara Barton, founder of the American Red Cross, began teaching school at the age of fifteen.

Ludwig van Beethoven, composer of nine outstanding symphonies, showed unusual ability at the age of four. When Beethoven was eleven, he could play the piano, organ, violin, had a good knowledge of harmony, and was already composing.

Wolfgang Mozart, composer of famous operas, played the clavier, an early piano, at the age of three and wrote music at the age of four. He went on a concert tour at age six.

Jesus, likewise, astonished His contemporaries at a very early age. As a boy of twelve, He stood in the center of a group of wise men in the Temple asking and answering questions, even to their amazement.

I can well imagine that Mary found it both difficult and challenging to mother such a precocious child. But mothers who seek to rear their children with God's help can do it, whether the child be precocious or otherwise.

265

Preparer

"I go to *prepare* a place for you" (John 14:2).

Have you ever served as chairperson of a building committee or a preparation committee? If so, you are well aware of the thought, effort, and attention needed to avoid mistakes and omissions.

Once, while I was president of Belmont College, we welcomed to our campus the vice-president of the United States. Such elaborate and complex preparations were made that I almost did not get into Massey Auditorium to welcome the vice-president.

Jesus serves as the one who is preparing a place for us for a special occasion. He is the architect, builder, decorator, and chairman of the welcoming committee, just for us.

I have been privileged to visit elegant buildings and fabulous structures: the Taj Mahal in India, the Schoenbrunn Castle in Vienna, and the Palace of Versailles near Paris. I assume the Taj Mahal is the most perfect building in every way.

But the place Christ is preparing for me and for all who claim Him as Savior and Lord will exceed all built by persons. People cannot build a perfect building. God and Christ are doing that very thing.

Above and beyond the place Christ is preparing, the better thing is that He will be present to greet us: "Your place is ready. Welcome! Do come in, and abide with me throughout eternity."

What an occasion! What elaborate preparations! Let us keep on preparing for what He is preparing for us.

Priest of the Order of Melchisedec

"Thou are a priest for ever after the order of Melchisedec" (Heb. 5:6).

Melchisedec was priest-king of Salem at the time of Abraham. His name meant "king of righteousness." He brought gifts to Abraham and bestowed blessings upon him. In return, Abraham gave a tenth of all booty, probably, unless it be of all his possessions.

The identical words of our verse for the day are recorded in Psalm 110:4. You would do well to read also most of the fourth and seventh chapters of Hebrews. The words referring to Christ as being of "the order of Melchisedec" are better understood when translated "after the likeness or manner of Melchisedec." Christ was not like Levitical high priests. He did not need to offer sacrifices for His sins. He had none. He had no need to offer sacrifices for the people day by day, for one offering of Himself was forever sufficient.

The priest-king Melchisedec introduced the elements of royalty and perpetuity into the priesthood, attributes of an ever-living king.

Christ followed the order, the manner, by being human and God appointed. He performed the duties of the priest by acting for others, representing God to people and people to God. He listened to the voices of His people so that they through Him might hear the voice of God. He heard their cries. He extended sympathy. He interceded on their behalf.

The perfection of Christ's priesthood makes every other priesthood, or order of priests, needless. He is our priest, always, and in all ways. We need not go to or through another.

Prince of Israel

"They shall smite the judge [*prince*] *of Israel* with a rod upon the cheek" (Mic. 5:1).

Christ came as the Prince of Israel, but, sadly enough, Israel did not receive Him. "He came unto his own, and his own received him not" (John 1:11).

But grateful are we that Paul made it very clear in his letter to the Galatians that the Israel of God is not those of the circumcision or of the house of Abraham, but those of the faith in the Son of God as Redeemer. Since that is the case, Christ is truly the "Prince of Israel."

Paul laid down some of the rules of the Kingdom over which the Prince of Israel rules. These are listed in chapter six of the Epistle to the Galatians.

Here are some of the rules—principles—of the Kingdom:

Bear ye one another's burden.

Do not be proud; pride is deceiving.

Prove your works.

Every man shall bear his own burden.

Let him that is taught in the Word communicate it to others.

A person reaps what is sown.

Do not be weary in well-doing.

Do good unto all men.

Glory only in the cross of our Lord Jesus Christ.

These principles have not been repealed or canceled. They are not in optional status.

As Christians, the Israel of God, let us be found faithful, walking according to these rules.

Prince of the Kings of the Earth

"From Jesus Christ, . . . the *prince of the kings of the earth*" (Rev. 1:5).

I am thinking today about who might be the most powerful princes or rulers of the earth. I thought of the following political figures:

Margaret Thatcher of Great Britain
Ronald Reagan of the United States
Konstantin Chernenko of Russia, and,
Deng Xiaping of China.

They are powerful. They have the destinies of many people under their power. Add to that list 136 more national leaders whose countries are members of the United Nations, put them all together, and Jesus Christ still remains the Prince of the kings of the earth. His arm has not been shortened or weakened.

But I can't keep from wondering how many of the leaders of the nations of the world leave Him outside, a total stranger.

Joachim Neander of the seventeenth century wrote a hymn, "Praise to the Lord, the Almighty," in which he recognized Christ Jesus the Lord as, shall we say, Prince of the kings of the earth.

> Praise to the Lord, the Almighty, the King of creation!
> O my soul, praise Him, for He is thy health and salvation!
> All ye who hear,/Now to His temple draw near;
> Join me in glad adoration!

And in the third stanza Neander wrote these words, "Ponder anew/What the Almighty can do."

A good admonition for us. Think, ponder, on your way, you kings of the earth and you people of the earth.

Prince of Life

"And killed *the Prince of life*, whom God hath raised from the dead" (Acts 3:15).

Peter spoke again. Let me dare a paraphrase. "Say, fellows. The one whom you deprived of life—Jesus, the Son of God—was Himself the one who gives life to all. A pretty stupid thing you did, don't you think?"

Weymouth's translation says "Guide of life" instead of "Prince of life" and throws extra light on the idea. The Prince of life was also to be the Guide of life, wanting to lead from darkness to light. His contemporaries gave Him a premature burial, and the same thing goes on today. Such stupidity.

How do we give Christ a premature burial? It can be done subtly and unconsciously by:

Putting Him under a clutter of self interests.

Burying Him beneath the archives of history.

Smothering Him with an air of indifference.

Sticking Him under a stack of files marked "Urgent."

Overdressing Him with the trappings of liturgical, habitual ritualism.

As the Prince of life, He came that we might have life and have it to the fullest—abundantly. He was no skinflint or Scrooge. He came to give and to share.

Peter softened somewhat by saying that they did it through ignorance, yet Peter reminded them that the prophets had uttered the fact that Christ should die for sin. He did not, however, back away from the fact, ignorance or not, that repentance was necessary.

Repentance is still necessary, and ignorance is still no excuse. The Prince of life should not be denied life.

Prince of Peace

"His name shall be called . . . The *Prince of Peace*" (Isa. 9:6).

It is sad, but so true, that around most peace tables of the past there has been a vacant chair. "The Prince of Peace" was not asked to join the peace conferences.

I guess the most striking illustration of His absence occurred on June 28, 1919, at Versailles, located just outside of Paris, France, when the Big Four—Lloyd George of Great Britain, Georges Clemenceau of France, Vittorio Orlando of Italy, and Woodrow Wilson of the United States—gathered to draw up a treaty after the defeat of Germany in World War I.

President Wilson was asked what Uncle Sam wanted, and the president stated that Uncle Sam wanted nothing for himself, but the downtrodden nations should have a chance. A halt needed to be called to the high-handed tyranny of dynasties that had made Europe a mortal hell.

But Clemenceau, the Tiger of France, would have none of that. Germany should be stripped of some of her territory and armaments taken away from her. Reparations totalling $33 billion were imposed, and her naval force was cut to a minimum. But these demands did not bring peace. Shylock's ghost of Shakespeare's *Merchant of Venice* stalked the conference, "Tell me not of mercy." And mercy disappeared as did peace.

The treaty became a hateful symbol to Hitler and his Nazi Party, and, in 1937, Hitler declared the treaty null and void. There was still no peace.

The Prince of peace, of love and mercy, had been left out. He was unwanted. Is He still unwanted?

Prince and Savior

"Him hath God exalted with his right hand to be a *Prince and a Saviour*" (Acts 5:31).

These were the words in the testimony which Peter gave to the captain and the officers in Jerusalem after he and other of the apostles had been released mysteriously from prison.

It was a good testimony, a far cry from the one Simon gave the maid who approached him as he sat by the fire after Jesus had been arrested and taken to the high priest's house. The maid said, "You were with him." Peter replied, "You are wrong. I know him not" (Luke 22:56-57, author's paraphrase).

Sometimes our testimonies are weak or sadly out of date. A minister called in a home and in the course of the conversation asked if the dear lady wished to share a testimony about Christ. "Oh, yes. Let me go up in the attic and get it. It is in my trunk."

Returning shortly with a downcast look on her face, she exclaimed, "Pastor, the mice have been in the trunk and have eaten up my testimony."

Such was not the case with Peter. He had moved from timidity and cowardice to courage and loyalty. He looked his audience straight in the eyes and said, "The God of our fathers raised up Jesus, whom ye slew and hanged on a tree. . . . And we are his witnesses of these things" (Acts 5:30-32).

"You know, Peter, from experience, how real Christ was. You came to the conclusion the hard way that Jesus was both Prince and Savior." Bravo, Peter! May your tribe increase. You know that Christ is worthy of our praise and adoration.

Prisoner

"Now at that feast the governor was wont to release unto the people a *prisoner*, whom they would" (Matt. 27:15). "He was taken from *prison* and from judgment" (Isa. 53:8).

Both by inference in Matthew's Gospel and by prophecy in the Book of Isaiah, Christ is called a prisoner. That is hard to swallow—man making God's Son a prisoner while human beings themselves are prisoners of sin.

But they did that to Jesus. They made Him a prisoner, placed Him under arrest and in the custody of the law. He was involuntarily restrained and made a captive. He became a common criminal, but as a prisoner He did a most uncommon thing: He forgave His captors.

There has been preserved for us a poem written by Madame Jeanne Guyon in the Bastille, France, at the turn of the eighteenth century, "A Prisoner's Song," which expresses the spirit of Christ while a prisoner.

> My cage confines me round;
> Abroad I cannot fly;
> But though my wing is closely bound,
> My heart's at liberty;
> My prison walls cannot control
> The flight, the freedom of my soul.

That was true also of John Bunyan who spent twelve years in a Bedford jail, but, while there, Bunyan wrote *Pilgrim's Progress* which was passed through those prison bars and has been translated into more languages and dialects than any book other than the Bible.

We have been freed from the prison of sin by the prisoner Christ! Now we can soar!

Prophet

"Many of the people therefore, when they heard this saying, said, Of a truth this is the *Prophet*" (John 7:40).

"The Prophet" in this context refers to the Prophesied One, the Coming One, the One inspired of God to speak for Him.

It has been said that when Augustine came to England as a missionary, he was met by King Ethelbert. After hearing Augustine speak, the king said, "All of us are like little birds that fly out of darkness into light. This man thinks he knows about the darkness from whence we come and the darkness into which we go." Jesus drew no diagram of life, heaven, and the world to come, but His prophecies and teachings spoke for God to humanity. He knew about the darkness.

Wordsworth's words:

> Mighty prophet! Seer blest,
> On whom those truths do rest
> Which we are toiling all our lives to find

apply appropriately to the Prophet, Jesus Christ.

As Prophet, Jesus announced future events, annunciated God's truths, and applied them to life.

He spoke of:

Goodness and mercy as enduring traits,

A light in the dark tunnel of death,

Not having to cross Jordan alone,

God's tomorrow being better than today,

A place prepared by Him for all who love Him, and

His return, the time of which is known only by the Father.

Beautiful words! Wonderful words!

Try to grasp their meaning.

Prophet of Nazareth

"The multitude said, This is Jesus the *prophet of Nazareth* of Galilee" (Matt. 21:11).

Some cities are not very well thought of for special reasons: economic conditions, types of people, lack of opportunities, reputation, and so forth. Nazareth was one of those cities during the time of Christ, and it was His hometown. There was a tendency to keep the town's name associated with Him either to cast some doubt upon His background or as a slight derision.

But wealth is no more a test of character than poverty. Both try a person. Poverty is not so much having nothing as in doing nothing. Christ had the job opportunity of a carpenter, a rather lowly but most honorable task.

I have seen the brightest minds and the most sterling character traits embodied in young people from undesirable and dismal surroundings and being from Nazareth did not depreciate Jesus' value or His sterling qualities. Smallness of purse is not half as bad as smallness of purpose. Maybe the contemporaries of Jesus didn't feel a prophet should come from Nazareth, but One did, and to some, that shock still exists.

Sara Henderson Hay, a contemporary American writer, in her poem "The Search," puts it very succinctly:

> We walked the world from sun to sun,
> Logic and I, with little faith;
> But never came to Nazareth,
> Or found the Holy One.

He is not solely in comfortable, cozy places. Look for Him in unexpected places. You just may find Him!

275

Propitiation for Our Sins

"He is the *propitiation for our sins*: and not for ours only, but also for the sins of the whole world" (1 John 2:2).

Propitiation is a big word with a bigger meaning. It carries the idea of atoning sacrifice, willingly made.

Since the creation of Adam in the garden, the sin-death principle has operated in humanity. It had to be destroyed by the obedience-life principle which was in Christ. Christ willingly became a propitiation for our sins by giving His life for all humankind.

He became the means whereby God could bestow the riches of His grace upon humanity through Him who identified Himself in His death with all humankind.

Dr. E. Y. Mullins, the great Baptist theologian, said about the propitiatory act of Christ,

It is the judgment of God against sin,
It put an end to the reign of death,
It appeased God's wrath against sin,
It broke the power of Satan, and,
It delivered to life eternal those that were held in his power.[24]

The words of Martin Luther King come to our ears and apply in meaning here, "Free at last, thank God, we are free at last."

Jesus was willing to do whatever it took to bring about such freedom. And it took plenty, more than the human mind can comprehend. It was the greatest act of giving with the greatest consequence the world has ever known.

24. Mullins, *The Christian Religion in Its Doctrinal Expression* (Nashville: Baptist Sunday School Board, 1917), p. 324.

Protector

"They come to Jerusalem: and Jesus went into the temple, and began to *cast out* them that sold and bought in the temple, and *overthrew the tables* of the moneychangers, *and the seats* of them that sold doves" (Mark 11:15).

It took a brave, courageous person, one sure of himself, to do what Jesus did on this occasion. It has been said that there are many nerves in the human body but none more sensitive than the one which runs from a person's brain to the pocketbook.

Money is an important item on the agenda of life. I have a book, *14,000 Quips and Quotes,* and there are more quips and quotations about money in this book than about any other subject. Jesus was touching a sensitive spot in turning over the tables of the money changers. He had done a similar thing three years earlier at the Passover (John 2:13-17). But people soon forget. They will salve their consciences and come right back to "the watering hole." You and I have seen that happen many times.

Jesus' act was an act of a king inspecting His capital and of His subsequent attempt to purify it. People were exploiting the place and the occasion. Foreign money was exchanged for the half shekels required for the temple tax. Doves were used as offerings made by the poor.

When Jesus saw what was going on, He set about to clean up the situation. His father's house was not to be a den of robbers. He had no assistance. The crowd looked on in awe.

Are we rightful guardians, providing the sacredness due His house? Does church membership become a matter of convenience and business-related advantage? Are we guilty?

Purchaser

"Take heed . . . to feed the church of God, which *he hath purchased* with his own blood" (Acts 20:28).

A good purchasing agent can save a corporation much money. The purchasing agent must know what to buy, when to buy, where to buy, and how much to pay for an item.

Let me relate here three different illustrations of purchases, historically speaking:

In 1626 the Dutch purchased Manhattan Island from the Manhattan Indians for $24 in bartered goods. The area, measuring two and one-half miles, now represents the world's largest concentration of business.

In 1803 the United States purchased 825,000 square miles from France known as the Louisiana Purchase at a cost of $15,000,000.

Today, Walt Disney Productions, which includes the theme parks, consumer products division, film studio, hotel business, and undeveloped land, is being sought by acquisitors for an estimated price of $3.5 billion.

Just for a moment, imagine you had been the purchaser in each of these cases. Wouldn't you consider yourself to be the world's top-notch purchaser? You would be justified.

But think of what Jesus did. He purchased our redemption. He bought the church with His own blood. Can you put a price tag on the worth of a soul? No, not when it is asked, "For what shall it profit a man, if he shall gain the whole world, and lose his own soul?" (Mark 8:36). Now, think of all the redeemed and those who will be redeemed.

Jesus paid it all, but no one knows how much is in the "all." There is no way to estimate the price tag. The blood of the Son of God is priceless.

Purifier/Refiner

"He shall sit as a *refiner and purifier* of silver" (Mal. 3:3). "For he is like a refiner's fire" (Mal. 3:2).

Before the day of blood transfusions and strong antibiotics, medical practices included bleeding of the diseased person and, in the case of boils, lancing the boil and removing the core—the slough in the central part of the boil. I had this latter procedure done to me while I was in high school in our country community. The principal took his pocket knife, sharpened it on the concrete steps, and plunged it into the boil on my elbow. Out fell the core and his instructions to me were, "Put some turpentine on it when you get home." Well I did, and well I got. The boil disappeared.

But to purify the soul, the spirit and the mind—things of spiritual nature—more drastic action is necessary. Fire cannot do it, even though fire is used to burn out the dross. Washing of water won't do it either, even though dirt can be removed with the much-advertised strong detergents. Antibiotics won't work either.

Blood transfusion is the best method of purging sin from the human soul. Christ did just this. His pure blood was transfused through His death on the cross into the impure human bloodstream, covering and reducing it to a pure state.

Like magnets moving over fine particles of sand drawing out the tiny pieces of metal, Christ continues to do His work of purifying and refining. He calls us to obey His commandments, to follow Him, and seek first His kingdom. We need to stay "hitched" to Him in transfusion relationships.

The Quencher

"Jesus answered and said unto her, Whosoever drinketh of this water shall thirst again: But whosoever drinketh of the water that I shall give him shall never thirst" (John 4:13-14).

Physical thirst on a hot day can become a serious matter. Dehydration must be avoided. Water is essential to life.

I guess the most thirst-tormented I ever was occurred about fifteen years ago while enroute from New Delhi in India to the Taj Mahal in Agra. The thermometer was way beyond 100 degrees. The bus we were riding in also got thirsty, and the driver had to put some of our orange pop in the radiator to keep it "purring."

I longed for that bottle of pop even though I was not as bad off as I thought I was. I wasn't sure of the water, and that accentuated my desire for the soda. I thought I would never quench my thirst, but I finally did and was none the worse off.

There are other kinds of thirst: mental, spiritual, and friendship. Jesus can supply every one of them.

In James 1:5, we are admonished by the brother of Jesus, "If any of you lack wisdom, let him ask of God, that giveth to all men liberally, and upbraideth not." In the Sermon on the Mount, Jesus said, "Blessed are they which do hunger and thirst after righteousness: for they shall be filled" (Matt. 5:6). Then in John 15:14 he said, "Ye are my friends, if ye do whatsoever I command you."

Physical water satisfies thirst temporarily. We must drink it again and again. When Jesus quenches our mental, spiritual, and friendship thirsts, His supply is adequate. So I admonish you as I admonish myself, "Ho, every one that thirsteth, come ye to the waters" (Isa. 55:1).

The Questioner

"He said unto them, *Have ye not* read what David did?" (Matt. 12:3).

Would you like to fill in a questionnaire compiled by Jesus? I wonder what kind of questions He would ask if He were conducting a modern Gallup poll? He was such a master at asking questions. There is an art to doing this, and He was an Artist, indeed.

With questions He could probe deeply into the human soul. With questions He could prick the consciences of His listeners. With questions He could evoke emotions. With questions He could bring forth hidden truths. With questions He could bring matters to "taw," the starting place for meaningful dialogue.

Questions make us think. They cause us to approach matters from the standpoint of the question and the questioner, rather than purely personal or selfish reasons.

Jesus still stands, looking straight into the deeper recesses of our souls, asking pertinent questions and expecting sensible, soul-searching answers:

You say you love Me, but do you really love Me?

Are you willing to go wherever I lead?

Will you tell others about Me?

Why do you put off important things for what you may think is a more convenient time?

May I have all the keys to every facet of your life?

He needs to have these answers from us. His ministry depends to a large extent on our answers. Can we pass the test in answering these questions? Think them over.

Rabbi

"The same [Nicodemus] came to Jesus by night, and said unto him, *Rabbi*" (John 3:2).

"Rabbi" means teacher, my master. It is a way of saying, "You are the teacher; teach me. I'm teachable."

Nicodemus recognized Jesus' right to be heard as a righteous teacher. He had respect for such teachers. He recognized that Jesus was a teacher come from God. He yielded to Jesus a great dignity as a heaven-sent messenger equal to the dignity and respect afforded rabbinical scholars. He was willing to agree that Jesus' doctorate was a heavenly diploma and not one from a rabbinical school. He was a sincere religious inquirer, a Pharisee though, who wanted safety to his own position.

He didn't go far enough. He did not recognize Jesus as the Messiah.

Nicodemus is heard today through those who compliment Jesus in a rather condescending way, recognizing His teaching credentials but not His messiahship, and that is wholly inadequate.

Jesus, in dealing with Nicodemus, pointed His finger at the deepest universal need, "Ye *must* be born again" (John 3:7, author's italics) and then went on to add another imperative, "Even so *must* the Son of man be lifted up" (John 3:14). He showed how both were linked together and the former is not possible without the latter.

This whole story about Nicodemus's coming to Jesus is a good illustration of the difference in the approach of a formalist, conceited by knowledge and a poor, penitent, perishing sinner. Nicodemus, "We know that thou art a teacher come from God" (John 3:2) and the sinner, "God, be merciful to me, a sinner. Save me or I perish."

Do we know the difference?

Rabboni

"She turned herself, and saith unto him, *Rabboni*, which is to say, Master" (John 20:16).

Rabboni is a good Aramaic word meaning "master." It is a term carrying the utmost respect, love, and reverence. This is the last time Jesus is ever called "Master" by any one of the disciples. Why?

From the resurrection on, the divine element in Him fills a larger place in their souls. He had triumphed over death and the grave, both requiring supernatural power. Up until this time there had been the Master-student relationship. Now He is their risen Lord, Master of both life and death.

Mary, in exclaiming "Rabboni," called Him by His previous title. Her gladness needed enlightment and expansion. What a difference there is between "Master" and "risen Lord."

This great truth began gradually to soak in, and the transition of affection, understanding, and comprehension began to dawn on them.

Later on, they gathered together upon the first day of the week to commemorate His resurrection, not to commemorate the remembrances of "Rabboni." He was out and beyond that stage now in their thinking.

It is not always an easy thing to elevate our estimate of one so quickly. It takes truth a bit of time to dawn upon us. Has it yet? Are we aware of the full significance of His death, burial, and resurrection? Do we pay Him the homage and respect due our risen Lord?

Raconteur

"And he began *to speak* unto them by parables . . ." (Mark 12:1). "And he *spake* this parable unto them, saying . . ." (Luke 15:1).

The world has had some great storytellers, Abraham Lincoln, Irvin S. Cobb, and Will Rogers, but Jesus was the greatest of them all. Even the officers sent out by the scribes and Pharisees to take Jesus (who came back empty-handed) agreed with this and reported of Him, "Never man spake as this man." They had heard Him speak and relate parables. This is why I am referring to Him as a "Raconteur," for He excelled in this art.

He didn't spin yarns or tell off-color stories. (A good hint to us.) He knew the power of a good story. He knew how to tell a good story. He could use stories to stimulate inquiry. When He wanted to stir up people's minds He came through with an appropriate parable. He seemed to prefer parables to allegories, folklore, or fables.

George Buttrick, in referring to Jesus as a master storyteller, asks, "Was ever a perception so instant, an imagination so rich, a discrimination so true? The life of His day poured through golden gateways into the city of His soul, there to be changed by a divine alchemy into matchless parables."[25]

Strangely enough, there were few parables after His day. His parables were flashes of light about the soil, servants and masters, the lost sheep, a lost coin, a prodigal son who had wandered far from home, the Kingdom of God, the Children of the Kingdom, and the love and judgment of God.

An incident is reported of Henry Grady, famous editor of the Atlanta *Constitution* of the previous century. When asked by an indignant caller why a certain article was printed, Editor Grady responded by inquiring if the article had been read. The response was affirmative. "Well," he said, "that is why I put it there."

Jesus told his parables to be heard, read, understood. And we are so much better off because of His "raconteurship."

25. Buttrick, George A., *The Parables of Jesus* (New York: Harper and Brothers, Publishers, 1923), p. xviii.

Ransom

"Who gave himself a *ransom* for all, to be testified in due time" (1 Tim. 2:6).

Shakespeare wrote, "The world's ransom, blessed Mary's son," and right he was.

There have been, however, several concepts as to the meaning of ransom as relates to Jesus. *Ransom* is a familiar word to us, appearing frequently in the papers in connection with hostages taken, hijackings, and kidnappings. The captors of persons who are taken captive demand a ransom, a money payment, and, usually, an exorbitant one at that before a release is consummated.

Early patristic theologians viewed the death of Christ a ransom, an amount paid by God to Satan to redeem those held captive by Satan. But this is not the correct emphasis. God doesn't deal or bargain with Satan.

Sinful humanity is morally bankrupt. Sinful humanity cannot break sin's power. Sin is against a Holy God and must be atoned for—forgiven. Captives in sin need to be released from sin. This is done only through God's love in Christ.

Only God can bestow forgiveness, remission of sin.

Only God can produce righteousness in the redeemed.

Only God can show forth to the world the supreme relationship between a Holy God, His self-giving Son, and a person made holy through the gift. Elizabeth Clephane's hymn "The Ninety and Nine" speaks to this matter:

> But, none of the ransomed ever knew,
> How deep were the waters crossed,
> Nor, how dark was the night the Lord passed through,
> Ere, He found His sheep that was lost.

But He found the sheep; He made the sacrifice and brought back His own. He is still doing it.

Reader

"[Jesus] stood up for to read" (Luke 4:16).

Some churches still have official readers, those who lead the church in this aspect of worship. I favor the practice of having the congregation stand when reading God's Word or when God's Word is read by others. There is a certain amount of respect and attention in this manner.

This may have been the only time Jesus stood up to read, but the Scripture infers that it was His custom to go to the synagogue and, therefore, possibly participated as a reader.

Scripture reading is important. It is a vital part of a worship service.

Jesus must have been a prolific reader. He must have been a good reader, but not all are good readers. He stood to read. I think He could have quoted what He read, but reading has a ring of authority, exactness, and importance. Accenting words, the tone of the reader's voice and the pace of the reading add to the impact made by the reading.

It is said that sound waves never die, only decrease in frequency. Do you think it would ever be possible to pick up the Sermon on the Mount as Jesus delivered it? I would love to have a record of His readings in the synagogue. But, you know, you and I do have a record, the Bible. We don't know what His voice sounded like, but we know that it was synchronous with His heartbeat. We can read about Him reading. We can read about His deeds of love. Let us read more and more, and the Bible is a good starting point.

Reaper

"The time is come for thee to reap" (Rev. 14:15).

Time may not be as acute with God as with us, but He fulfills His schedule on time. His word has informed us that there is a time to sow and a time to gather in, to reap.

Until now, death has been the reaper.

> There is a Reaper whose name is Death,
> And with his sickle keen,
> He reaps the bearded grain at a breath,
> And the flowers that grow between.

And we know not the hour when that reaper will call for us.

Sometime in the future, Christ is coming to gather us together, to reap a harvest. To the redeemed it will be a joyous reunion, a homecoming. We do not know when He will return, and it is folly to try to predict that time. It isn't folly, however, to prepare for His coming, and if He doesn't come before death calls, then we will be well prepared to answer death's call.

To those who are without Christ as Savior, the time of reaping will be a somber, serious event. Their hope will be gone. Their opportunity for salvation will have passed. For them it will be a separation and a commitment to eternal life apart from Christ. It will be a casting out and a casting into hell.

In the meantime, our work is cut out for us. The fields are white unto harvest. God has work for us to do. Society needs Christian witnesses. The church needs involved members. Maybe our home needs a little more of the Christlike spirit. There is plenty to do.

Rebel

"Ye have heard that it was said by them of old time" (Matt. 5:21). "But I say unto you" (Matt. 5:22).

Those words sounded as if they were spoken by a full-fledged rebel. For, as you know, a rebel is one who breaks from the usual, the customary, the traditional, and even to a rebellious state.

I have never read anything outside the Bible that points Jesus up as the greatest rebel who ever lived quite like that written by Henrik Ibsen, a Norwegian dramatist of the past century.

Maximus: "Were Constantius and death your worst terror? Think."

Julian: "No, you are right. The priests. My whole youth has been one continuous dread of the Emperor and Christ. Oh, he is terrible, that mysterious—that merciless god-man. At every turn, wherever I wished to go, he met me, stark and stern, with his unconditional, inexorable commands."

Maximus: "And these commands—were they within you?"

Julian: "Always without . . . If my soul gathered itself up in one gnawing and consuming hate towards the murderer of my kin, what said the commandment, 'Love thine enemies!' If my mind, athirst for beauty, longed for scenes and rites from the bygone world of Greece, Christianity swooped down upon me with its, 'Seek the one thing needful' . . . All that is human has become unlawful since the day when the seer of Galilee became ruler of the world. With him, to live means to die."[26]

26. Henrik Ibsen, "Greatest Rebel that Ever Lived," *Behold the Man,* ed. Ralph L. Woods (New York: The Macmillan Company, 1944), p. 394.

Receiver

"If I go and prepare a place for you, I will come again, and *receive you* unto myself; that where I am, there ye may be also" (John 14:3).

Is it fair to say that Jesus has a welcome sign hanging on the outside of the door of heaven, ready to receive and welcome us home?

Seven years ago when my wife and I disembarked in Seoul, Korea, we saw amid the crowd a sign saying, "Welcome, Dr. and Mrs. Gabhart." It was a good thing to see in a strange land. It was being held high by the brother of one of our students who entertained us graciously.

Within a week from now I will fly with my tour group to Frankfurt, Germany. We will be met at the airport by our receiver, our escort, who will remain with us throughout our sixteen days in Europe. Our escort will welcome us, then proceed to guide us to interesting places and rewarding sights.

Jesus has prepared a place for us. He waits to receive us in gloryland. I can hear Him saying, "Welcome! Come right on in. Come with Me, and I will take you to your heavenly home. Please feel free to ask Me any questions you wish. I know your stay is going to be most enjoyable. I will do all I can to make it so."

A German, Erdmann Neumeister, wrote an eighteenth-century hymn, "Christ Receiveth Sinful Men." I like the fourth stanza:

> Christ receiveth sinful men,
> Even me with all my sin;
> Purged from ev'ry spot and stain,
> Heav'n with Him I enter in.
>
> Sing it o'er and o'er again;
> Christ receiveth sinful men.

Let us make that message clear and plain.

Reconciler

"To wit, that God was in Christ, *reconciling* the world unto himself" (2 Cor. 5:19).

A reconciler is one who is able to bring back harmony among persons of diverse thoughts and action. When this transpires, there is restoration of fellowship, a healing of the breach in the gap.

Christ did this for us because God was reconciling the world to Himself and doing it in Christ. We are admonished to continue the work of reconciliation among ourselves. In the Sermon on the Mount, Christ taught His disciples that efforts of reconciliation must begin with them, and with us. We are not to wait until our adversary or dissenting friend comes to us. As Christians the initiative belongs with us.

David Livingstone, who wrought so well in Africa, received a letter—well-meaning, I am sure—with this question: "Have you found a good road to where you are? If so, we want to know how to send other men to you."

Dr. Livingstone sent back this message, "If you have men who will come only if they know there is a good road, I don't want them. I want men strong and courageous, who will come if there is no road at all."[27]

Maybe that wasn't a too reconciliatory reply, but the reply did underscore a great truth: reconciliation and oneness of purpose and aim are likely to cost someone, and faith and courage are component parts of the effort.

Due to Christ's role of reconciliation, we have a good standing with God. Let us share that same spirit with our friends.

27. *Positive Power for Successful Salesmen,* ed. Bill Glass, Garry and Jack Kinder, William Arthur Ward (Atlanta: Drake House, 1972), p. 45.

Redeemer

"I know that my *redeemer* liveth" (Job 19:25).

We have referred many times to Christ as Redeemer and to His eternal atoning work. However, I don't want to overdo this to the extent that the impression is given that once a commitment is made to Christ in faith for His redeeming grace, everything is all over. We have been too prone to insist that the great transaction is done, so we dip them in the baptismal water and "drap" them. There is more to it than that, even though we sing:

> Redeemed, how I love to proclaim it!
> Redeemed by the blood of the Lamb;
> Redeemed thro' His infinite mercy,
> His child, and forever, I am.

If proclaiming it is all, we might agree with a statement made by Evil Knevil, the motorcycle daredevil, who upset some people when he said that he was going to let God caddy for him on a celestial golf course.

However, this is not a new idea to many people today. It is absolutely amazing how many of us expect God to "caddy" for us. We think it is His job to assume all the responsibilities and provide for every need while we are busy playing our games throughout life.

As Redeemer, Christ has a right to expect from us unswerving loyalty, unwavering faith, and unassuming love.

He paid the price and finished His redeeming work, but don't you think we should respond to His love through devotion and service?

He is no caddy. He is our captain.

Reformer

"But I say unto you, Love your enemies . . ." (Matt. 5:44).

In Jesus' day, anyone who said, "Love your enemies," must have possessed the soul and spirit of a reformer. It was such a strange and radical departure from the normal feeling toward an enemy.

It is said that Martin Luther, while climbing the twenty-eight steps of the Sanctus Scala of Saint John's Lateran on his knees, was prodded by other monks to hasten his climb and shorten his prayers while going up. Haste came from Luther, not to his climb, but to his mind and soul: the just shall live by faith, not by law, and ritual, and step climbing. Luther got up from his knees and went out to later tack his ninety-five theses on the chapel door at the University of Wittenberg. The Reformation was on its way.

Jesus Christ started a reformation with His strange and radical teachings which impacted people who yielded to His teachings to the extent of a spiritual transformation.

Some of those radical, strange teachings were:

Love your enemies; that is the way to destroy them.

Love your neighbor as yourself; that is the way to get along.

All persons are equal; there is no favorite with God.

The human soul is of utmost worth, far more than money.

Death, in closing one door, opens another; enter it without fear.

A wag remarked recently, "We are so much concerned about reforming horse races. We should spend our time trying to reform the human race."

I will go along with that person if that reformation of the human race in the final analysis becomes a transformation through Christ, our Savior.

Reigning One

"He must reign, till he hath put all enemies under his feet" (1 Cor. 15:25).

I want to tie two other passages into our verse for today. The first one is, "Why do the heathen rage, . . . He that sitteth in the heavens shall laugh: the Lord shall have them in derision" (Ps. 2:1-4). The second verse, "The kingdoms of this world are become the kingdoms of our Lord, and of his Christ; and he shall reign for ever and ever" (Rev. 11:15).

Now *I want to say most emphatically*:

He's alive. He lives. The tomb is vacant. He is on His throne of glory, ruling and reigning as our risen Monarch. His kingdom has already come. It is within us. He is King of kings and Lord of lords, NOW!

Let me raise a few questions:

Should I be discouraged and downhearted? Sakes alive, no! He is working at His job.

Should I act as if I had to go it all alone, without help? No! I can call His number. He is not out on a hunt.

Since he has won our eternal redemption with his unutterable love and unbounded charity, should I not give to him unlimited fidelity? Yes, indeed!

I'm in the army of the reigning One whose Kingdom shall not perish. I am a soldier of the risen One. He calls the signals.

He rules with love, not hate; with mercy and grace, not rawboned justice.

Lead on, O King Eternal. I'm going along!

Restraining One (Preventer)

"When he was come into the house, Jesus prevented [restrained] him, saying . . ." (Matt. 17:25).

Two experiences have "stuck in my craw" over the years. While a young minister in the seminary, I observed the tendency of some to want special privileges and favors because of being ministers. On many occasions, while president of the college, I had persons ask for special concessions, even to the forgiveness of unpaid bills. "This is a Baptist college, and I am a Baptist. Won't you cancel my debt?" Is this the same as trying to exploit noblesse oblige, and don't Baptist colleges need to collect their past due accounts?

On the occasion of his last visit to Capernaum, Jesus instructed Simon Peter with regard to similar matters. He told Peter that He wanted to speak first. He anticipated Peter's approach to the matter of Jesus' paying the Temple tax.

I think Jesus said something like this: "Peter, you are right to a point, but let us look at the total picture. Yes, as the Messiah, I could expect respect in avoiding the tax, but I want to be careful not to usurp that privilege so that others would have no occasion of misapprehending me."

Jesus took pains to keep the law in order not to cause someone to stumble. He was careful not to exploit his divinity for material, human gain.

There are times when we need to be restrained by the Master in order to hear Him speak. His words of wisdom will set us straight. And, of course, we should not exploit any privileges of noblesse oblige but realize that greatness is in serving and sharing.

Resurrection and Life

"Jesus said unto her, I am the *resurrection* and the *life*: he that believeth in me, though he were dead, yet shall he live" (John 11:25).

Lazarus of Bethany was dead. He had been dead for four days when Jesus said to Martha, "I am the resurrection and the life." Martha was Lazarus's sister, and she was discussing his death with Jesus. The occasion afforded the ground of belief in the resurrection from the dead.

"Martha, I am the ground for your belief, the source of that belief and I have the power to perform the raising of the dead."

Those were powerful, pointed words—unusual claims that needed proof and verification, and Martha and her sister, Mary, did not have to wait long.

Jesus loved this family of Mary, Martha, and Lazarus. He had frequented their home on occasions. He was emotionally affected by the emotions and concerns of the sisters. He also wept.

Standing with them at the graveside of Lazarus, Jesus, in a prayer of gratitude, expressed to God His assurance of His presence and, with a loud voice, said, "Lazarus, come forth" (v. 43). The dead man obeyed the voice of the living Lord and came forth. The Resurrection and the Life had spoken with authority.

A soldier of World War II was heard to exclaim while on duty, "When I die, don't sound taps, but sound reveille, the morning call, the summons to rise!"

Why could the soldier say that, and why can you and I say the same thing? Jesus *is* the resurrection and the life. He said so, and He proved it.

Revealer

"The Father loveth the Son, and sheweth him all things that himself doeth: and *he will shew him greater works than these, that ye may marvel*" (John 5:20).

"To reveal" means to take the lid off, to bring into clearer focus, to open a door in order to see larger things, and to draw back the curtain that has concealed truths and hidden sources. It is like the first glimpse of a child that has been restless in its mother's womb.

Jesus, as revealer, came from the central depths of the unseen, wise and loving, to reveal the heart of God and the possibilities of life in Him through His Son.

He revealed the truths of God in a new light.

He revealed the power of God, available to the redeemed, through Him: a cure for evil.

He revealed Himself as a model of pure and holy living, the best of human life.

He revealed the best of the divine life accessible to His followers.

These truths embodied in His disciples made them lovers of all men and doers of good.

All of His revelation of God was for all people. As the embodiment of this revelation, He was approachable and sympathetic to the poor, the ignorant, the rich, and the learned.

His revealing act was like the dawning of the day, as the morning light reveals an emerging landscape from the darkness of the night: a clearer vision of what was to come.

Revolutionary

"I say unto you, That except your righteousness shall exceed the righteousness of the scribes and Pharisees, ye shall in no case enter into the kingdom of heaven" (Matt. 5:20).

We have previously referred to Jesus as a "Rebel," and now we call him a "Revolutionary." But He wears those hats quite well.

As a spiritual revolutionary leader, He was one with a compass in His head and a magnet in His heart. He taught the people of His day, and of that age at least three revolutionary ideas and teachings still remain somewhat revolutionary to us, in practice at least.

He taught the universal love of God, the fatherhood of God, without ethnic favor.

He taught the brotherhood of humanity in Christ without respect of persons.

He taught the coming of the kingdom of heaven.

These three went beyond the greedy and exclusive narrowness of the Jewish mind.

His doctrine of the kingdom of heaven was nothing less than a bold and uncompromising demand for a complete change and cleansing of life, both inner and outer. The demands of His subjects called for total commitment, selfless service, and purity of mind and heart.

Morally, as a hunter, His revolutionary ideas pricked and prodded His followers out of the snugness of their burrows of self-centeredness and thrust them into a world of self-giving and sacrifice.

We follow in their train, and the demands are the same.

Rewarder

"Without faith it is impossible to please him: for he that cometh to God must believe that he is, and that he is a *rewarder* of them that diligently seek him" (Heb. 11:6).

I want you to think of some award or reward that you have gotten. Think of why you received it, what it meant to you and how you treasure it. I've always enjoyed the presentations of awards at commencement.

Once, during a fund-raising campaign, our consultant told me, while we were in New York on such a mission, that he would buy me a very colorful sport coat if I would raise $50,000 in a certain way in a limited time. I succeeded and have the coat. It is almost too colorful to wear, but it reminds of something precious.

Jesus Christ knows our frame. His rewards are predicated on a strong personal commitment that builds confidence in things hoped for. Incentives are there to challenge us, and His rewards will come only on the prayers of faith. They are not automatically bestowed.

The author of Hebrews tells us that our prayers, longings, and efforts must be linked to faith. We must work hard but leave it all in faith with Christ.

Our prayers of faith must be fervent, coming from a soul afire with intensity.

The rewards may not come as a result of our first prayer or effort. Persistency must be practiced.

Won't it be great to receive a reward from Him!

Righteous Judge

"Which the Lord, the righteous judge, shall give me at that day" (2 Tim. 4:8).

In the summer of 1984 our country hosted the games of the XXIII Olympiad in Los Angeles. The television showed many thrilling moments of victory. But there was some question from the Koreans regarding the judges of the boxing matches. The Koreans felt there might have been some tilting of judgment toward the United States in a match or two.

Judges can and do make mistakes. Human beings are not without error.

In our Scripture focus for the day, the apostle Paul was relating to Timothy a brief biography of his life as a Christian. "I have fought a good fight, I have finished my course [race]." And one day Paul would hear from the righteous Judge, "Well done." There was reserved for Paul a "crown of righteousness" [gold medal] which he would receive at the day of judgment (2 Tim. 4:7-8).

A crown of righteousness was a symbol of excellence and glory and a recognition of righteousness achieved by the wearer. It was acceptable in the court of royalty.

To Paul, life was a race to be won, a battle to be fought in the presence of a great multitude of witnesses. He willingly gave the race his second wind. He struggled hard and patiently to cross the finish line. Even though Paul faltered at times, he pressed on toward the mark.

To him the reward, the crown of righteousness given by the righteous Judge, would be worth it all.

Let us keep running. There are other crowns! And it will be worth it all.

Righteous Man

"Now when the centurion saw what was done, he glorified God, saying, Certainly this was a *righteous man*" (Luke 23:47).

After hearing Jesus utter His last saying on the cross, the centurion in charge of the soldiers who smote Jesus, put stripes on His back, and placed a crown of thorns on His head before nailing Him to the cross, made a very interesting statement.

He tried to appease God by saying, "Certainly this was a righteous man." Some light began to dawn in the centurion. His participation in the sordid tragedy of the cross aroused some sense of perception.

The centurion's mind told him that he was dealing with a very special person. Maybe there was a tiny crack in the door of his heart. Matthew wrote that the centurion said, "Truly this was the Son of God" (Matt. 27:54).

Whatever the correct statement or the depth of it, there is not sufficient evidence to establish any credence that the centurion went any further than verbal acknowledgment of Jesus. He did not go all the way, only halfway.

It would be hard to see a person act as Jesus acted under such adverse and cruel circumstances and not be terribly impressed. He was bound to be a good man, a righteous man, for who else could pray, "Father, forgive them; for they know not what they do" (Luke 23:34)?

But recognition of Jesus as good, as righteous, and even as the Son of God was not enough. Confession of sin and acceptance of Him as Savior and Lord are necessary. Let us be careful that our verbal expressions do not exceed our soul commitments.

300

Rock of Ages

"Unto thee will I pray, O Lord my *rock*" (Ps. 28:1).

I want to use the title of Augustus Toplady's eighteenth-century hymn "Rock of Ages, Cleft for Me" as the central theme for today. The rock, which is Jesus, still stands like a mighty Rock of Gibraltar as a haven for sin-weary souls. It has provided shelter and salvation for thousands through the ages.

Toplady wrote:

> Rock of Ages, cleft for me,
> Let me hide myself in Thee;
> Let the water and the blood,
> From Thy wounded side which flowed,
> Be of sin the double cure,
> Save from wrath and make me pure.

Who is there among us who has not felt, while singing that stately hymn, that the words and even the melody struck receptive chords in our lives? There just seems to be something in the hymn that reaches deep down inside.

Some of the names and titles which I have used in this book have a special beauty in them. Four, "Lily of the Valley," "Rose of Sharon," "Bright and Morning Star," and "Rock of Ages" stand out, appropriately so, and with a special message. Maybe this is because the heart is the fountain of beauty.

Inflation cannot affect the wages of sin, that is death; nor can it affect the gift of God, the Rock of Ages, which is free.

Rock of Offence (A Stone of Stumbling)

"A stone of stumbling, and a rock of offence" (1 Pet. 2:8).

The Greek word for "offence" originally carried the idea of a "trapstick." I had one such stick in my rabbit boxes during my teen years as I tried to trap rabbits. It was a stick baited with some enticing food that rabbits liked, and when the little animal nibbled at the food, the stick would release, and the trap would be sprung.

Jesus does not try to trap us; we trap ourselves in several ways:

First, by refusing to obey His Word. He has spoken. His commandments are clear, yet we refuse to give credence to His Word and His commandments.

The next step after refusing to obey His Word is the rejection of Him as well as His Word. This rejection springs the trap and closes the door to salvation.

After refusing to heed His Word and rejecting His overtures of grace, then repentance becomes difficult, and we are trapped in sin.

It is in this way that offence and stumbling occur.

"Thy word is a lamp unto my feet, and a light unto my path" (Ps. 119:105), and if His Word is hidden within my heart, I will not stumble. I can walk uprightly. I have been created a creature with an upward look.

It may sound paradoxical, but it is true that the best and safest way to walk over treacherous ways is with head held high . . . eyes fixed on Christ. Looking down, we may become dizzy and lose balance, trapped in fear by our weakness.

Keep looking up!

Root of Jesse

"Again, Esaias saith, There shall be a *root of Jesse*" (Rom. 15:12).

In referring to Jesus as being from the root of Jesse, we are establishing His family and ethnic relationships. We shall refer to Him additionally on the following page as the *rod and Branch of Jesse*. In that respect we shall talk of His fruit bearing—service—rather than family ties.

Like David, Jesus was an offspring of Jesse. He would reign over the Jews and Gentiles with a more extensive and lasting reign than David, the son of Jesse.

One theologian remarked that the reference to David as the son of Jesse was because an upstart is always contemptuously referred to under His father's name, both in the courts and in society. And, to many, David was just a young upstart until he proved his mettle and displayed his leadership qualities.

Jesus, too, could be called a young upstart even at a much earlier age than David—at twelve in the Temple. At thirty, when He began His active ministry, He was unseasoned in the trials of theological controversy.

Family lineage was then and is now of importance. It is good to know from whence we came. Our heritage should challenge us, whether good or bad. If good, to live up to, and, if bad, to live so as to improve the family line.

But Paul was using this family lineage of Jesus to stress the value of prophecy in marking Jesus as one who would minister to the Gentiles. I am one of the recipients. Aren't you?

Rod and Branch

"There shall come forth *a rod* out of the stem of Jesse, *and a Branch* shall grow out of his roots" (Isa. 11:1).

The verses which follow this prophecy of Isaiah tell of the "fruits" which the branch produced. The fruits are in the nature of "the spirit of wisdom and understanding, the spirit of counsel and might, the spirit of knowledge and of the fear of the Lord" (v. 2).

Other fruits are: "With righteousness shall he judge the poor, and reprove with equity for the meek of the earth: and he shall smite the earth with the rod of his mouth, and with the breath of his lips shall he slay the wicked" (v. 4).

We can follow up on this by turning to Isaiah 61:1 *ff.* "The spirit of the Lord God is upon me; because the Lord hath anointed me to preach good tidings unto the meek; he hath sent me to bind up the brokenhearted, to proclaim liberty to the captives, and the opening of the prison to them that are bound. To proclaim the acceptable year of the Lord, . . . to comfort all that mourn; . . . to give unto them beauty for ashes, . . . [to give them] the oil of joy for mourning, the garment of praise for the spirit of heaviness" (vv. 2-3).

What a basket of fruit, or what a bunch of graces! These are some of the fruits that are still being produced on the Branch of the rod of Jesse, Jesus Christ.

As He bore fruit abundantly, He expects us to bear fruit. He showed great displeasure with the barren fig tree (Luke 13:7 *ff*). It should be our prayer that we, personally, bear much fruit and that such continues out of our house and lineage in the years to come.

Rose of Sharon

"I am *the rose of Sharon*, and the lily of the valleys" (Song of Sol. 2:1).

Many are those who have applied the name in this reference to our Lord Jesus Christ. I gladly accept that application.

Some of my friends have said on many occasions that when I think of flowers I think only of roses. They are about right, as usual. There is just something about a rose and a lily. Maybe it is the fragrance of the rose and the soft whiteness of the lily.

Dr. G. Campbell Morgan tells of being entertained in a home which he visited occasionally. Each time he entered a certain room of the house he detected a strong fragrance of roses, but he could see no roses in the room. When he inquired about the aroma of roses, Dr. Morgan was told by his host that ten years previously he had bought a small tube of attar of roses in the Holy Land. Upon returning home, while unpacking it, Dr. Morgan had broken the bottle. But he put the contents and the cloth wrapping around the tube into a lovely vase which had a lid on it and placed it on the mantle. The fragrance had permeated the clay of the vase and saturated the room with its pleasant odor.

Dr. Morgan would use this to illustrate the fact that if Christ is given the preeminence in one's life, the sweet Spirit of the Rose of Sharon, Jesus Christ, will infiltrate one's entire life, causing others to be conscious of His presence.

He is the Rose of Sharon, beautiful in mind and heart, whose sweetness and gentle fragrance blesses all who breathe the fragrance and think His thoughts after Him.

305

Sacrificer

"Walk in love, as Christ also hath loved us, and hath given himself for us an offering and a *sacrifice* to God" (Eph. 5:2).

An old legend tells of three lovely ladies discussing which had the most beautiful hands. One of them dipped her hands in the pure stream, another plucked berries till her fingers were pink, and the third gathered flowers whose fragrance clung to her hands. An old, haggard woman passed by and asked for some small gift, but all refused her. Another woman, with no claim to beauty of hands, supplied her need. The old woman then said, "It is not the hand that is washed in the brook, nor the hand tinted with red, nor the hand garlanded and perfumed with flowers that is the most beautiful, but the hand that ministers to the needy." As she spoke her wrinkles vanished, her staff was thrown away, and she stood there an angel from heaven.

Think of the nail-scarred hands of Christ, marked as a sacrifice for us. He was the perfect priest and the perfect sacrifice. He freely and voluntarily gave of Himself. He made Himself an offering for the sins of the world. He renounced everything for us. To sacrifice, then, is to forget the cost to self, to think of others, and to offer all of self to God.

His sacrifice for us was so generous, self-effacing, and significant that it should evoke from each one a sacrificial, self-giving to His glory.

Salesman

"After these things the Lord appointed other seventy also, and *sent them two and two* before his face into every city and place, *whither he himself would come*" (Luke 10:1).

I was asked to offer the invocation at the International Sales and Marketing Convention during the summer of 1984. Just before going to the podium, this thought came to me which I expressed in the prayer, "Lord, Thou who art the greatest salesman in the world, You sent Your sales representative, Christ, our Savior, to earth to enlist recruits." I still think the statement appropriate to use about Christ.

Christ sent seventy out, two by two, to represent Him. They were to proclaim, "The kingdom of God is come nigh unto you" (Luke 10:9). They were to persuade people to follow Him. They became His "sales reps." It was said about His representatives, "These that have turned the world upside down are come hither also" (Acts 17:6).

But let us think of Jesus, Himself, as a super salesman. Several times in the Gospels, the statement is made that His fame spread abroad. Crowds followed Him. They sought for that which He was giving away: healing, food, and peace.

We are in the selling business. We are His "sales reps" today. He has no other ones to represent Him. We are His hands, His feet, and His voice. We represent His products. We offer to the world what He has offered to us and in us. Ours is the task of ringing doorbells in His Name. I go with the sales manager who said, "A green salesperson is better than a blue one."

Salvation of God

"Mine eyes have seen *thy salvation*" (Luke 2:30).

I want to refer again to the Passion Play in 1984 in Oberammergau, Germany. Words are wholly inadequate to express my feelings and thoughts as the play unfolded, and the chorus and actors became involved in the drama. After the sentencing and condemnation of Jesus, the chorus sang:

O people of God! O people of God!
The blood of the Lamb purifies you of all guilt;
It gives you forever surely God's grace.

That's the message the world still needs to hear—Christ, the Salvation of God.

I have a friend who is an outstanding Christian surgeon. Recently, his father and niece were killed when their car was hit by another driver. My friend told me that he was going to conduct his father's funeral himself. He wanted to share with his friends and the friends of the deceased who came to the service that Christ is the Salvation of God, and His mercy and saving grace still abound.

What courage, what faith, and what a testimony! And yet, in one sense, what a celebration.

But, after all, my physician friend knew the Great Physician and stood at that emotional time to pay homage to the Salvation of God.

The application of this to me is: I must understand fully what the Quaker meant who, when asked by a visitor who had sat for a long time during the meditation period "And when does the service begin?" replied, "After the benediction, sir, for that is when service begins." The arena of life is where it must happen.

Samaritan

"Then answered the Jews, and said unto him, Say we not well that thou art a *Samaritan, and hast a devil"* (John 8:48).

The word "Samaritan" made the paper: "Samaritan Act Possible Death Trigger" appeared on the front page. The article talked of how an attempt by a restaurant manager to aid others likely caused his own death.

The Jews, in referring to Jesus as a Samaritan, did not think of him in such a context of helpfulness. It was a term of derision, a burst of mockery. How much lower could one get than being a Samaritan? They said in essence, "Even with your lofty assertions, you are no better than a Samaritan, the most hated neighbors." They said Jesus was not worthy of being called a member of God's Family even though He lived in Israelite territory.

They were smarting under His rebukes and struck back in resentment. Resentment is from two Latin words, "to fail again." Resentment is when one allows negative emotions at the time of hurt to recur over and over long after the event.

But it is most remarkable the special attention and kindness Jesus showed toward Samaritans. He used the parable of the Good Samaritan to show His disciples the meaning of neighborliness. He took a derisive term and goldplated it with a deed of unselfishness and mercy.

Oh, that the Jews could have understood the spiritual parable of the Good Samaritan rather than trying to cast Him into a role that was such a mismatch.

Jesus was the Good Samaritan, not the Samaritan of Jewish concept of His day. He taught us how to be a good neighbor and forever reflected good light on a Samaritan deed.

Sanctifier

"Of him are ye in Christ Jesus, who of God is made unto us wisdom, and righteousness, and *sanctification,* and redemption" (1 Cor. 1:30).

Well do I remember a neighbor who rented a farm next to our farm. He was a self-styled preacher. He claimed to be perfect. He said he was sanctified, and to him that meant sinless perfection. As a lad I shied away from him, somewhat suspicious.

A few weeks after our neighbor preached his self-perfection and sanctification, my uncle, then deputy sheriff of the county, arrested him for stealing five turkeys from another neighbor. Had the preacher never heard of the Commandment of God: "Thou shalt not steal"? Certainly his perfection and sanctification were not above this commandment.

As sanctifier on our behalf, Christ was perfect, but from our standpoint to be sanctified does not mean sinless perfection. It means an unfolding in the redeemed life of its potentialities of moral purity and spiritual beauty. It is one of the fruits of faith and comes about through a new relationship with God and the subsequent new character formed by that relationship.

To be sanctified by Christ means to be set apart for a special task, to be totally dedicated to that task, and to perform that task unselfishly. Jesus said, "Sanctify them through thy truth: thy word is truth" (John 17:17).

So, as His people we are told in His word that we are to be His witnesses, we are to work for the night comes and we are to worship God in the beauty of holiness.

I am sanctified in Christ, but I am not perfect. I've gotta keep working at it. What about you?

Savior

"Of this man's seed hath God according to his promise raised unto Israel a *Saviour*, Jesus" (Acts 13:23).

It has been said about Michelangelo, the great Italian sculptor, "With him the very rocks seem to have life; they cast away the dust and scurf; they rise and stand upon their feet."

Did not Jesus come into the world to declare and to prove that what Michelangelo could do to a rock, God could and did for us in Him?

He came to do this for the Jews. He fulfilled a promise to them that a Messiah would come. He tried to give Nicodemus a clear, concise knowledge of Himself as the Messiah and what was expected of the Jews if they were to become partakers of the Savior's redemption.

Christ came to do this for the Samaritans—half Jews—of His day. In John's Gospel, chapter four, we read of his encounter with the Samaritan woman at Jacob's well. It was less than an ideal situation. He was tired. He was hungry. Being a rabbi he was not supposed to talk in public with a woman, much less a Samaritan. She was of questionable character, having already had too many husbands. Then, too, she seemed to want to dispute with the preacher-prophet. That indicated her intended use of such a person. But Jesus kept bringing her back to the essentials. Finally, she raised an eyebrow, and asked, "Is not this the Christ?" (John 4:29).

He came also as Savior for the whole world. His commission to His disciples clearly stated they were to go into all the world.

He is Savior for one, and He is Savior for all.

Sceptre Out of Israel

"There shall come a Star out of Jacob, and a Sceptre shall rise out of Israel" (Num. 24:17).

A sceptre is the ceremonial emblem of the outward authority of a sovereign. It denotes full investment of power and authority upon an individual by a state or nation. A sceptre in one's hand is indicative of authority, both vested and accepted by the one bearing the sceptre.

Jesus as the Sceptre of Israel never carried any sort of mace or sceptre, nor did He ever wear anything on His garments to indicate that He was possessed of power and authority. He saw no purpose nor reason to do so.

Rather, He chose to display His emblem of power and authority in the lives of a cleansed leper, a blind man with restored sight, and a forgiven harlot, and by the act of raising persons from the dead.

He displayed His power by driving out demons from a tortured soul, by calming a troubled sea, and by feeding over five thousand people with five loaves and two fishes.

At no time did He instruct His disciples to erect monuments in His honor or collect memorabilia for a museum or library. Rather, He instructed them to go into all the world "and teach all nations, . . . Teaching them to observe all things whatsoever I have commanded you" (Matt. 28:19-20).

It is interesting to note that rather than ask that something of a material nature be done for Him, He stated that He was going to prepare a heavenly place for us. One day the Sceptre of Israel will sit on a great white throne, "And he hath on his vesture and on his thigh a name written, King of Kings and Lord of Lords" (Rev. 19:16).

Scholar

"He taught them as one having authority, and not as the scribes" (Matt. 7:29).

It would be very easy to dismiss this consideration of Jesus as a scholar by saying that He was omniscient, possessor of all knowledge, but that is too simplistic a way to deal with this title.

I want to refer your mind and heart to seven scriptural references which point up His distinctive scholarship.

He early had a *penchant* for learning as seen in His visit to the Temple at the age of twelve, where He both heard and asked the doctors of the law questions (Luke 2:47).

He was a *perceptive* learner. In response to the one with great possessions, Jesus quickly perceived where the rich man's heart was and told him to go, sell what he had, and to come, follow Him. But that didn't happen (Luke 18:18-23).

The *profundity* of His knowledge and skill also amazed His onlookers. In replying to the Sadducees about the resurrection, He astonished the multitude who were listening to the discussion (Matt. 22:33).

He was *persuasive* in His use of His knowledge. Many were astonished at His teaching, following His raising of Jairus's daughter (Mark 5:42; 6:2).

He was a *prodigious* scholar. "He hath done all things well" (Mark 7:37).

He was a *precise* scholar in stating what would happen to those who heard Him and obeyed, and those who heard and disbelieved (Matt. 7:21 *f.*).

He was a very *punctilious*, observant scholar. Sensing the temperament of the chief priests, He went out of their city (Mark 11:18-19).

Thank God, He had plenty of gumption, also. He was not an intellectual snob.

Seed of Abraham

"Now to *Abraham* and his seed were the promises made. . . . And *to thy seed, which is Christ*" (Gal. 3:16).

Abraham was a great man. Look at him from any angle. He was a man of faith, courage, and commitment. He has been called the father of the Jews, Moslems, and the Christians. It was promised to Abraham that through his seed, "All the families of the earth [shall] be blessed" (Gen. 12:3).

Christ came of that heritage. He was the glory of Abraham's spiritual seed. He was the channel of that blessing as well as the unifying power of all true believers. Abraham's spiritual seed are those of faith, not those of circumcision or physical inheritance.

Christ, the seed of Abraham, came in fulfillment of that faith and to bring the individual's faith to fulfillment. What the law had hoped to do for those prior to Christ's coming was done now through Christ. He became the schoolmaster, the teacher of "the way, the truth, and the life" (John 14:6).

There is a lesson for each of us to learn. We who are now in Christ are Abraham's seed also. The promises made to Abraham have been fulfilled, and we have become heirs according to the promise.

"The just shall live by his faith" (Hab. 2:4) and not the law. "There is neither Jew nor Greek, there is neither bond nor free, there is neither male nor female: for ye are all one in Christ Jesus" (Gal. 3:28). That means that we are all spiritual seed of Abraham—all one through Christ who has redeemed us. There are no special groups, no firsts because of inheritance, just sinners saved by grace.

314

Seed of Woman

"I will put enmity between thee and the *woman*, and between thy seed and *her seed*; it shall bruise thy head, and thou shalt bruise his heel" (Gen. 3:15).

This is a dim but first prophecy concerning the coming of Christ to earth in human flesh. Even though dim, it was a certain and unmistakable proclamation. It was like a slight ray of sunlight through a heavy bank of clouds.

Our verse for the day tells us three things. First, the guile of the serpent. Second, humanity will be saved from the serpent. Third, the Seed of woman will become the conqueror. In this case the conquered will become the conqueror.

Since the "Eden experience," there has been constant antagonism between the tempter and the seed of woman. The hostility that began between the serpent and the seed of woman has continued through their descendants.

It would take a different type of "seed of the woman" to free the descendants of the "seeds of the woman." Jesus, the Seed of the woman, came to destroy the works of the devil. In so doing, the Seed of the woman would bruise the head of the serpent, and He would receive a bruised heel—a wound.

It might be well just here to mention the slyness of the tempter prior to this prophecy of destruction in order to keep us on our toes. His approach to Adam and Eve was twofold: "Do it, it will do you no harm," and, "You are cheating yourselves out of something good by not doing it" (Gen. 3).

The same approaches are still very much with us, often garbed in colorful attire. And the Seed of the woman is still able to bruise the head of the serpent.

Whosoever shall call upon Him shall be saved, even unto eternal life.

Sent One

"When the fulness of time was come, God *sent forth his Son*" (Gal. 4:4).

It is never easy to send a loved one away from home. When our youngest daughter went off to college it was a lonesome time for us. All of the "chicks had flown the coop." I think there was also some homesickness on her part.

What was God's feeling when He sent his Son to earth? What was the feeling of the Son when He left his Father's heavenly home? In leaving God's presence, He left the glory which He had before the world was.

But He was sent at the right time. It was the hour of supreme need. It was a time when the world was specially prepared for His coming, the best possible moment. *Jesus was sent.* He came on a mission.

But in sending Jesus, God gave His Son, gave Him up, for the time being, to a hostile world. That was not an easy thing to do. It indicated deep love on the part of the Father. *Jesus was given.*

Jesus said, "I came forth from God" (John 8:42), indicating a willingness to come on His part. He came with a purpose. He had a task to perform, a mission to accomplish.

He came to redeem us from the law. The law was no longer a part of redemption. The Fulfiller of the law had come.

He came that we might receive the adoption of sons and daughters into the family of God. He had the adoption papers in His heart.

He came to open the door of participation to us in the mission He was sent to accomplish. Are we enrolled? Are we carrying our part of the load?

316

Servant

"Even as the Son of man came not to be ministered unto, but *to minister,* and to give his life a ransom for many" (Matt. 20:28).

Someone said, I don't remember who, "Service is the rent we pay for the space we occupy on earth," and it is so true.

The role of service, or of a servant, is not an easy one to fulfill. Both smack of the connotation of servitude, blind obedience, and strict adherence to the order of a superior. But, thank God, Christ gave the servant role a new dignity, a new meaning, and a new significance. He did not mind getting His hands dirty for others. He set the example by washing His disciples' feet. Early in life, He stressed His role of doing His Father's business and committed Himself to working the works of Him that sent Him. With Christ, service was love in action in work clothes. He never asked that special services be done for Him.

Sometimes we are prone to think of service as a lower role and want to serve only in an advisory capacity.

The words of James Russell Lowell, in his poem "The Vision of Sir Launfal" are familiar to us, yet still very uplifting:

Not what we give, but what we share,
For the gift without the giver is bare;
Who gives himself with his alms feeds three,
Himself, his hungering neighbor, and Me.

Doesn't it behoove each one of us to have our work clothes on and our tools sharp and ready, for God will find plenty of work for us to do, and the joy will be unbounded, if we are ready to perform.

317

Servant of the Lord

"Behold *my servant,* whom I have chosen" (Matt. 12:18).

Make no mistake about it, Jesus let it be known early in His ministry that He was here to work for God. His mission was to do the Father's will, to bear the Father's message, to represent God. He was the "servant" of the Lord God.

I may be wrong, but I somehow think that Christ will be at heaven's gate to welcome us home and will say, "Come right in. Is there something I can do for you? My Father and I have been expecting you."

The prophet Isaiah wrote centuries before Christ came to earth, telling his readers that there was a coming servant of the Lord who would bring forth judgment into truth (Isa. 42:1). He predicted furthermore that this servant would not fail in His mission. He would come conquering and to conquer.

I feel most of us, at times, want to play the servant role. As Christians we want to serve God. We want to be loyal and faithful servants. But, gratefully, there is a spin-off from such service— gladness.

B. B. McKinney caught this connection between service and joy in his hymn "Serve the Lord with Gladness":

"Serve the Lord with gladness,/In our works and ways,
Come before His presence/With our songs of praise;
Unto Him our Maker/We would pledge anew
Life's supreme devotion/To service true."

Let this be our theme today!

318

Righteous Servant

"By his knowledge shall my *righteous servant* justify many; for he shall bear their iniquities" (Isa. 53:11).

Servants can be trouble makers, perhaps the hired ones more so than those who serve at their own bidding.

A servant once called his employer to relate to him that he was in jail and could not appear for duty. The employer inquired as to the reason the servant had been incarcerated. When told the reason, the employer replied, "Well, they can't put you in jail for that."

"But, boss," responded the servant, "I am in jail. I am here."

God never had to intervene on behalf of Christ. He did not intervene when Christ, struggling with the approaching experience of the cross, prayed, "Father, if it be possible, let this cup pass from me" (Matt. 26:39). He did not ask to be bailed out of prison the night before His crucifixion.

Our Savior was a righteous servant. He devoted His life to righteousness. He came to convict the world of righteousness, to show the path of right and good.

Howard Walter's hymn "I Would Be True" is a challenge to us to strive to be righteous servants of God.

> I would be true, for there are those who trust me;
> I would be pure, for there are those who care;
> I would be strong, for there is much to suffer;
> I would be brave, for there is much to dare.

May we be ever giving and forget the gift, serving the Lord with gladness and in righteousness.

Suffering Servant

"He began to teach them, that the Son of man *must suffer many things*" (Mark 8:31).

As Jesus faced the suffering of the cross, taking upon Himself the sins of the world, it would have been an almost forgivable human act to go "AWOL." But He never turned aside due to any fear of suffering, pain, or death.

His servant role thrust Him into conflict with the pious and self-righteous as well as with the forces of evil. His purity of character and His Messiah mission were just too much for total consumption.

His heavy servant role did not cause Him to complain that He was overworked or overloaded. He never claimed that He was being unfairly discriminated against by His Father or even by those He came to save. He suffered with dignity and love.

Saint Francis of Assisi, the Italian monk of the thirteenth century who devoted his life to the service of the poor and the afflicted, is remembered for one of his prayers:

For it is in giving, that we receive;
It is in pardoning, that we are pardoned;
It is in dying, that we are born
To eternal life.

When death comes, we leave the land of the dying and go to the land of the living because the Suffering Servant, "who for the joy that was set before him endured the cross" (Heb. 12:2), for all our sakes.

320

Seven Spirits of God

"Unto the angel of the church in Sardis write: These things saith he that hath the *seven Spirits of God*, and the seven stars" (Rev. 3:1).

Sardis was a church where deadness, complacency, and lifelessness were prevalent. It was not a flagrantly corrupt church, there was just no spiritual pulse. Only a faint spark remained among the ashes. The church seemed oblivious to its stale and listless condition.

Christ, as Lord of the seven Spirits, denoting His completeness and perfection, brought back life to the church. He helped remove the load, the pressure, of the unconsciousness of their lethargic state. According to our Scripture passage, He did this through the seven stars, held in the Lord's right hand, the officers of the churches, by sounding a "wake-up" call. By filling the leaders of the seven churches with His Spirit, thus causing them to be warmed and aflame, the cold and dying embers of the Sardis church could be revived.

The church needed to realize that it had come to its status quo condition through a monotonous routine that had stifled its sensitivity to the need of becoming alive. Only the Lord of the seven Spirits could lift that dead weight. This is reminiscent of the little lad helping his dad remove some stones from a ditch. "Dad," said the lad, "this stone is so big I have done my best, but I can't remove it."

"Oh, son, don't say you have done your best. You have never done your best until you have asked your father to help you."

Many of our churches today are descendants of the Sardis church and need desperately to call upon the Lord of the seven Spirits of God to revive them.

The Good Shepherd

"I am *the good shepherd:* the good shepherd giveth his life for the sheep" (John 10:11).

Shepherds are like servants—there are good ones, fairly good ones, and poor ones. They come in all kinds.

Good shepherds are committed to looking out for the security and safety of their sheep. They carry staffs, and many carry slings to ward off wild animals and thieves. A good shepherd will even lay down his life for his sheep—a very strong commitment.

Alexcenah Thomas wrote a hymn in the nineteenth century, "Bring Them In," which speaks in good terms about the intensity of the shepherd searching for the sheep.

> Hark! 'tis the Shepherd's voice I hear,
> Out in the desert dark and drear,
> Calling the sheep who've gone astray,
> Far from the Shpeherd's fold away.

And, in the last stanza, Thomas makes it very personal:

> Out in the desert hear their cry,
> Out on the mountains wild and high;
> Hark! 'tis the Master speaks to thee,
> "Go, find My sheep where'er they be."

A good shepherd will be constantly on the lookout for greener pastures for his flock. He searches out the watering holes and the good grazing areas.

Jesus, as our Good Shepherd, is also our Bread of life and Water of life. He provides for us as a shepherd cares for the sheep. And He gave His life, the supreme sacrifice, for our sins. He did it all.

How much are we doing?

Shepherd, the Great Chief

"Now the God of peace, that brought again from the dead our Lord Jesus, the *great shepherd* of the sheep" (Heb. 13:20). "When the *chief Shepherd* shall appear, ye shall receive a crown of glory that fadeth not away" (1 Pet. 5:4).

What a Shepherd Christ was of the flock of God. He, like all good shepherds, was willing to lay down His life for His sheep. He knew the green pastures and the still waters, and His sheep gladly responded to His voice.

Henry Baker wrote in the mid-nineteenth century a very beautiful hymn "The King of Love My Shepherd Is" which suggests the warm and meaningful relationship between the Chief Shepherd and His sheep. Stanzas 1 and 5 are especially relevant here.

Stanza 1:

> The King of love my Shepherd is,
> Whose goodness faileth never;
> I nothing lack if I am His
> And he is mine forever.

In designating Christ as the Chief Shepherd, was Peter inferring that Christ was head of all the flocks of the elect? I think He was because He was anticipating a crown of glory at the end of the road.

It is the privilege of the Good Shepherd to give out the awards at His appearing. Maybe Peter was thinking of the wreath of flowers given in token of victory at the Grecian games, but Peter couched his words to convey also that bliss of heaven which will be the life of God poured into the redeemed souls through Christ.

Stanza 5:

> And so through all the length of days
> They goodness faileth never:
> Good Shepherd, may I sing Thy praise
> Within thy house forever.

Shield

"Thou, O Lord, art *a shield* for me" (Ps. 3:3).

A shield is a defense mechanism, a defensive armor.

I remember about thirty years ago while on a preaching mission in Jamaica, I slept at night under a net to shield me from the insects and mosquitos. It was a welcomed shield, probably no longer in use.

David, a man of war, spoke of Christ as his shield. A rather interesting statement, don't you think, by a man of war? But it was not a shield of metal that David thought of but a shield of the spirit.

Christ shields us, as He did David, from the fiery darts of the wicked (Eph. 6:16). The wicked ones, under the control of Satan, have cleverly devised stratagems and subtle ways.

Christ shields us from the wiles of the devil (Eph. 6:11). The devil—that crafty evil one—is always on the job. He never lets up.

C. S. Lewis, in his book *Screwtape Letters,* imagined Satan writing to Wormwood, one of his henchmen, urging him to keep reminding the new church members of the disappointments that will come early, that his neighbors, whom he wishes to hitherto avoid, are sitting near him. He also chides Wormwood for downplaying gluttony.[28]

The use of every ruse and wile possible are the devil's ploys. How true! How true! But Christ is our shield.

Christ will also shield us from the sting of death. His resurrection produced that shield.

28. C. S. Lewis, *Screwtape Letters* (New York: The Macmillan Company, 1942), pp. 16, 86.

324

Shiloh

"The sceptre shall not depart from Judah, nor a lawgiver from between his feet, until *Shiloh* come" (Gen. 49:10).

This verse has been much discussed. The dilemma seems to be whether the author means "until he comes to Shiloh, a town of Ephraim," or, "until Shiloh [the Messiah] comes." There is a strong enough acceptance of the latter idea to justify our referring to Christ as "Shiloh." The word is used nowhere else in the Old Testament.

The term indicates peace, rest and tranquillity. Sin had brought to humankind the curse of labor. Unrest replaced rest. There was no more peace. The coming of Shiloh, the Messiah, would change that horrible plight.

Shiloh would come to redeem humankind from sin by bearing the sins in His own body. He would come to gather His own unto Himself. He would come to teach the redeemed His way of life.

His coming would establish His kingdom over which He would reign with love and righteousness.

His coming would bring to humankind the climactic gift of eternal victory.

The good thing is that Shiloh did come, and He came bringing all those things humankind needed to be freed from the curse of sin and its entanglements.

And equal to His coming 2,000 years ago, and a part of His total plan, is the fact that He is coming again.

Shiloh was expected. Shiloh came. Shiloh is expected to come again, and one day Shiloh will come again. Labor will have ended. Unrest will become rest, and peace will have its day. The plan is working itself out. Let us be ready.

325

The Silent One

"Jesus yet answered nothing; so that Pilate marvelled" (Mark 15:5).

Jesus knew the fine distinction of when silence should be golden or yellow. He knew it wise to say nothing when nothing needed to be said. He knew when to say something when something needed to be said. And that is both an art and wisdom.

It would have been very easy for Jesus to give Pilate a lengthy discourse on His kingship and mission, but He chose to remain silent and told Pilate much in that manner. He felt that His actions would speak louder than His words. And what wise dignity He showed!

Silence is a word that one can't say without breaking it. So don't break it unless you can improve on it.

It would be well for us to know when to keep silent.

Let us listen when God speaks. Let us be silent when we are angry or attempting to judge another in public. Let us keep silent when ill-chosen words are being tossed at another's character.

It would be wonderful for us to know when to speak up: when God's name is taken in vain, let us express our displeasure; when evil needs denouncing, it is yellow to remain silent; when a good cause is lacking for support, someone should speak; and, when sins need confessing, we should not be silent before God.

The tongue is a tricky member, and we should learn how to hold it and how to use it.

"A word fitly spoken is like apples of gold in pictures of silver" (Prov. 25:11).

Sin Bearer

"Who his own self *bare our sins* in his own body on the tree" (1 Pet. 2:24).

Savonarola, the fiery fifteenth century Italian monk, who preached with zeal against the wickedness of the world and who suffered a martyr's death for his convictions, wrote:

> Jesus, refuge of the weary,
> Treasure of the spirit's love,
> Fountain in life's desert dreary,
> Savior from the world above;
> O how oft Thine eyes, offended,
> Gaze upon the sinner's fall!
> Yet upon the cross extended,
> Thou didst bear the pain of all.

The load of sin that Jesus carried must have been very heavy, almost back breaking and soul destroying, but He too replied, "The weight is borne because of My commitment to My purpose to redeem all who come unto Me."

B. B. McKinney caught completely the idea of Jesus as sin bearer:

> All the sin of the world
> On the Savior was hurled,
> As He knelt in the garden alone;
> Hear His soul-burdened plea,
> Let this cup pass from Me,
> "Even so, not My will, Thine be done."

Yes, Jesus bore our sins alone. No angel aided Him in doing it. In Gethsemane an angel ministered to Him only in order that He might bear the load alone. He bore our sins in His soul upon the cross in the sense of suffering for what God accepted in place of our deserved penalty. *He bore our sins in love.*

Smitten One of God

"Yet we did esteem him stricken, *smitten of God,* and afflicted" (Isa. 53:4).

Have you ever looked upon a distasteful scene and tried to justify indifference by saying, "That's none of my business," yet, realizing all the time that you and I were involved? I am guilty.

It is embarrassing to be punished by peers. The old, public whipping block was a hideous, heinous sight and deed. But think of being smitten of God as Jesus was for our sins.

Do we have any emotional or guilt reaction when we read about His being smitten by soldiers during His trial? Do we get a little upset when we review the account of his being spat upon? Do we cringe when we think of the crown of thorns that was pressed down upon his head? Do we cry out when we reread the account of the sword's piercing his side? How do we react to the Gethesemane experience when Jesus' sweat "was as it were great drops of blood" (Luke 22:44)?

The next question is this: Do we hurt Him now? Are we so indifferent and unconcerned as to pierce His heart? Do we neglect to minister to those in need, grieving Him sorely? Are we such off-again, on-again Christians as to leave Him stranded, without laborers for the fields white unto harvest? Are we more interested in getting all we can from Him that we give so sparingly that His causes suffer heavily?

I am afraid that the smiting goes on. We are in the continuous drama just as we were in on the crucifixion.

Let us receive His mercy and allow it to bring forth from us a greater commitment.

328

Solitary One

"Then said Jesus unto the twelve, Will ye also go away?" (John 6:67).

In some respects Jesus lived a lonely, solitary life. He did not have many close friends: the twelve disciples, and Mary, Martha, and Lazarus. He had no place to lay His head. The crowds that, at times, seemed to acclaim Him were fickle crowds, looking mostly for bread. The religious people were critical and jealous of Him. He had to make four withdrawals with His disciples to avoid both the crowds and the religious groups.

It is rather paradoxical. Jesus spent His life building bridges instead of walls. He did everything for others, never for self. Yet He was almost a "man without a country." He came unto His own, but they did not receive Him. To many He was just a poor, wayfaring stranger.

He was also just an itinerant preacher. He held no formal assignments or pastorates. He wrote no books nor taught at any university. He was not a world traveler, journeying no more than 200 miles from the place of His birth.

He was not hard to get acquainted with. He loved children. He went about doing good, but in so many instances He stood alone. Why? Was it because His peers could not comprehend fully His mission, His task, and His unfathomable love?

Another paradox: His great love and unselfish service have warmed the hearts of millions through the centuries and driven from their hearts loneliness and alienation.

He made much of solitude. He found strength in silence, and out of such solitude and silence came peace and joy. A good example for Christians when practiced judiciously.

329

The Son of the Blessed

"Again the high priest asked him, and said unto him, Art thou the Christ, the Son of the Blessed? And Jesus said, I am" (Mark 14:61-62).

Our Scripture reference for the day is most interesting. Jesus was being grilled by the high priest. In a rather condescending manner, the high priest asked Jesus if He was the Son of the Blessed. Without hesitation, Jesus said, "I am." Then the high priest goes off the deep end of bigotry and narrowness by accusing Jesus of blasphemy. What an inappropriate conclusion!

The term *blessed* is one used most often by the Jews as a title for God. Therefore, as the "Son of the Blessed" Jesus is saying that he is the son of God. Mary, in the Magnificat (Luke 1), says that she will be called "blessed." So on the maternal side Christ is the son of the blessed. Thus He was highly favored. He was therefore a dispenser of blessings.

Our blessings as Christians come from the Son of the Blessed. Christ knew His relationship to every aspect of God and never hesitated to perform whatever role such relationships demanded.

He does not withhold good things from those who love him. His blessings abound.

The hymn "Count Your Blessings" by Johnson Oatman, Jr., pays tribute to the Son of the Blessed, the Dispenser of blessings:

When upon life's billows you are tempest tossed,
When you are discouraged, thinking all is lost,
Count your many blessings, name them one by one,
And it will surprise you what the Lord hath done.

Should it be such a surprise when we understand the nature of the Son of the Blessed? No. Not as much of a surprise as an occasion of gratitude!

330

Son of David

"The book of the generation of Jesus Christ, *the son of David*, the son of Abraham" (Matt. 1:1).

Matthew laid the genealogy of Jesus right on the line. He begins with the pedigree of Jesus, showing what a distinguished ancestry He had.

Our family has had a great deal of pleasure reading the genealogy of my grandmother's family, the Davenports. I think Matthew took great pride in relating Jesus' noble ancestry to the Jews.

Jesus—from the Hebrew word *Joshua* means "Jehovah is helped." Like the Joshua of old who led Israel into the Promised Land, Jesus was to be the leader and ruler of His people, the captain of their salvation (Heb. 2:10; 4:9).

Christ—the Hebrew for the Messiah, the Anointed One, and the Jews looked for the Messiah to be born of a certain family, thus:

Son of David—David was the founder of the royal line (2 Sam. 7:13-16). As son of David, Jesus fulfilled all the prophecies that the Anointed One would descend from David and from Abraham.

Son of Abraham—Abraham was head of the covenant nation and the one to whom the promise was made that in him all the nations of the earth would be blessed. (See Gen. 17:1-5.) Thus, as son of Abraham, Jesus would fulfill the new covenant and would fulfill the role of the One who would become a blessing to all nations.

Jesus was exceptionally wellborn. He provided us with exceptional born-again privileges.

Son of the Father

"When Jesus had cried with a loud voice, he said, "*Father,* into thy hands I commend my spirit" (Luke 23:46).

Did Jesus ever cry again unto God, His Father, while on earth when He hurt on occasion? It is the nature of a son to go to his father when in need and distress. I did.

The son desires also to fill his father's shoes, to follow his father's leading. I well remember as a lad putting on my dad's shoes and wishing that I could fill them and wear them, but they were too large. I was sad.

Jesus bore an acute consciousness of His duties as the Son of His Heavenly Father. At the early age of twelve, while in the temple reasoning with the wise men, he responded to Mary and Joseph, "Wist ye not that I must be about my Father's business?" (Luke 2:49). Again Jesus, in speaking to his disciples as he was ministering to the man born blind, said, "I must work the works of him that sent me, while it is day" (John 9:4). (See also John 5:19,36; 17:4.)

Then, while on the cross, Jesus cried unto His Father "with a loud voice, he said, Father, into thy hands I commend my spirit." It was a statement of calm and filial trust to His Father, saying, in essence, "As your son I have accomplished the appointed work which you gave me to do."

Jesus was a family man, both of earth and of heaven. We are, happily, a part of the family of God through Him who loved us and gave His life for us. Good friends, we cannot rest in the shade of our family tree of spiritual inheritance. Neither do we want our spiritual family tree to have a crop failure due to our apathetic efforts. We, too, must work the works of Him who sends us into the fields!

332

Son of Joseph

"They said, Is not this Jesus, the *son of Joseph,* whose father and mother we know?" (John 6:42).

Usually a son bears a very close and unique relationship with his father. In the case of our Lord it was a very unusual and delicate relationship since He was the Son of God and of Mary, while Joseph was the husband of Mary and generally known as the father of Jesus.

I can't keep from wondering if such a unique relationship ever caused any undue strain on either Joseph's or Jesus' part. Did Jesus ever mildly chafe under the "stigma" of being identified as Joseph's son?

The Jews had long known of Him as the son of Joseph and Mary, and they were shocked to hear Him claim that He was from above. The miracles He was performing were not in line with that of a carpenter's son. So their question relating to His lineage was one of unbelief rather than perplexity. Joseph, Mary, and Jesus never tried to explain His miraculous birth and the Jews certainly were skeptical, if it ever came to their minds.

The question asked by these murmuring Jews, after Jesus had claimed to be the Bread of life, was one of doubt, contemptuous surprise, and dissatisfaction.

But Jesus was always loyal to His parents and extremely loyal to the higher sonship of God. He performed well as Joseph's son and as God's son. He was not ashamed of His family connection, and He rejoiced in the sonship relationship He bore with His Heavenly Father.

What about our performance?

333

Son of Mary

"Now the birth of Jesus Christ was on this wise: When as *his mother Mary* was espoused to Joseph" (Matt. 1:18).

A large billboard at a busy intersection in Nashville, Tennessee, carried these words: "God still makes house calls."

Aren't we glad that He still does? We are most grateful that He made His first house call to the humble home of His mother, the virgin Mary of Nazareth, because He came to live with her and her husband, Joseph, for thirty years.

Sons are special to mothers and vice versa. I remember the sacrifices and prayers of my mother. Just this week, I watched the glow on our daughter's face as she showered love upon their first son. It was so natural, so special.

Jesus' mother was given special interest by both Matthew and Luke. Luke tells us of her call to be the mother of our Lord, her maidenly fears, her loyal submission, and her outburst of sacred joy. Matthew speaks of the shame and suspicion which she initially had, causing humiliation but ultimately vindication.

Mary was a typical Jewish believer of the best sort. She was a typical mother with deep devotion to her child, pure in heart, and one who pondered many things in the deep recesses of her soul regarding her Son.

There seemed to have existed a strong tie of love, understanding, and respect between Jesus and His mother.

And as Mary's son He still makes house calls. It is my hope and prayer that we will receive Him with that same joy and devotion that His mother received Him long ago. I hope He is no stranger when He knocks. We must be sure to let Him come in.

334

Son, the Only Son

"Nathanael answered and saith unto him, Rabbi, thou art *the Son of God*" (John 1:49).

Just as there is something special between a mother and her son, there is something extra special between a father and his only son.

The New Testament underscored this fact in incidents related in Luke 7:12 and 9:38. In both cases the only son is considered important to father and mother.

The father tends to see in his only son a continuity of the family name, the posterity of the family. The only son gives strength and security to the family, especially to sisters and more especially if the sisters are unmarried. The only son is looked upon to carry on the work of the father, to preside over family affairs in lieu of the father. As God's only Son, Jesus filled all of these roles admirably. He has borne His Father's name with dignity and honor. He has given strength to all the children of God and has provided security —eternal life—to all them. He continues to preside over the activities of the kingdom of God with infinite wisdom and everlasting love.

If the old saying "The glory of the father is in the son" is true, then God has been glorified through His Son, Jesus Christ. The prayer which His Son prayed while on earth indicated the Son's desire to accomplish just that, "I have glorified thee on earth: I have finished the work which thou gavest me to do" (John 17:4). And the son went on to say, "I have manifested thy name" (v. 6); "I kept them in thy name" (v. 12); "I have given them thy word" (v. 14); "I also sent them into the world" (v. 18); and, "I have declared unto them thy name" (v. 26).

What a wonderful Only Son!

335

Sower

"Behold, a *sower* went forth to sow" (Matt. 13:3).

In this chapter of parables, the first one being the parable of the sower, Jesus identified Himself as the sower. He had been sowing for many months. His seed—his holy words—had taken deep root in some; in others, no root at all.

There are several things I learned about sowing seed while a lad charged with sowing the watermelon seeds each year in the patch prepared by my father. It was important to have good seed. There must be good sowing, hills prepared, and the seed placed in the hills. Good soil was important as watermelons need fertile and moist soil. Then the weeds must be kept out, and the young plants properly cultivated. If all of this was done, the reward would be luscious watermelons, and they never tasted better than when pulled early in the morning with the cool, refreshing dew on them.

Through us Jesus is still the Master Sower. We are to scatter the seeds of His Holy Word. It is still true that some may fall on stony ground, but that does not relieve us of sowing. We are to prepare the soil, sow the seed, and cultivate the young plants, but only God can give the increase.

The first stanza of Knowles Shaw's hymn "Bringing In the Sheaves," written over one hundred years ago, reminds us:

Sowing in the morning, sowing seeds of kindness,
Sowing in the noontide and the dewy eve;
Waiting for the harvest, and the time of reaping,
We shall come rejoicing, bringing in the sheaves.

May we be sowers of the Word, hearers of the Word, and doers of the Word.

Spiritual Rock

"They drank of that *spiritual Rock* that followed them: and that Rock was Christ" (1 Cor. 10:4).

The rock spiritually typifies Christ as the source of living water. As water is essential to life, so Christ is essential for spiritual life.

In typifying Christ, the Rock is the sure foundation preventing people from sinking into the sands of sin. It is the foundation stone upon which faith is grounded and built. It is the foundation upon which hope is anchored, and love is erected.

In the nineteenth century Edward Mote captured this thought of Christ as the "spiritual Rock" in the hymn "The Solid Rock":

My hope is built on nothing less
Than Jesus' blood and righteousness;
I dare not trust the sweetest frame,
But wholly lean on Jesus' name.
On Christ, the solid Rock, I stand;
All other ground is sinking sand.

The ancient world thought of the world as resting on the back of an elephant with the elephant standing on the back of a turtle. To them this concept was one of security, strength, and adequacy of foundation.

I prefer to build my case, place my life, upon the solid Rock, the spiritual Rock Christ. He is able and trustworthy.

Star of Jacob

"There shall come a Star out of Jacob" (Num. 24:17).

Jesus Christ came into the world as the brightest Star out of the galaxy of Jacob.

Jacob was the grandson of Abraham and the father of twelve sons who established the house of Jacob, known also as the children of Israel, the totality of the seed of promise. Jacob was spiritually sensitive and capable of growth in faith and goodness.

The "star" is the symbol of power, and, in referring to a person, it denotes one possessed with brilliant and attractive qualities with drawing power. Jesus possessed such power. "I, if I be lifted up from the earth, will draw all men unto me" (John 12:32). A star is the recognized chief person at social gatherings. Jesus again qualifies: "This beginning of miracles [turning of the water into wine at the wedding feast] did Jesus in Cana of Galilee" (John 2:11). A star is a leader or outstanding performer at special events. Jesus again manifests His "star" qualities: "They straightway left their nets, and followed him. . . . Multitudes . . . from Galilee, and from Decapolis" (Matt. 4:20,25).

As a star comes into the heavens dispersing darkness by bringing light, Jesus came into a world of darkness as the Light of the world. After coming He has continued His work of dispersing darkness from the souls of the peoples of the world.

The Star of Jacob was welcomed into the world on that first Christmas night by the star of the East, which guided the Wise Men in their visit to the Christ child.

May we follow the Star of Jacob out of darkness into His glorious light.

338

Stone

"Jesus saith unto them, Did ye never read in the scriptures, *The stone* which the builders rejected, the same is become the head of the corner?" (Matt. 21:42).

It has been said that the early Christians were *excluded* from the synagogues and the Temple because Christianity *included* any and all who by faith and repentance became followers of Christ, the chief Cornerstone of the kingdom of God.

As the Stone, the Chief Cornerstone, the Living Stone, elect and precious, Jesus Christ, the Messiah, became the One on whom depended the existence and support of the Kingdom. As a cornerstone is placed at the base and holds two walls together, Christ wanted to unite Jews and Gentiles into one fellowship of believers. In so doing, however, He became the Stone which the builders rejected.

The Jews, who prided themselves as builders of God's temple, rejected the precious Chief Cornerstone, but the Architect interfered and pushed them aside and had the true and precious Stone used in the new temple built in the hearts of regenerate people.

Rejection of the Chief Cornerstone through ignorance, contempt, and prejudice caused the stone to become to those rejecting it a stone of stumbling, a rock of offense. It produced a millstone around their necks as they drowned in the sea of hopelessness and contempt.

But the rejected stone was to be elevated to the Chief Stone, and here is the prediction of ultimate victory.

In the building of our lives we would do well to build upon the Chief Cornerstone, and in that way, our house will be built upon a rock, not upon sand.

339

Stranger In Jerusalem

"And the one of them, whose name was Cleopas, answering said unto him, Art thou only a *stranger in Jerusalem,* and hast not known the things which are come to pass there in these days?" (Luke 24:18).

Jesus a stranger in Jerusalem? How could it be? His horrible crucifixion was only a few days old. So soon forgotten?

News of His resurrection was slowly spreading; however, the two of His disciples on the way to Emmaus, a short distance from Jerusalem, were engrossed, talking about the previous events, when Jesus locked step with them and asked, "What manner of communication are these that ye have one with another?" (v. 17). Cleopas, one of the disciples, replied hastily, "Don't you know what has happened in Jerusalem? Aren't you aware of the events which have transpired? Aren't you then a stranger here?"

They were so full of the previous events that they wondered how anything of such import could escape Him. It hadn't escaped Him, only them. Had their eyes been beholden so they did not recognize Him? Luke says so, which inferred a divinely ordered impediment to their recognizing Him. I think also there was some lack of faith in them regarding His resurrection. He was a stranger to them. They had never before seen the Risen Lord.

Jesus began to converse with the two disciples, asking about the things which had happened. Their response was a full detail of the events. His response to them was a review of the prophecies concerning Himself. He was no longer a stranger. Faith had opened their eyes.

Is He still today a stranger to many?

There's a stranger at the door,
Let Him in,
He has been there oft before,
Let Him in.
Let Him in, ere He is gone,
Let Him in the Holy One,
Jesus Christ, the Father's Son.

Become acquainted with this Stranger in Jerusalem.

340

Stricken One

"For the transgression of my people was he *stricken*" (Isa. 53:8).

Referring to Jesus as the "Stricken One" means that He was incapacitated, bruised, wounded, and smitten. It is hard to think of the righteous Son of God ever receiving such horrible treatment. But he did.

James Gregg, a minister in Nashville, Tennessee, speaking at the pastors' conference, talked about the wounds of Christ. He stated that, medically speaking, there are five types of wounds: contuse, lacerated, penetrating, perforated, and incised, and Jesus suffered every one of these.

In Pilate's court, when the soldiers struck Him on the head, He suffered contuse wounds. The skin was not broken, but it was badly bruised.

During the scourging before Pilate, He suffered lacerated wounds when He received thirty-nine blows.

The penetrating wound came when a crown of sharp thorns was pressed on His brow.

As He was nailed to the cross, His hands and feet were pierced with nails, thus the perforated wounds.

Incised wounds are made with knives or razors, or spears. Jesus received this wound from the soldier's spear which entered His side.

I wonder how many of these wounds I have had a part in putting on Jesus. We were all there at the crucifixion.

Forgive us, Lord.

We somehow at times seem to lose our concern and love for others who hurt. It is easy to strike a wounded one who can't strike back. Do forgive us!

341

The Stronghold

"The Lord is good, a *strong hold* in the day of trouble" (Nah. 1:7).

Several years ago we became a nation looking at bomb shelters as our main source of protection. Today, the forces of destruction make even bomb shelters most inadequate.

A stronghold is a fortified place, a place of security in the day of trouble. It must meet at least three standards. First, it must be adequate in strength and amply secure, well guarded. Second, it must be accessible to all and easily available. Third, it must be abiding, capable of service through the years.

Jesus Christ is our stronghold. He possesses the royal attributes of omnipotence, omniscience, omnipresence and the godly character traits of faithfulness, godliness, and righteousness. He is adequate. He is available for all, for he said, "Him that cometh to me I will in no wise cast out" (John 6:37). His stronghold is abiding for even "the gates of hell shall not prevail against it" (Matt. 16:18).

The prophet Isaiah gives a good picture of the ideal stronghold (25:4). It is strength to the poor, strength to the needy in distress, a refuge from the storms of life, and a shadow from the searing heat. Job adds yet another, one who comforts the mourners (29:25).

Looking at eternal life, I had rather have Jesus as my stronghold than all the well-built bomb shelters. He is so adequate, accessible, and abiding. He has made ample provision for our needs. I can shelter, rest, and be at peace in Him.

He has never had a fatality, a casualty, among those who have entrusted themselves to Him. His stronghold is sinproof.

342

Successful One

"In the world ye shall have tribulation: but be of good cheer; *I have overcome the world*" (John 16:33).

There are many books, magazines, and articles published today on how to be successful. We are a success-oriented society. This is nothing new, just more accentuated.

Men have sought to be successful in conquering the world. Alexander the Great tried it, but died in 323 BC, in a drunken stupor. Themistocles wrote of him, "Greater in genius than in character."

Napoleon, after devastating Europe, met disaster in Russia in 1812, died with a cancer in exile on the island of Saint Helena in 1821.

Hitler, one of the most ambitious and ruthless of all dictators, probably took his own life when he saw his empire crumbling and died on May 1, 1945.

The Great Depression of the 1930s wiped out many financially successful persons. Success is not easy to come by and far more difficult to maintain.

I once read in a fund-raising book about an Episcopalian bishop who called on a Presbyterian layman twenty-six times in quest of a gift, and received a million dollars after being turned down twenty-five times. Risk and tenacity are both very important ingredients in success.

Jesus had all the qualities as the Successful One. He conquered the citadels of people's souls. He staked His life against the forces of evil, sin, and death and gambled it against the promises of His Father's word of triumph over the last enemy: death.

He not only overcame the world but promised His followers that "one jot or one tittle shall in no wise pass from the law, till all be fulfilled" (Matt. 5:18). He kept His word.

343

Surety

"So much was Jesus made a *surety* of a better testament" (Heb. 7:22).

We can sing Fanny J. Crosby's hymn:

Blessed assurance, Jesus is mine!
Oh, what a foretaste of glory divine!
Heir of salvation, purchase of God,
Born of His Spirit, wash'd in His blood

because Jesus was made our surety.

A "surety" is one who confirms, makes sure, and guarantees our faith commitment in the new covenant of grace. It is a pledge made by one on behalf of another. This guarantee is not for 50,000 miles or five years, or even ten years; it is for all eternity.

As our high priest—surety—Christ brings God's assurance to His people. He is not only our intercessor and advocate for us before God, but He brings God's promises and hope to us.

If you want to decorate the center of your heart with a little "sweet p" bouquet, try this one:

As our surety, Christ is our *perpetual* high priest of the New Covenant. No one will ever take His place.

He is the *principal* high priest. There are none superior to Him. He has the final say.

He is the *perfect*, unfailing high priest as our Surety. He makes no mistakes. He is guilty of no errors of judgment or service, and He stands ever available.

Place the bouquet of certitude in your heart and sing with joy: *Blessed assurance, Jesus is mine!*

Teacher from God

"We know that thou art a *teacher* come from God" (John 3:2).

"A Teacher come from God!" What credentials! There never was any better teacher certification than that. Such a statement would look good on a prospective teacher's dossier or vita.

Nicodemus accepted Jesus as such a teacher, even acknowledging that He had come from God. Nicodemus did not ask Jesus about any credentials from a rabbinical school even though He called Him "rabbi." He did not ask for any record or certification as a teacher. Jesus had proven Himself to Nicodemus through the miracles He had performed.

Jesus had served His apprenticeship with the Father before coming to earth. As a teacher come from God, He came:

To teach us about God—His love, mercy, and grace. He came to teach as the way to God and how to pray to God.

To turn us from our sinful ways onto the right path. The turning was both a conversion (transformation through grace and faith) and an inversion (the turning of the selfish self inside out).

To train us how to become good stewards in the kingdom of God by serving God first, others second.

His disciples, those closest to Him, called Him "Teacher" more than by any other title. He was different. He called for a new order by new persons with new principles. He still does! We can learn much if we go to His school.

345

The Tempted One

"The Pharisees also with the Sadducees came, and *tempting* desired him that he would shew them a sign from heaven" (Matt.16:1).

Temptations will knock on the door of our hearts, but we, like Jesus, don't have to invite them in. Even little temptations will come for admission and, if admitted, will soon return bringing bigger ones.

Jesus, as the Son of God, was not immune to temptations. He was tempted forty days in the wilderness (Matt. 4:2); by the Pharisees asking Him which is the greatest commandment (Matt. 22:35-36); by the lawyer asking what one should do to inherit eternal life (Luke 10:25); and by the Sadducees, after the Herodians had asked about tribute money to Caesar, asking, "In the resurrection whose wife shall she be of the seven? for they all had her" (Matt. 22:28). The author of Hebrews says that He was tempted in all points "like as we are, yet without sin" (Heb. 4:15).

The scribes, Pharisees, Herodians, Sadducees, and others, set their traps for Him. They wanted a sign from heaven as proof of His power. Unusual signs had been performed by Moses, Joshua, Samuel and Elijah, and now it was His time.

His answer to them wasn't what they wanted to hear. He told them to read and understand the signs of the time. Prophecies about Him were being fulfilled. The miracles that He was performing were all indications, signs, of His Messiahship and mission. Their hope was that He would be unable to show "flashing" signs, but He foiled their hopes. Temptations beset Him, often and strongly, but He overcame them.

May we find in Him power to overcome our temptations.

The Terrible Meek

"I am *meek* and lowly in heart: and ye shall find rest unto your souls" (Matt. 11:29).

Meekness is frequently thought of as weakness. But not so in the life of Jesus, for He was both the meekest and strongest man who ever lived, strong like gravitation that makes no noise.

Meekness is a mixture of humility, lowliness, and courage. Jesus called the attention of His disciples to this character trait in His life. Meekness is the thread He added personally to the tapestry of His character.

He was not meek as a lamb but virile as a strong shepherd. He was the most God-tamed, God-tempered and God-molded person who ever lived. He portrayed that "invincible might of meekness" which Milton spoke of. He was so humble, lowly, self controlled, and strong as to appear meek.

Charles Rann Kennedy wrote a one-act play entitled *The Terrible Meek*. The three characters in the play are a peasant woman, an army captain, and a soldier. The captain speaks to the woman, " 'I tell you, woman, this dead son of yours, disfigured, shamed, spat upon, has built a kingdom this day that can never die. The living glory of him rules it. The earth is his and he made it. . . . The meek, the terrible meek, the fierce agonizing meek, are about to enter into their inheritance.'

"The woman speaks, 'My peasant lad, a king? Yes. And more yet. He was what he said he was. He was God's Son.' "[29]

What more can I say? The Terrible Meek! Our Terrific Master!

29. Charles Rann Kennedy, *The Terrible Meek* (New York: Harper and Brothers, 1912), pp. 39-40.

The Terrifying Realist

"Whosoever will be chief among you, let him be your *servant*" (Matt. 20:27).

One day a young woman visited the battlefield of Gettysburg, and, after looking the area over carefully, she said in almost surprised horror, "This is the first time in my life that I even realized that the Civil War was not just reading matter." A visit there had made the Civil War for her a terrifyingly realistic event.

And that is so true in life. We have to come face-to-face with some things and some people to realize that they are for real.

In our Scripture focus for the day, the mother of Zebedee's children came to Jesus asking Him to grant a special privilege to her two sons. She asked that one might sit on His right hand and the other on His left hand in His kingdom.

In this experience she found that Jesus was a terrifying realist. He did not cover actual situations with ideal phrases. He saw the real, raw world. He saw the real, selfish heart. He could see the pluses and the minuses, the ups and the downs, the successes and the failures, the shame and the glory, and the desires for special favors and the opportunities of service.

His enthusiasm never blinded Him to what makes the spiritual world tick. His tears of concern and disappointment did not change His mind regarding the place of service and submission in the kingdom of God.

He has a special way of keeping the realities of life before us. He seems to be ever pointing them out to us. The stark realities of life don't go away.

348

Testator

My good friend of forty years ago, Hugh Peterson of The Southern Baptist Techological Seminary, tells this story in his book *A Study of the Gospel of Mark:*

"When the great evangelist, George Whitefield, was getting the people of Edinburgh out of their beds at five o'clock each morning to hear his messages, a man on his way to the tabernacle met David Hume, the Scottish philosopher and skeptic. Surprised at seeing the skeptic going to an evangelistic service, especially at such an hour, the man said, 'I thought you did not believe in the gospel.'

"Hume tersely replied as he hurried on, 'I don't, but he does.' "[30]

Jesus Christ believed so much in the New Covenant that He sealed it with the shedding of His own blood. He proclaimed to be a new and better covenant than the Book of the covenant, comprising the Ten Commandments.

It was decidedly better because He, as the Testator, had put the power of His sinlessness back of it. He had put the strength of His godliness into it. The force of His righteousness was supporting it.

As the Lamb of God who taketh away the sin of the world (see John 1:29), He was saying, "I believe in it enough that I will willingly lay down My life to give the New Covenant validity, viability, and eventual victory for all who ascribe to it."

As Testator, His death underwrote all the promises made. There is enough to honor all the bequests in His will, and you and I are in His will.

30. Hugh R. Peterson, *A Study of the Gospel of Mark* (Nashville: Convention Press, 1958), p. 21.

349

That Holy Thing

"Therefore also *that holy thing* which shall be born of thee shall be called the Son of God" (Luke 1:35).

Jesus was begotten of the Holy Spirit. His mother, Mary, was with child and yet she had not known a man.

So the child thus conceived by the Holy Spirit within the virgin Mary could be rightfully called "that Holy Thing" or "Son of the Holy Spirit."

My small, finite mind is pleased with the belief that no normal human conception of man and woman could produce *That Holy Thing*. Such an one needed to have both holy and human parentage. He was born in a virgin's womb and buried in a virgin tomb.

I cannot explain adequately His physical birth; nor can I explain adequately one's spiritual birth in Him. Both are mysteries to me, but both I accept without question and in faith. To me, faith makes better company than doubt, and I will feed my faith and thereby starve my doubts.

Philip Bliss has expressed in song my prayer regarding "that Holy Thing, Christ":

More holiness give me,/More striving within;
More patience in suffering,/More sorrow for sin;
More faith in my Savior,/More sense of His care;
More joy in His service,/More purpose in prayer.

True God

"This is the true God, and eternal life" (1 John 5:20).

Christopher Morley is credited with once remarking, "I had a thousand questions I wanted to ask God, but when I met Christ, they all vanished."

Christ was the true God. That statement made by John in his epistle harmonizes with statements made about Christ in the Gospels and in Revelation. If Christ had been anything less than true God, a half God for instance, He would not be God. God is totality and never just a part. Jesus was not just part man and part God. He was both truly man and truly God. When tempted, the temptations came to Him as a whole man, and when He overcame them, He was both man and God.

I believe Christopher Morley was saying that when he met Christ, he saw Him as the true God and found in Him all the answers to all His questions.

It is hard to worship the true God standing on question marks, yet the true God is willing to listen to our sincere inquiries. He willingly entertains all who seek for truth. In fact, He has promised that His Spirit will guide us into all truth. (See John 16:13.)

In life we are frequently disappointed when for the first time we meet someone who has been much heralded. But I doubt if anyone, including Morley, has ever been disappointed in meeting Christ. Even those who during His time on earth wondered if any good thing could come out of Nazareth were deeply impressed when they met Him. He is most impressive!

True Idealist

"Ye have heard that it hath been said, Thou shalt love thy neighbour, and hate thine enemy. But I say unto you, *Love your enemies*" (Matt. 5:43-44).

It is most difficult for a person to be a terrifying realist and a true idealist. But the mixture of these elements in Jesus' life was smooth and well balanced without one emasculating the other.

Jesus, our Heavenly Physician, was much like an earthly doctor who, when asked how he could endure so much disease and suffering in his patients, replied, "I always look at the disease from the curative standpoint."

Jesus saw the potential in people. He saw sin as harmful, but He knew the curative plan. Sins could be forgiven and overcome, even the last enemy, death.

The natural impulse is to love a neighbor and dislike an enemy, but Jesus never veered away from the spiritual ideal of loving one's enemy. In this respect His idealism was a far better way than acting as a terrifying realist.

In His challenge to be perfect as our Father in heaven is perfect (Matt. 5:48), He was throwing out what we might consider an impossible ideal, but not the relevancy in the attempt. He stressed the ideal elements of love, kindness, purity, and brotherliness, yet His ideals have never been fully accepted, comprehended, or practiced.

Idealists are the dreamers of dreams, the music makers, the movers and the shakers of the world, even sometimes the losers and the forsakers of the world.

Yet the price is not too high. Living idealistically doesn't come cheap. It is worth the price!

The Truth

"Jesus saith unto him, I am the way, *the truth*" (John 14:6).

Thomas a Kempis of the fifteenth century, and author of *The Imitation of Christ,* made this profound statement: "Without the way there is no going, without the truth there is no knowing, without the life there is no growing." Jesus is the truth in knowing about God.

Through the centuries, seekers have sought for truth. Some critics have called such a search "a wild-goose chase." To them there seemed to be no absolute truth, only relative. Pilate was not the only one to ask, "What is truth?" (John 18:38). He might have been prompted to ask that by seeing in Jesus a ray of the infinite source of truth. In Christ truth flows from God like an ever-streaming fountain.

Life is a continuous search for truth: scientific truth, spiritual truth, and moral truth. A scientific truth can be tested in a laboratory. A spiritual truth can be tested by the teachings of Christ under the leadership of His Spirit. Moral truth is rooted also in Him and tried in the arena of life.

Following truth exactly is hard. John Milton, in *Paradise Lost,* wrote:

Hard are the ways of truth,
And rough to walk.

We cannot order free and easy truth from a warehouse. We must go for it. We must pay the price and upon finding it, we may find that it does not inflate vanity but to the contrary deflates it on the altar of service. All Christian truth brings seekers to the foot of the cross where submission and commitment are requested.

The Transfigured One

"[He] was *transfigured* before them: and his face did shine as the sun, and his raiment was white as the light" (Matt. 17:2).

During World War II an airman lighted a match and, holding it in his hand, said to his chaplain, "Tell me, man to man, do we go on living, or," and pausing to blow out the match, he added, "is that what happens to us?"

The transfiguration of Jesus while on the mountain with Peter, James, and John gives us a glimpse of certainty that death doesn't blow out the candle of our eternal lives. While on the mountain Jesus was transfigured: His form was changed with His face becoming as the sun, and His garments were, as Luke said, "white and glistening" (9:29). It is said in Exodus 34:29 that the face of Moses "shone," and, while Stephen faced the council, the council members "saw his face as it had been the face of an angel" (Acts 6:15). But neither Moses nor Stephen, during those experiences, was transfigured.

Moses and Elijah appeared with Jesus on the mountain and conversed with Him while He was in the form of personal glorification. Also, a voice out of the cloud spoke, "This is my beloved Son, in whom I am well pleased; hear ye him" (v. 5). In this unusual way God stamped His approval upon Jesus: His life, teachings, and actions. Two other times a similar stamp of approval was given Him: at his baptism (Matt. 3:17) and while He was speaking to His disciples, telling them that His hour had come and that the Son of man should be glorified (John 12:28).

The Light is still burning in heaven's gate, awaiting the arrival of earth's weary pilgrims. Let us march on in confident faith.

354

Transient

"Jesus said unto him, Foxes have holes, and birds of the air have nests; but *the Son of man hath not where to lay his head*" (Luke 9:58).

As far as we know, Jesus had no organization or headquarters during His three years of active ministry. He did spend some time in Capernaum, Bethany, and other places. He owned no condo or apartment. He had no mail outs asking for support.

We doubt that He had any regular source of income, no bank account, and, of course, there was no unemployment compensation available to Him. There is no record that He ever took an offering for His subsistence.

He was entertained by friends and was the receiver of the hospitality of others.

Even though we can track some of His itinerary during those three years, it does not appear that He had any set plan. He seemed to go where the need was and where the situation demanded.

If there ever was an intinerant minister, He was one. The writings do not infer, however, that He was ever an imposition on anyone's hospitality or graciousness. To the contrary, His presence was warmly welcomed, and He seemed to be a very gracious recipient of other people's cordiality.

He did not, to our knowledge, even carry a suitcase. His earthly possessions were at a minimum. He spent His time making it possible for others to receive heavenly possessions. He came not to fill wardrobes but to make it possible for us to be clothed in righteousness and immorality.

We will all go to our rewards empty-handed. That's the way it is—but our hearts will be loaded with faith and hope!

355

A Verb

"In the beginning was the [Verb], and the [Verb] was with God, and the [Verb] was God" (John 1:1).

Marilee Zdenek and Marge Champion wrote a beautiful book in 1974 entitled *God Is a Verb!* The book is written because the Spanish of the Scripture verse in John 1:1, "En el principeo era el Verbo, y el Verbo era con Dios, y el Verbo era Dios," uses literally the word *verb* for the word *word*. It provides an interesting and suggestive idea.

There is no doubt but that Christ was and is a verb in the present as well as the past tense. He had been active in

creating,
redeeming,
guiding,
sustaining, and
loving—

all verb forms of intense action.

He has provided the energy, the movement, and the force that has brought life and immortality to depraved persons.

Let me therefore suggest an appropriate prayer:

Lord, *squeeze* love for the unlovely out of our hearts. *Tune* our minds to sing Thy grace. *Place* our hands on the handles of the plow as we prepare new soil for a planting. *Shake* loose any residual lethargy that may be clinging to our souls. Continue to *stir* us with Thy truths and *move* within us so that we may not become complacent. *Keep* us abnormally restless in Thy service and *sharpen* our yearning and longing for a closer and fuller relationship with the Verb, and the goals of your Kingdom.

356

The True Vine

"I am the *vine*, ye are the branches" (John 15:5).

Branches cannot live disassociated from the vine. They will wither and die. Branches must draw life from the vine. It takes a relationship of oneness of association and relationship.

A minister friend of mine related the occasion of a wedding where a football player was getting married. He had written part of the ceremony. After promising many things in sacred vows to his bride, the minister then gave the clincher: "Jane," he intoned, "I promise you that even with my back against the goal line, I will not punt on fourth and ten." What a promise of attachment to his bride! Are we willing to make a similar one to Christ, the True Vine?

In the relationship of branches to the vine, the Bible speaks of three types of branches. *First,* the fruitless branch which bears no fruit: it will be severed from the branch. *Second,* the withered branch which is not properly attached to the vine or is diseased: those branches will be gathered up and burned. *Third,* the fruit bearing branches: they are those that bear the fruit of the spirit: love, joy, peace, longsuffering, gentleness, goodness, faith, meekness, and temperance (Gal. 5:22-23) will be pruned and purged so that they may bear more fruit.

Jesus spoke of this relationship between the vine and the branches as "Abide in me, and I in you," and, "He that abideth in me, and I in him, the same bringeth forth much fruit. (See John 15:4-5.)

We must stay very close to the True Vine, the Water of life, and the One who gives the increase. His request for our abiding in Him is followed by His promise, "Ye shall ask what ye will, and it shall be done unto you" (John 15:7).

A good harvest is possible!

Wanderer

"Jesus said unto him, Foxes have holes, and birds of the air have nests; but the Son of man hath not where to lay his head" (Luke 9:58).

Many times my mother would say to the preacher of the little community church where we worshiped during my early years, "Pastor, our home is your home. Come any time you wish. You are always welcome, and there is a plate at the table for you." Later, as a young preacher myself, such an invitation was more meaningful, especially when arriving on the church field without knowing where I would spend the night or have my meals. I wish more of that basic hospitality still existed.

Did Jesus have such invitations? I assume He was always welcome in Bethany with Mary, Martha, and Lazarus. There were homes in Capernaum open to Him, but, basically, He was a vagabond, an itinerant preacher, a peripatetic teacher. He had no office to call headquarters. As far as we know, He earned no stipend while preaching, nor do we have records of any monetary gifts He might have received.

Did this Wandering Minister have any three-month, five-month, or yearly plans? Did He set any goals for Himself and His disciples? His movements did appear to have casualness about them, but He was not an idler or wastrel.

There are at least three good things about His type of ministry while on earth. First, He shared the drifting life of the most homeless and hopeless of the poor. Today the police would have moved Him on, maybe arresting Him for having no visible means of subsistence.

Second, no group or city had exclusive rights on Him or His ministry. That was good. He was for the world.

Third, He placed little, if any, emphasis on material things. He trusted His Father to provide. Not bad!

The Happy Warrior

"Think not that I have come to send peace on earth: I have come *not to send peace, but a sword*" (Matt. 10:34); "Who for the *joy* that was set before him, endured the cross" (Heb. 12:2).

In these two passages we see very clearly that Jesus was a warrior against sin, but a happy warrior, willing to endure the cross and the shame heaped upon Him in the struggle. He knew the fierceness of battle, but He also knew the incomparable joy that awaited Him at the right hand of the Father.

William Wordsworth wrote a poem "The Happy Warrior," which gives descriptive lines of who a happy warrior is:

A constant influence, a peculiar grace;
But who, if he be called upon to face
Some awful moment to which Heaven has joined
Great issues, good or bad for human kind,
Is happy as a Lover; and attired
With sudden brightness, like a Man inspired;
And, through the heat of conflict, keeps the law
In calmness made, and sees what he foresaw;
Or if an unexpected call succeed,
Come when it will, is equal to the need.

I am glad Jesus was a happy warrior, and a successful one.

Old John Newton, well-known hymn writer, rector of Saint Mary Woolnoth of London and known as one of the most influential of the evangelical leaders of the eighteenth century, used to say, "If you think you see the ark of the Lord falling, be sure it is due to swimming in your own head."

And let me add that the Happy Warrior won't let it fall. (See Gen. 3:15.)

359

Watchman

"While I was with them in the world, I kept them in thy name: those that thou gavest me *I have kept*" (John 17:12).

There is a riddle that made the rounds years ago which goes like this, "A watchman said, 'I dreamed last night.' He was fired. Now, why was he fired?" The answer is that he slept on the job.

A watchman is supposed to be alert, open eyed, and aware of all that is going on. He is to provide security and protection from intruders for those asleep. He is to watch and warn if danger lurks near.

David, the good shepherd of his sheep, wrote in Psalm 121:3-4: "He will not suffer thy foot to be moved; he that keepeth thee will not slumber. Behold, he that keepeth Israel shall neither slumber nor sleep." He was aware of the watchful eye of the Almighty. He felt secure and safe under the care of His Heavenly Father.

Just as a lion watches over her cub and a mother watches carefully over her newborn babe, Christ takes care and precaution over His own. He watches over His own.

I think you will be blessed by reading the words of the hymn "My Father Watches Over Me" by W. C. Martin:

> I trust in God wherever I may be,
> Upon the land or on the rolling sea,
> For, come what may,
> From day to day,
> My heav'nly Father watches over me.
> The valley may be dark, the shadows deep,
> But O, the Shepherd guards His lonely sheep;
> And thru the gloom
> He'll lead me home.

The Way

"Jesus saith unto him, *I am the way*" (John 14:6).

Jesus cleared the way to God by becoming the Way. He called it a strait and narrow way, the only way.

A few days ago, I, along with my wife and six-year-old granddaughter, was looking for a certain recently opened restaurant in Louisville, Kentucky. We asked directions three times, all to no avail. No one seemed to be able to tell us the way exactly. We did not have the address, just an approximation as to location. Finally, in desperation I entered a beauty salon and asked a customer awaiting her turn. She gave me explicit directions, and we found the restaurant immediately. The granddaughter spoke up, "I guess it is located here where robbers can't find it." Touché! But not too bad after all. Robbers would be very unwanted there.

But in Christ the difference is so much difference. If robbers want to find the way to God, they can be asking Jesus, the Way. It is not off limits to robbers nor to any other seeking earnestly and with repentance of sin and faith in Him. The search for God ends with Jesus.

In reply to Thomas's inquiry about the way, Jesus gave Thomas a very short and correct answer. He knew exactly. He didn't say, "I kinda know, but I am not quite sure." He replied, "I am the way. Follow me."

It seems that in life similar experiences come in twos or threes. Three weeks prior to the above experience I was running late for a speaking engagement in Hamilton, Ohio, on the outskirts of Cincinnati. Finding myself in bustling downtown Cincinnati, I asked a fellow motorist. He said, "Follow me, and I will show you the right road." What a relief! And that is exactly what Jesus does. He leads. Ask him; then follow. He will show you the way.

Weatherman

"There shall be *signs* in the sun, and in the moon, and in the stars; and upon the earth *distress of nations*, with perplexity; the sea and the waves roaring" (Luke 21:25).

Jesus was a good weatherman. He could read the signs of the sky and of the times. He was much better than the one my wife chuckles about when remembering, "Either it will rain tonight, or it won't," he said. He was right. He couldn't miss, but he didn't say anything for sure. He didn't even measure up to the one who said that he predicted darkness for the night.

I learned to consider the weather as a child. Rain was needed to moisten our farmland. A windstorm struck one evening, tearing down two of our barns. As a child I memorized the poem,

Rainbow at night, sailor's delight,
Rainbow in the morning, sailor's warning.

So the skies said something to me. I watched for the rain clouds, the wind clouds, and the rainbow, which was a promise made by God to Abraham, "I do set my bow in the cloud, and it shall be a token of a covenant between me and the earth. . . . the waters shall no more become a flood to destroy all flesh" (Gen. 9:13-15).

Jesus said that signs of the sky—eclipses, comets, and meteors— would be witnessed before the destruction of Jerusalem, and similar events would occur before His coming again. There would be distresses of earth also, as heralds of His coming.

While on earth He sounded a weather watch, "Look up and when you see these signs, you will know that your redemption is near." There is no need of a storm shelter. We are safe in Him.

The Weeping One

"When he was come near, *he* beheld the city, and *wept* over it" (Luke 19:41).

Do tears coming from the heart of a strong man turn you off or on? Do you consider that one a weakling, one who has given way to his feelings? How long has it been since you had a good cry?

When Jesus approached the city of Jerusalem enroute from Bethany during His last days on earth, He saw it in its glory and grandeur and magnificence. As He crested the hill just outside the city, He was about two hundred feet above the Temple, and the panoramic view roused in Him an outburst of adoration and sympathy. He broke into a passion of lamentation, giving vent to an overpowering awareness of the plight of the city and her inhabitants.

The Greek word used here for "wept" means a loud expression of grief. It was more than sobbing. At the grave of Lazarus He shed silent tears, but here His tears were accompanied by loud verbal expressions.

Jesus loved the city of Jerusalem. It was a royal city, in some ways, a holy city. He was inwardly torn by an awareness of the potentiality of the city in comparison to its actuality. He grieved for the city, knowing what would befall it when Titus came.

His agony was enhanced over the lostness within it. The city had become hardened in ignorance. There was apathy and scorn for His words, methods, and aims. He had tried, but He had failed—foiled by their rejection of Him.

And He still weeps over our cities. He still has tears for them, tears of tender compassion and concern. Do we care enough to cry over our cities? If so, let them be tears of strength and commitment.

363

The Worthy One

"For this man [Christ Jesus] was counted *worthy* of more glory than Moses" (Heb. 3:3). (See also Rev. 5:12.)

Leaders make demands of their followers, even unto death.

One of the most appalling and distasteful things I have read recently described the unholy war between Iran and Iraq. The author states that Ayatollah Khomeini tells young boys, who have been given plastic keys to heaven, that if they are killed on the battlefield in the war between Iran and Iraq, they will go directly to heaven. Khomeini told them, as he lined them up by the hundreds and commanded them to march over land planted with mines in order to explode the mines before his soldiers came, "The purest joy in Islam is to kill and be killed by Allah."[31]

Khomeini is not worthy of such power, nor has he the power to give young lads a plastic key to heaven.

Christ, the founder of the New Covenant, earned His worthiness. It was not self-bestowed. He earned it by giving of Himself, and in return, worthiness was bestowed on Him by His Father.

John, in writing the Book of Revelation, spoke of the voice of multitudes upon multitudes of angels saying with a loud voice (and loud indeed with so many voices), "Worthy is the Lamb" to receive:

"power" (indicating His Almightiness)
"riches" (in Him all the fullness of the Godhead dwelt)
"wisdom" (infinite knowledge)
"strength" (more than needed)
"honor" (from God)
"glory" (bestowed by God) and,
"blessing" (of God).

What a worthy tribute to the One who holds the keys to heaven.

31. David Reed, "The Unholy War Between Iran and Iraq," *The Reader's Digest,* Aug. 1984, p. 124.

Yokefellow

"Take my *yoke* upon you, . . . For my yoke is easy, and my burden is light" (Matt. 11:29-30).

It is wonderful to be invited to become yoked with Christ. That is indeed a rare opportunity.

Richard Wurmbrand, a former Communist, tells in his book *Tortured for Christ* how one of his friends became a yokefellow of Christ. " 'Jesus has won me by his politeness,' Piotr [Peter] said."[32] Later, Piotr was imprisoned for his faith where neither politeness nor an easy yoke were available.

The term *yoke* in our Scripture passage refers to a type used on oxen to fasten to the load being pulled. Linguistically in our Scripture context, rather than literally, it means an agreeable and serviceable yoke. A yoke that doesn't gall or irritate, restrict or impede, freeness in drawing the load.

Spiritually, the yoke relates to a pleasant association: one that calls us to be submissive, reponsive, and cooperative to the instructions and leadership of Christ.

The irritation or galling, if there is any, would come from holding back or failing to keep in rhythm with His movements.

Being yoked denotes that our companionship with Christ is continual and well preserved if we submit our wills to His authority.

Frankly, I had never thought of one being won to Christ by the Savior's politeness as Piotr said was in evidence in the account of Jesus after His resurrection conversing with the two disciples on the Emmaus road. But Jesus deals with us in gracious love, not with force and sternness.

32. Wurmbrand, Richard, *Tortured For Christ* (Old Tappan: Fleming H. Revell Company, 1969), p. 28.

Omega

"I am Alpha and *Omega*, the beginning and the ending" (Rev. 1:8).

So, we come to the end of our journey through 365 names and titles of our Lord. I hope you get the feeling with me that it is like viewing from a hilltop a great city in all its splendor—like Moses, viewing the Promised Land from Mount Nebo, or like a 365-piece orchestra coming to a majestic crescendo and ending of a stirring masterpiece.

I have not been able to do justice to that Name which is above every name, but I hope that you, my readers, will see in the name "Omega," the last letter of the Greek alphabet, a crowning gesture of affirmation of Jesus Christ as:

The end of faith, as its Author,

The end of wisdom, as its Beginning,

The end, epitome, of love, as its Greatest Lover,

The summation of all truth,

The consummation of all mortal hope,

The culmination of all joy,

The termination of our hopes and fears of all the years, and that there is,

Nothing longer than His outreach,

Nothing higher than His ideals,

Nothing deeper than His grace, and

Nothing wider than His beneficence.

I ask you, as I ask myself, to give yourself more fully to Christ so that the flame of eternal faith, hope, and love that is rooted and grounded in Him whose Name is above every name will burn even more brightly.

366

Blessed Be the Name
(for Leap Year)

"[Job] said, Naked came I out of my mother's womb, and naked shall I return thither: the Lord gave, and the Lord hath taken away; *blessed be the name* of the Lord" (Job 1:21).

The beautiful hymn "Blessed Be the Name" begins with these words: "O for a thousand tongues to sing." It would take at least a thousand tongues to express the fullness of the blessed name of Jesus.

If, therefore, a thousand tongues cannot fully express the praise and glory due "that Name which is above every name," it is quite certain that 365 names fall far short. The name of Jesus Christ is inexhaustible. Right now you are probably thinking of a name that I have not used. If not, let your mind shift into overdrive and you will, no doubt, come up with one.

So let me, for this three hundred and sixty-sixth day, quote the first stanza of Charles Wesley's grand hymn: "Blessed Be the Name:

> O for a thousand tongues to sing,
> Blessed be the name of the Lord!
> The glories of my God and King,
> Blessed be the name of the Lord!
>
> ....
>
> Blessed be the name of the Lord!

On and on—366 ways or 1,000 ways or even 2,000 ways—still the Name remains inexhaustible. The Bearer of those names is the matchless, *sans pareil,* Son of God who is the second person of the Trinity, and all of the accolades say, "ne plus ultra"—"more beyond."

The end is not even in view.

Epilogue

The Name of Jesus

The name of Jesus is so sweet,
  I love its music to repeat;
It makes my joys full and complete,
  The precious name of Jesus.

I love the name of Him whose heart
  Knows all my griefs, and bears a part;
Who bids all anxious fears depart—
  I love the name of Jesus.

That name I fondly love to hear,
  It never fails my heart to cheer;
Its music dries the fallen tear:
  Exalt the name of Jesus.

No word of man can ever tell
  How sweet the name I love so well;
Oh, let its praises ever swell,
  Oh, praise the name of Jesus.

"Jesus," O how sweet the name!
  "Jesus," every day the same;
"Jesus," let all saints proclaim
  Its worthy praise forever.

—Rev. W. C. Martin

Index

(Numbers refer to devotional sections instead of pages.)

Bibliography

Angus, S. *The Environment of Early Christianity.* New York: Charles Scribner's Sons, 1932.

Auden, W. H. "For the Time Being—A Christmas Oratorio," *The Collected Poetry of W. H. Auden.* New York: Random House, 1945.

Blair, George. "The Carpenter of Nazareth," *The Story of Jesus in the World's Literature,* ed. Edward Wagenknecht. New York: Creative Age Press, Inc., 1946.

Brunner, Emil. *Our Faith.* London: SCM Press, Ltd., 1936.

Champion, Marge, and Marilee Zdenek. *God Is a Verb!* Waco, Texas: Word Books, 1974, 1975.

Cobb, Irvin S. "Greatest Gentleman That Ever Lived," *Behold the Man,* ed. Ralph L. Woods. New York: The Macmillan Company, 1944.

———. "Ladies & Gentlemen," *Behold the Man,* ed. Ralph L. Woods. New York: The Macmillan Company, 1944.

Crowley, Arthur E. "Worship Opens Blind Eyes," *Treasury of the Christian Faith,* ed. Stanley Stuber and Thomas Clark. New York: Association Press, 1949.

Fairbairn, Andrew Martin. *The Philosophy of the Christian Religion.* London-New York: The Macmillan Company, 1928.

Flint, Annie Johnson. "Jesus Christ—and We," *1000 Quotable Poems,* comp. Thomas Curtis Clark and Esther A. Gillespie. Chicago-New York: Willett, Clark and Company, 1937.

Glass, Bill, Garry and Jack Kinder, and William Arthur Ward, eds. *Positive Power for Successful Salesmen.* Atlanta: Drake House, Hallux, 1972.

Guyon, Madame Jeanne. "A Prisoner's Song," *Masterpieces of Religious Verse,* ed. James Dalton Morrison. New York: Harper, 1948.

Hay, Sara Henderson. "The Search," *Masterpieces of Religious Verse,* ed. James Dalton Morrison. New York: Harper, 1948.

Holmes, Oliver Wendell. "The Chambered Nautilus," *1000 Quotable Poems,* comp. Thomas Curtis Clark and Esther A. Gillespie. Chicago-New York: Willett, Clark and Company, 1937.

Hosmer, Frederick. "The Indwelling God," *1000 Quotable Poems,* comp. Thomas Curtis Clark and Esther A. Gillespie. Chicago-New York: Willett, Clark and Company, 1937.

Hovey, Alvah. *An American Commentary on the New Testament,* Vol. III. Philadelphia: American Baptist Publishing Society, 1881.

Ibsen, Henrik. "Greatest Rebel that Ever Lived," *Behold the Man,* ed. Ralph L. Woods. New York: The Macmillan Company, 1944.

Kennedy, Charles Rann, *The Terrible Meek* (play). New York: Harper, 1912.

Kipling, Rudyard. *The Light that Failed.* New York: Grosset and Dunlap, 1890.

——. "Recessional," *Poems with Power to Strengthen the Soul,* comp. James Mudge. New York-Chicago: The Abingdon Press, 1907, 1909.

Lacordaire, Jean Baptiste. "The First Gentleman in the World," *Behold the Man,* ed. Ralph L. Woods. New York: The Macmillan Company, 1944.

Lewis, C. S. *Screwtape Letters.* New York: The Macmillan Company, 1942.

Longfellow, Henry Wadsworth. "The Builders," *Poems with Power to Strengthen the Soul,* comp. James Mudge. New York-Chicago: The Abingdon Press, 1907, 1909.

Lowell, James Russell. "The Vision of Sir Launfal," *1000 Quotable Poems,* comp. Thomas Curtis Clark and Esther A. Gillespie. Chicago-New York: Willett, Clark and Company, 1937.

MacLaren, Alexander. Book of Joshua, *Exposition of the Holy Scriptures.* Grand Rapids: Wm. B. Eerdmans Publishing Company, 1932.

Markham, Charles Edwin. "Outwitted," *1000 Quotable Poems,* comp. Thomas Curtis Clark and Esther A. Gillespie. Chicago-New York: Willett, Clark and Company, 1937.

McClure, A. K., ed. *Lincoln's Own Yarns and Stories.* Chicago-Philadelphia: The John C. Winston Company.

Mead, Frank S. *The March of Eleven Men.* New York: Grosset and Dunlap, Inc., 1931, 1932.

Millay, Edna St. Vincent. "Renascence," *W. L. Symphonic Sermons,* ed. Stedges. New York: George H. Doran Company, 1924.

Milton, John. *Paradise Lost.* Chicago: Encyclopedia Britannica, 1955.

Moody, Dwight L. *The World's Greatest Sermons.* New York: Garden City Publishing, 1943.

Mullins, Edgar Young. *The Christian Religion in Its Doctrinal Expression.* Nashville: The Baptist Sunday School Board, 1917.

"Napoleon I." *The Treasury of the Christian Faith,* ed. Stanley Stuber and Thomas Clark. New York: Association Press, 1949.

Otto, Rudolph. *Contemporary Thinking About Jesus,* comp. Thomas S. Kepler. New York: Abingdon-Cokesbury Press, 1944.

Peterson, Hugh R. *A Study of the Gospel of Mark.* Nashville: Convention Press, 1958.

Pope, Alexander. "The Universal Prayer," *Poems with Power to Strengthen the Soul,* comp. James Mudge. Chicago-New York: The Abingdon Press, 1907, 1909.

Reed, David. "The Unholy War Between Iran and Iraq," *The Reader's Digest,* August 1984. Pleasantville, New York: The Reader's Digest Association, Inc.

Sandburg, Carl. "Prayer of Steel," *1000 Quotable Poems,* comp. Thomas Curtis Clark and Esther A. Gillespie. Chicago-New York: Willett, Clark and Company, 1937.

Schweitzer, Albert. *Contemporary Thinking About Jesus,* comp. Thomas S. Kepler. New York: Abingdon-Cokesbury Press, 1944.

Slessor, Mary. *Sources of Power in Famous Lives,* ed. Walter C. Erdman. Nashville: Cokesbury Press, 1936.

Sockman, Ralph. *The Higher Happiness.* New York: Abingdon-Cokesbury Press, 1942.

Studdert-Kennedy, G. A. "Indifference," *1000 Quotable Poems,* comp. Thomas Curtis Clark and Esther A. Gillespie. Chicago-New York: Willett, Clark and Company, 1937.

——. "The Carpenter," *The Story of Jesus in the World's Literature,* ed. Edward Wagenknecht. New York: Creative Age Press, Inc., 1946.

Tabb, John Banister. "The Boy Jesus," *The Story of Jesus in the World's Literature*, ed. Edward Wagenknecht. New York: Creative Age Press, Inc., 1946.

Tillich, Paul Johannes. *The Shaking of the Foundations*. New York: Charles Scribner's Sons, 1948.

Westcott. *The International Standard Bible Encyclopedia*, Vol. III, ed. James Orr, Grand Rapids: Wm. B. Eerdmans, 1949.

Whitman, Walt. "O Captain! My Captain!" *1000 Quotable Poems*, comp. Thomas Curtis Clark and Esther A. Gillespie. Chicago-New York: Willett, Clark and Company, 1937.

Wurmbrand, Richard. *Tortured for Christ*. Old Tappan: Fleming H. Revell Company, 1969.